D1564232

COREY VILLAGE AND
THE CAYUGA WORLD

The Iroquois and Their Neighbors

Christopher Vecsey, *Series Editor*

COREY VILLAGE
AND THE
CAYUGA WORLD

Implications from Archaeology and Beyond

Edited by JACK ROSSEN

Syracuse University Press

∞ The paper used in this publication meets the minimum requirements of the American National Standard for Information Sciences—Permanence of Paper for Printed Library Materials, ANSI Z39.48-1992.

For a listing of books published and distributed by Syracuse University Press, visit www.SyracuseUniversityPress.syr.edu.

ISBN: 978-0-8156-3405-8 (cloth)   978-0-8156-5334-9 (e-book)

Library of Congress Cataloging-in-Publication Data
Rossen, Jack.
    Corey Village and the Cayuga world : implications from archaeology and beyond / edited by Jack Rossen. — 1st edition.
        pages cm. — (The Iroquois and their neighbors)
    Includes bibliographical references and index.
    ISBN 978-0-8156-3405-8 (cloth : alk. paper) — ISBN 978-0-8156-5334-9 (ebook)
1. Cayuga Indians—Antiquities.   2. Cayuga Indians—History.   3. Cayuga Indians—Religion.   4. Excavations (Archaeology)—New York (State)—Cayuga County.   5. Indians of North America—New York (State)—Cayuga County—Antiquities.   6. Cayuga County (N.Y.)—Antiquities.   I. Title.
    E99.C3R67 2015
    974.7'6800497554—dc23   2015017772

Manufactured in the United States of America

This book is dedicated to the Cayuga people, with the hope that it helps them reconnect with the past and walk steadily into the future.

In memory of
Gahsënihsa:s
"Name Searcher"
Bernadette "Birdie" Hill
(1944–2015)
Cayuga Heron Clan Mother who led her flock back to the homeland

Contents

Illustrations

Tables

Acknowledgments

I am enormously grateful to all the people who have helped on the Corey project. The lists below cannot express my sincere thanks and sense of wonder at the range and scope of friendships and collaborations that occurred and continue to inspire me.

The Corey site was excavated as joint field schools of Ithaca College and Wells College. The 2003 crew included Jason Addams, John Ellison, Karen Goetsch, Stephen Moragne, Jessica Murray, Nina Rogers, and Martin Smith. The 2005 crew included Hannah Bailey, Holly Buchanan, Garrett Byrnes, Kristi Corrado, Nidal Fakhouri, Delilah Heshmat, Jody Klue, Jamie Mazzeo, Martin Smith, Sarah Steiner, Naomi Stockwell, and Bobbi Jo Wilson.

In administration, we thank Kim Milling of Ithaca College and Terry Martinez of Wells College.

Ithaca College supported the project with Academic Project Grants, Dana Internships, equipment, supplies, and laboratory facilities.

The Funk Foundation supported analysis and special studies.

Specialists included April Beisaw, Macy O'Hearn, David Pollack, Michael "Bodhi" Rogers, Martin Smith, Wes Stoner, Sarah Ward, and Joseph Winiarz.

In the herb study, we thank Kelly Keemer and Amanda Williams with Brooke Hansen.

Matt Gorney and Ithaca College Digital Media Resources provided graphics.

Theodora Weatherby drew the Tree of Peace pipe stem.

The eclipse map (figure 12.1) is reproduced with permission from the NASA eclipse website, calculations by Fred Espanek, NASA/GSFC.

For guidance and wisdom, we thank Birdie Hill (Cayuga, Heron Clan Mother), Chief Norman Hill (Seneca, Wolf Clan), Freida Jacques

(Onondaga, Turtle Clan Mother), Ada Jacques (Onondaga, Turtle Clan), Dan Hill (Cayuga, Heron Clan), Karl Hill (Cayuga, Heron Clan), Chief Sam George (Cayuga, Bear Clan), Chief Chuck Jacobs (Cayuga, Heron Clan), Donna Silversmith (Cayuga, Snipe Clan), Peter Jemison (Seneca, Heron Clan Faithkeeper), Richard Hill Sr. (Tuscarora, Beaver Clan), Tadodaho Sidney Hill, and Tony Gonyea (Onondaga, Beaver Clan Faithkeeper)

The liaison with Wells College was Ernie Olson. The neighborhood liaison was Paul Mitchell.

Thanks for the hard work and useful comments of the anonymous and semianonymous reviewers, such as Kurt Jordan.

Siobhan Hart helped me organize my thoughts on dominant narratives by organizing the session "Whispers, Screams and Echoes: Creating, Recreating and Challenging Archaeological Narratives" at the New England American Studies Association Conference, Plymouth, MA, November 2010.

Douglas Perelli helped with access to the Marian White notes and artifacts at the Marian White Anthropology Research Museum, University at Buffalo.

Thanks to Peter Whiteley for permission to publish an excerpt from his e-mail in the epilogue.

Special thanks to Deanna H. McCay at Syracuse University Press for her faith and encouragement of this volume and to Annette Wenda for the hard work of copyediting.

Special thanks to Eli Thomas (Onondaga, Wolf Clan) for use of his mural art on the cover.

Special thanks to Wayne and Patricia Bowman!

Special thanks to the Closet Chickens!

Love, patience, criticism, and support: Brooke Hansen!

COREY VILLAGE AND
THE CAYUGA WORLD

Introduction

The Corey Site and Its Contexts

JACK ROSSEN

Before coming to Ithaca College, I was primarily an Andeanist, perform-
ing archaeological research and teaching in Peru, Chile, and Argentina. I
arrived in central New York as a temporary replacement for their South
American archaeologist. While driving around the area, I became fasci-
nated with the Cayuga landscape, including mounds, earthen embankments, sacred landmarks such as the Great Gully, and historical plaques.

The Cayuga are one of the original Five Nations (now six) of the
Haudenosaunee Confederacy (figure I.1). More commonly known as the
Iroquois Confederacy, Haudenosaunee, meaning "People of the Longhouse" or "People Building Longhouses," is the name they use, and thus
that name will be used throughout this book. The Haudenosaunee Confederacy, with their nations stretched across the landscape like an enor-
mous geographic longhouse, was a powerful alliance of nations when
encountered by Euro-American missionaries, explorers, settlers, and soldiers. The origins of the confederacy have been much debated, and the
issue is discussed in chapter 11 and the epilogue, including substantial
disagreement among historians, archaeologists, and Native oral histories.

The most conspicuous historical markers in the Cayuga Lake region
commemorate the destruction of the Cayuga Nation in September 1779
during the Sullivan Campaign. As the Revolutionary War ground on and
the US Continental army established the upper hand in military operations, George Washington sent nearly one-third of the army to destroy the
Haudenosaunee Confederacy. This scorched-earth expedition included

1

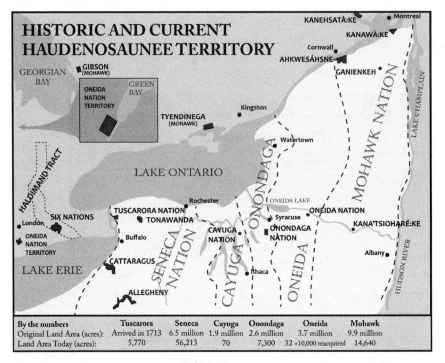

HISTORIC AND CURRENT
HAUDENOSAUNEE TERRITORY

By the numbers	Tuscarora	Seneca	Cayuga	Onondaga	Oneida	Mohawk
Original Land Area (acres):	Arrived in 1713	6.5 million	1.9 million	2.6 million	3.7 million	9.9 million
Land Area Today (acres):	5,770	56,213	70	7,300	32 +10,000 reacquired	14,640

I.1. Map of the Haudenosaunee Confederacy territories. (Courtesy of Lindsay Speer/Two Row Wampum Campaign, Honorthetworow.org)

burning at least forty-three settlements and the destruction of crop fields (Cook 2000 [1887]).

The William Butler detachment of the campaign peeled off from the main force to the west in Seneca territory and burned the Cayuga settlements, forcing most people to flee northwest to Niagara and Canada, while remnant groups stayed behind. Oral histories include a dramatic recounting of Cayuga women and children hiding in Great Gully (near present-day Union Springs) as soldiers burned the nearby village of Chonodote, known as Peachtown to the Americans, and destroyed a fifteen-hundred-tree peach orchard. The Cayuga were spared because their screams echoed off the gorge walls, leading the American soldiers to believe there were warriors threatening ambush. The Great Gully is thus credited with saving the Cayuga people (Tobin 2002). Despite a dominant narrative that the Cayuga were punished for supporting the British during the American Revolution, documents suggest that the Cayuga were primarily neutral, though some may have fought with both sides (Mann 2005; see also the epilogue).

What were the reasons for the Sullivan Campaign? Like many military actions, this series of events is complex, and there are many perspectives on why it occurred. The United States was nearly bankrupt from the long war, and the area was viewed as a site for potential land-grant payments to soldiers (Flick 1929). This payout is indeed what ensued after the war, as the "military tract" was divided among officers, soldiers, and land speculators. Some view the campaign as a training exercise for an army with problems such as poor organization, including nonfunctional chains of command and supply lines (Fischer 1997). There were certainly geopolitical considerations for Washington in removing a perceived strong Indian confederacy in the path of potential westward expansion (Flick 1929). The Sullivan Campaign ultimately led to the Erie Canal, proposed in 1807 and constructed from 1817 to 1825 (Finch 1998 [1925]).

In the immediate region of the Corey site, Cayuga County, the destruction of villages in existence two hundred years after Corey was occupied meant the shift of the area from the center of one nation to the peripheral outskirts of another. The Sullivan Campaign began a period of more than two centuries in which the Cayuga were displaced from their homeland. Besides the social fragmentation, one effect of the displacement is that the Cayuga have relatively little knowledge of the location, organization, or ambience of their ancestral villages. The Corey site, with its sixteenth-century materials, represents the last period of Cayuga florescence before European contact. Corey is even more spectacular for its relatively intact environmental setting. Perched on a triangular finger of land against steep cliffs, it has a dual earthen embankment with a ditch along one-fifth of its boundary. The site is farmed today, but the surrounding areas are wooded. A pathway leads down a cliff side from the site into the gorge of Paines Creek, where an unusual variety of medicinal herbs grow. I will suggest later that medicinal practices occurred at the site and that perhaps there was at least partial occupational specialization there.

The Haudenosaunee and Archaeologists

Most archaeological research in Haudenosaunee territory, particularly excavation of cemeteries, has been conducted without the consent or knowledge of Native leaders (Benedict 2004). As early as 1903, even the Seneca archaeologist Arthur C. Parker focused on cemeteries, fending off Native protests of his work on the Allegany Seneca Reserve (Colwell-Chanthaphonh 2009, 65–90). One dark landmark of regional archaeology was the 1939–40 excavations at Frontenac Island on Cayuga Lake, near Union Springs (Ritchie 1945; Trubowitz 1977). William A. Ritchie excavated the island cemetery with hundreds of individuals, producing a graphic report and dispersing the human remains to various public and private institutions and individuals. In 2003 some remains from these excavations unexpectedly turned up in a small private museum and were quietly repatriated to the Cayuga.

This history has created a justifiable atmosphere of Haudenosaunee mistrust of archaeologists. The adoption of the Native American Graves Protection and Repatriation Act (NAGPRA) in 1990 opened an opportunity for reform of the discipline and a new partnership between Native people and archaeologists (McManamon 1995). Today, a few archaeologists working in Haudenosaunee territory work actively with Native leaders, while others do not. The central Cayuga heartland, an area I define as a ten-mile-diameter area along the central eastern shore of Cayuga Lake, has had little archaeological research done in recent decades. Marian White of the University of Buffalo worked at Corey and other nearby Cayuga sites from 1968 to 1970 (see chapter 1). Prior to that time, work was conducted by Harrison Follett in the 1930s and '40s (Follett 1957) and Arthur C. Parker in the 1920s (Parker 1922). I was amazed at the nearly thirty-year absence of professional archaeology in this zone when I first explored the area in 1998.

Indigenous Archaeology

From a Native perspective, much of the history of Haudenosaunee archaeology is a regrettable series of exploitations and abuses of Native peoples ("Theft from the Dead" 1986; Benedict 2004; Mann 2003). A few Native archaeologists, such as Arthur C. Parker, worked in the margins between traditional academic archaeology and a Native perspective (Colwell-Chanthaphonh 2009; J. Porter 2001), and a few non-Native archaeologists, including Marian White, were deeply concerned with contemporary Native issues. By the 1970s, Haudenosaunee scholars Oren Lyons, John Mohawk, G. Peter Jemison, Salli Benedict, and Richard Hill Sr., along with publications such as *Akwesasne Notes*, were at the forefront of reframing scholarship toward Native perspectives and knowledge systems (Lyons, Mohawk, and Deloria 1992).

It was not until the 2000s that a true countermovement known as indigenous archaeology began to develop into a serious minority contingent within the Society for American Archaeology, the professional organization that guides policies, publications, and the national archaeology conference (Watkins 2000). The indigenous archaeology movement involves both Native and non-Native archaeologists such as myself and has become an international phenomenon (Bruchac, Hart, and Wobst 2010; Colwell-Chanthaphonh and Ferguson 2008; C. Smith and Wobst 2005; Silliman 2008). It is a multidimensional perspective that values and encourages Native participation and requires the permission and guidance of Native leaders. At its finest, indigenous archaeology shares power with and has positive cultural and practical benefits for Native people. Within the Haudenosaunee, archaeologists such as Donna Silversmith, Corinne Hill, and Curtis Lazore, as well as Dan Hill and Karl Hill of the Cayuga Council and Tony Gonyea, the Onondaga faithkeeper, are developing a greater activism toward archaeology and cultural resources.

My view of indigenous archaeology is that practitioners should strive to have projects and friendships outside of archaeology that advocate for Native issues and help their communities. I have called this idea of the broader responsibilities to living communities "expanded identity" (Hansen and Rossen 2007; Rossen 2006b, 2008). As examples, we have brought a Native filmmaker to a reserve school to teach middle school Onondaga students to use video equipment and tape short films, including stories of their elders and Native humor. More closely related to archaeology, at the request of Native leaders, we conducted ground-penetrating radar at a cemetery to map unmarked graves and prevent their disturbance by new burials. Last and most ambitious is the Cayuga-SHARE Farm, a seventy-acre organic farm that was purchased in 2001, operated as an educational center for five years, and then transferred to the Cayuga Nation (Hansen and Rossen 2007; LaDuke 2005, 154–60; Rossen 2006b, 2008).

The archaeology itself can have benefits for Native people, such as establishing affiliation between ancient sites, artifacts, and human remains and Haudenosaunee groups such as the Cayuga and Onondaga to aid NAGPRA-based repatriation of human remains from the New York public museums. Repatriation has been a difficult process in New York, primarily because of state-mandated limitations on what constitutes cultural affiliation and how far back in time it can be established. In Cayuga territory there was a general hiatus of professional archaeology, particularly in the central homeland area east of Cayuga Lake. Three decades of inactivity promoted the idea that nothing of consequence had happened there, leading some local residents and members of the anti-Indian organization Upstate Citizens for Equality (UCE) to believe that the Cayuga homeland was elsewhere (Hickman n.d.; Pettingill n.d.). This concept was promoted by a professional archaeologist paid by New York State in the Cayuga Land Claim hearings of 2001 that were held in Syracuse. I found that my mere presence in the area raised new awareness of the history of the Cayuga heartland.

I feel that non-Native archaeologists benefit too from practicing indigenous archaeology and striving to overcome the colonialist history of the discipline. The most rewarding aspect for me is making great friends in Indian country and hopefully helping them in a variety of projects. There are several aspects of interpretation of Corey and other sites that I will attribute to my conversations with Native people. Students excavating at Corey through the Ithaca College–Wells College archaeological field schools all spent time doing service learning at the Cayuga-SHARE Farm, doing basic farmwork, planting the Three Sisters, and preparing the grounds for the annual Cayuga Nation Picnic. Practicing indigenous archaeology means learning, understanding, and respecting how the Haudenosaunee view life as well as archaeology and archaeologists. There are interrelated key tenets to this understanding, all of which will be discussed below: the good mind, the Two Row Wampum, spiritual danger, archaeologists as conduits, and the problem of English.

The Good Mind

The good mind is a fundamental Haudenosaunee concept governing personal conduct and interactions with people and nature. The idea refers to acting and speaking with a clear mind and thoughts and thinking beyond immediate needs to consider the impact of our decisions for seven generations (Jacques 1991). Haudenosaunee leaders such as Onondaga Turtle Clan Mother Freida Jacques constantly remind us to keep the good mind, which diffuses difficult interactions and requires developing what Peter Jemison, Heron Clan faithkeeper of the Seneca Nation, refers to as "seven thumbs of skin" (Jemison 2013). My interpretation of the good mind (constrained by my dependence on English, as discussed below) is that it is embodied in self-control, maintaining inner peace within the turmoil of the world, and negotiating complex situations to arrive at compromise.

I often think of the potential role of the good mind in archaeology. It can alter how we approach archaeological sites, as the Haudenosaunee view the earth as a living organism and sites as places where ancestral spirits reside. It emphasizes the archaeological site, along with all the inhabitants of the environment, as relatives instead of resources to be harvested (Kimmerer 2013). This emphasis places archaeologists more in the position of companion, or maybe surgeon, with responsibilities to care for and heal the site following excavation. I also contemplate archaeology conferences, which can be very contentious. In those contexts, the good mind reminds us to try to frame our work and responses to others' ideas in nonconfrontational ways. The fact that archaeologists often state that we are "arguing" a point suggests that academics can benefit from this frame of mind. I will not pretend to be an expert practitioner of the good mind, but I am certainly an admirer of the concept. I understand that some people will disagree with concepts and issues that I will address in this book, such as the origins of the Haudenosaunee Confederacy, and I will endeavor to use the good mind as much as possible in the inevitable forthcoming debates.

The Two Row Wampum

The Two Row Wampum belt represents one of the first treaties between Euro-Americans and Native people, in this case between the Haudenosaunee and the Dutch around 1613. Two rows of purple beads represent the two peoples: Native people in their canoe and Euro-Americans in their ship, traveling side by side down the river of life in friendship, respect, and mutual noninterference. The treaty included specific references to separation of beliefs and laws (R. Hill 2013). The three rows of white beads between the purple rows represent the need for communication and the mutual responsibilities to care for each other and the environment. This idea is the most pervasive indigenous concept pertaining to Haudenosaunee relations with arriving outsiders. Throughout 2013, the four hundredth anniversary, the Two Row Wampum Renewal Campaign was staged. This joint Native and non-Native effort organized numerous events, including an enactment paddle down the Hudson River from Albany to New York City, arriving at the United Nations on the International Day of Indigenous Peoples. The Two Row is a living ideal for the present and future of Native–non-Native relations, regardless of the painful historical realities. It defines useful supporting roles for non-Native allies. The Cayuga-SHARE Farm described above, along with allied community organizations like NOON (Neighbors of Onondaga Nation) and festivals, powwows, and shared events are living examples of the vibrant Two Row concept.

The practice of indigenous archaeology is a Two Row–style reform of archaeology. It emphasizes the incorporation of Native people and concepts into archaeology. Also significant is the maintenance of open communication lines to ensure that research is properly conducted and respectful. It encourages the development and incorporation of Native people and the infusion of Native ideas of space, time, and material culture into archaeology. Recognition of the value of oral history is also a key aspect of Two Row relations within archaeology (George-Kanentiio 2000, 26).

Spiritual Danger

In the Haudenosaunee belief system, there is spiritual danger present throughout the archaeological research process of excavation, analysis, public presentation, and publication. The correct sites must be selected and approved. Cemeteries and other sacred zones are the most spiritually dangerous, but some danger is present in all excavations. Even particular artifacts may be dangerous or benign, and only Native specialists or seers can ascertain the difference (T. Porter 2008, 116). Probably the most famous case is that of Handsome Lake, the Seneca prophet whose Good Message (*Gaiwi:yo*) brought Longhouse religion and social change to the Haudenosaunee. Handsome Lake was killed in 1815 by a knife that he left at a clearing, which had become cursed when it was retrieved (Thomas 1994, 122–24). Spiritual danger extends beyond excavation to handling materials in the lab, taking photographs, and presenting images in public presentations. Recognition of this constant threat of spiritual danger and the presence of signs that reflect positive or negative energy is important to a successful project.

The presence of spiritual danger means that archaeological excavations can take rapid and unexpected turns. My excavations at a site not discussed in this report were quickly and quietly ended when human remains were surprisingly encountered. This decision by the clan mothers and chiefs was made for the protection of everyone involved, and private ceremonial arrangements were made to calm the disturbed spirits. It is important for archaeologists to sincerely respect these beliefs and follow through by seeking and allowing Native guidance to handle delicate situations.

Archaeologists as Conduits

Haudenosaunee people believe that archaeologists are conduits of information, receiving it when the time is socially or politically correct. Important sites that have not been located have just not yet revealed themselves. For the clan mothers, it is not a matter to worry about. Some stories must be told repeatedly and regularly, such as the story of the Peacemaker, who along with Hiawatha and the woman Jigonsaseh united the five nations of the Haudenosaunee Confederacy. The story of Handsome Lake, the Seneca prophet who brought new social rules to the Haudenosaunee at the beginning of the nineteenth century, is also told regularly (Parker 1990 [1913]; Thomas 1994). In contrast, some stories should not be told. I have been instructed to avoid sites associated with tragedy, including the Sullivan Campaign. Some stories should be told only when the time is right, including the story of the Corey site (and other sites I have worked on that are currently being analyzed, such as the Levanna and Myers Farm sites).

Current events make it necessary for both Native and non-Native people to know more about the Cayuga. As mentioned above, one assertion made during the 2001 hearings of the Cayuga Land Claim is that the Cayuga homeland was not near Cayuga Lake but only in Canada, near Montreal (Hickman n.d.; Pettingill n.d.). The excavations provided immediate local visual evidence of the Cayuga in central New York. When I excavated a portion of a heavily disturbed longhouse behind a house in Aurora Village, I could state that, in contrast to the courtroom statement, the "Cayuga lived literally in your backyard" (Shaw 2002).

The Problem of English

Haudenosaunee leaders often speak of the problem of English, including but not limited to translation, even in basic communications. Recitations of the daily Thanksgiving Address, the "words that come before all else," which thank the Creator for everything provided for us on earth, are often offered to mixed Native and non-Native audiences at public events (George-Kanentiio 2000, 35–39; Haudenosaunee Environmental Task Force n.d.). Native speakers such as Chief Jake Edwards of Onondaga Nation emphasize before and after recitation how much is lost in the translation to English (2013). Tom Porter, Mohawk Bear Clan elder, describes the poetics and multidimensionality of Haudenosaunee languages in comparison with English, using the contrast of "3-D Technicolor versus a little six-inch black and white television set" (2008, 91–96). Peter Jemison describes English as a "cruel" language that unintentionally hurts people through its lack of nuance (2013).

What are the implications of the problem of English for archaeology? Some aspects of the richness of daily life, material culture, and circulations of the sixteenth-century Cayuga must be lost in the translation and conventions of archaeological reporting in English. In particular, the language problem transfers into misunderstanding of Native scientific principles or traditional environmental knowledge (Kimmerer 2011, 2013). My goal is to guide the reader through a sixteenth-century Cayuga village just prior to European contact. This trip is organized through references to the layout, occupations, and activities of the site; the circulations of people and materials; and the landscape and neighboring peoples. My use of English blocks aspects of ideology and what we imperfectly refer to as spirituality in daily Cayuga life. English is an isolating language, while Cayuga and most Native languages are heavily agglutinating and polysemic (Comrie 1990). That is, these languages can be described as containing "hidden meaning," or "multiple meanings." Native Hawaiians refer to this as *kaona*, or hidden and multiple meanings that express the inherent beauty of everyday activities connecting people to nature, folklore, sky signs, and the ancestors (Low 2013, 295, 308–10).

Working toward an Ideal

The development of indigenous archaeology is a long-term process of working toward an ideal. Despite their approvals of my excavations, the Cayuga are reluctant. In a recent talk, Dan Hill of the Cayuga Council stated, "We would prefer that there are no digs, but we have to approve some because our history has been taken away, people deny our homeland, and we are not given credit for our oral history" (2013). There are stages of the process of developing indigenous archaeology in any region, and there may come a time when the archaeology is considered unnecessary or undesirable by Cayuga leaders. Toward the ideal of Native control of their cultural resources, I envision five stages of development. The present work with the Cayuga people has developed to Stage 3.

Stage 1: Embracing the concepts and seeking out and developing relationships. In this beginning stage, archaeologists ask themselves how research questions are chosen and pursued and whether research questions mesh with issues that interest Native people. This stage also includes reaching out to Native leaders for their input on a humane archaeology and conditions for participation. Non-Native allies learn local and regional Native concepts for conducting their professional lives. In central New York, this understanding includes the concepts of the Two-Row Wampum and good mind discussed above.

Stage 2: Working out a local-regional model and developing expanded identities. Because each region has different circumstances and, as explained above, particular social and political contexts, a model for collaboration must be developed that accounts for local conditions. For example, are cultural resources located on private, state, or Native-controlled lands? Do local and regional museums cooperate with or actively or passively resist collaboration and repatriation efforts?

Stage 3: Active participation and field collaboration. This stage is fundamentally about active partnerships in fieldwork and lab work. It also includes releasing publications explaining the local model of indigenous archaeology. In an early stage of collaboration, archaeologists may have to deal with what Dorothy Lippert refers to as "silencing techniques" (2010). These overt and covert actions occur at professional conferences, in the publication review process, and in the workplace. At this stage Native interpretations and ideas appear in publications as personal communications, although Native authors may not be present. I would classify the present work as reflecting this local stage of development of indigenous archaeology.

Stage 4: Collaboration in reporting and publication and cooperation of all local-regional institutions. Stage 4 moves collaboration to a higher level, with cooperation in analysis, interpretation, and publication of materials. At this stage all local institutions (colleges, universities, museums, and others) actively cooperate toward Native-defined goals of research (both protocol and reporting) and repatriation. I have had conversations about the future inclusion of Native-written essays on Cayuga archaeology with several collaborators. "When we add our words and stories to it," Dan Hill says, "it will make a little more sense" (MacCarald 2014).

Stage 5: Native control of cultural resources. At Stage 5 all archaeological research and curation are controlled by Native peoples with the help of non-Native allies. A few western groups like the Diné (Navajo) are in the process of achieving this stage through the founding and development of the Navajo Nation Archaeology Department, an agency of the Navajo Nation government (Two Bears 2006, 2008). Another region that has made remarkable strides toward this stage is Hawai'i. Increasing numbers of Native Hawaiians and non-Native allies are establishing and practicing protocols of tradition, collaboration, and respect in all aspects of archaeology, ranging from excavation to community service, curation, restoration, and public education (Kapuni-Reynolds 2014; Lima et al. 2014; Wichman, NeSmith, and Wellman 2014). Ideally, at some point, we will interpret the Cayuga past through their worldview, integrating Western and indigenous paradigms to fully understand their past.

The Corey Site and Its Contexts

The Corey site is located just outside the boundaries of the Cayuga Land Claim area. From 1980 to 2006, the Cayuga Indian Nation fought in the courts to regain access to its reservation lands (sixty-four thousand acres) in a horseshoe-shaped area surrounding the northern end of Cayuga Lake in what are now Cayuga and Seneca Counties of New York. Through the late 1990s and during the time that Corey was excavated (2003–5), the claim was active, with dramatic court hearings, and communities were divided. An anti-Indian organization called Upstate Citizens for Equality fought land rights for the Cayuga through signs, parades, and protests, including historical revision that denied the Cayuga their New York homeland (Hansen and Rossen 2007; Hickman n.d.). The SHARE Farm was being operated by a group, including myself, as an educational center on Native issues in preparation for its transfer to the Cayuga as their first homeland foothold in two centuries.

Birdie Hill, the Cayuga Heron Clan Mother, first visited the Corey site in the spring of 2003. She lay in the grass for a while and pronounced that the place was powerful and she would have to think about whether it should be excavated. Around that same time, I also met with Freida Jacques, who told me she thought I was dealing with an unusually powerful site. She asked if the site was triangular in shape and if there was a confluence of energy there. The site is indeed triangular, and Paines Creek and its two unnamed tributaries meet in the gorge below the site. She too stated that it is a site of unusual power that demands unusual care and respect. A few days later Birdie Hill voiced her misgivings but also her trust in me to work respectfully and carefully, watching for signs of danger. She would visit the site three more times during fieldwork, asking the crew members for their feelings and observations of the land and creatures in the area. Freida Jacques later visited the site twice to personally experience this place of power.

The role of the local nonindigenous farmers in this research should not be overlooked. Growing corn, soybeans, and hay in a chronically depressed economic area is difficult and relentless work. Local farmers identify with the Cayuga as the people who worked the same land before them. They proudly view themselves as land stewards. Farmers throughout the research area have been supportive and interested, especially given the complex political environment. At the political moment in time that I worked at Corey, it was a courageous act for farmer Wayne Bowman and his schoolteacher wife, Patricia, to allow site excavation on their property that would highlight Cayuga history.

In summary, the Corey site excavations took place in a complex atmosphere of Native cultural revitalization, an archaeologist learning collaborative indigenous archaeology on the fly, a politically charged land claim, and a proud local farming culture. Within this experience, my hope was to rekindle an interest in Cayuga archaeology for local communities, to respect Native beliefs, and to incorporate their input about archaeology. Furthermore, my goal was to produce scientific results with attention to special studies and types of artifact analysis that are not often presented in the Haudenosaunee homeland. I hoped to perform research that was in some ways positive and beneficial to the Haudenosaunee people, as opposed to the dominant and tragic local history of archaeology.

1

Site Setting, Description, and Excavations

JACK ROSSEN

The Corey site lies above the protected gorge of Paines Creeks, an eastern tributary of Cayuga Lake. Paines Creek and its two unnamed tributaries lay transverse to the flow of glacial ice during the Pleistocene, and thus have stratified sediments as old as thirty thousand years (Muller and Caldwell 1986). The site is situated immediately above hard fossiliferous and calcareous shale cliffs, "almost an impure limestone," about one mile east of the lakeshore (Cleland 1903, 24). The site is surrounded by the gullies of the creek tributaries on its north and south sides and the 40-foot gorge of Paines Creek on its west, but is open to the east (figures 1.1 and 1.2). The site is located on and surrounded by Honeoye silt loam soil, the most fertile agricultural soil in New York State. This soil type, constituting only 18 percent of Cayuga County, is highly valued enough to be the official state soil type of New York (Hutton 1971).

The first recorded mention of the Corey site was made in 1829 by James Macauley in his massive work, *The Natural, Statistical and Civil History of the State of New York in Three Volumes*: "Those [fortifications] in Cayuga [County] are in the towns of Aurora and Auburn. That in Aurora is two miles southeasterly from the village. The area is of a triangular form and contains nearly two acres. Two of its sides were defended by precipitous banks and the other by a bank and ditch. Fragments of earthen vessels and the bones of animals have been found here enveloped in beds of ashes" (111).

The above description was repeated verbatim by Ephraim G. Squier (1849, 37), William Beauchamp (1901, 39–40), and Arthur C. Parker (1922, 505). There is some sentiment among local aficionados that Squier visited

1.1. Air photo of the Corey site. (Courtesy of Natural Resources Conservation Service, Auburn, NY, office)

1.2. General view to the northwest of the Corey site. (Courtesy of Jack Rossen)

the Corey site. It appears, however, that he surveyed and mapped only one site in Cayuga County, located on a promontory surrounded by 175-foot ravines. This site is probably what is known today as Great Gully Fort (Niemczycki 1984, 117; Squier 1849, 63, fig. 13). Beauchamp added slightly but significantly to the description of Corey by mentioning that the site existed on two levels, both above and below, within the Paines Creek gorge. Alanson Skinner visited and described several sites in Cayuga County (1921, 41–45), but Corey was not among them.

Marian White at the Corey Site

Marian White conducted limited excavations at the Corey site during the three summers of 1968 to 1970. She was distinguished as the first woman to receive a doctorate in anthropology from the University of Michigan, in 1956, and began a teaching position in 1958 at the State University of New York (SUNY) at Buffalo, now the University at Buffalo (Bender 1994, 1999). In 1968 she cleaned up three small pits dug by landowner Rick Corey and local high school biology teacher Paul Thomas, finding eroded potsherds and flakes in plowed topsoil.

White received a National Science Foundation grant in 1969, to continue the research at Corey and other area sites, which was linked to the study of warfare. She proposed to categorize village movements as orderly or disorderly to understand the nature and relative intensity of warfare during the period of AD 1200–1600. This proposal included an assumption of a peaceful average settlement movement of two miles as a baseline to place the Corey site within a village sequence to assess warfare locally and in comparison with Jefferson County, in northern New York. Peaceful village movement is presumably the product of the depletion of soil, game, and other resources in the immediate area. Within this model, the location of the Corey site was assumed to have been defensive, including a hypothetical movement of villages from low-lying floodplains to higher cliff-line locations as warfare increased (White 1969). William Engelbrecht worked with White in those years:

> Two "Big Ideas" in Iroquoian archaeology in the 60's were: 1) the regular
> movement of communities over space, and 2) disruption of that pattern

must mean something. I'm not sure who came up with #1, but I think it was probably a consequence of Charles Wray's work on Seneca villages [Wray et al. 1987]. Jim Tuck noted the movement of two Onondaga communities close to one another and suggested that this marked the birth of the Onondaga as a nation [Tuck 1971]. Marian was using these ideas in this application to address broad anthropological questions. She hoped Earl Sidler would flesh out the Jefferson County sequence, but unfortunately that never happened. (personal communication, 2012)

It appears that White's primary interest was to gather information on a range of sites in the area. The same summers as the Corey tests, she conducted major excavations at the Mahaney site, a seventeenth-century village and cemetery, and conducted lesser excavations on at least two more sites, Underwood and Weir. Her work in Cayuga County raises unanswered questions. Why did she move her investigative focus into Cayuga territory after long committing her research career to the western New York Niagara region? White faced numerous difficulties as a woman archaeologist in a then male-dominated profession. Her intensely local focus and commitments to community involvement and public education, along with time spent working for site protection with the Highway Department and developing relations with the Seneca Nation, may have slowed her research and unfairly repressed her legacy (Bender 1999). Her work included collaborating with the Seneca on the salvage of sites and burials prior to the tragic construction of the Kinzua Dam that flooded one-third of their reservation territory (Bilharz 1998; Fenton 1976). White was not motivated by traditional academic career accomplishments. This perspective makes the shift away from the Niagara area of western New York to central New York more interesting.

The 1969 and 1970 excavations at Corey were conducted with her students. The 1969 excavations occurred on August 12 and 14, with at least five students present during the excavation of three test units. Three cigar boxes of materials are curated at the University at Buffalo, including faunal remains, 12 incised sherds of the Cayuga Horizontal type, and 1 Madison projectile point. The 1970 excavations were conducted on July 10 and 23, with at least six students present, including William Engelbrecht. The 1970 work produced more materials, with six cigar boxes of material curated at the University at Buffalo. Included are 186 plain and cord-marked pottery sherds, plus 30 decorated sherds and rims of the Richmond Incised and Cayuga Horizontal types. Two trumpet-style ceramic pipe-bowl fragments were recovered from the "potter's backdirt in the ravine midden" (White, excavation notes).

Stephen T. Mocas also worked with White on the project:

> There was a narrow cleft over the edge of the bluff where the edge was going to slough off (given enough millennia). I remember a precipitous drop to a stream beyond it. I guess it was Paines Creek. The aboriginal inhabitants had come to the edge of the bluff and thrown stuff into the fault. I have a little Polaroid photo of the area, because just as I was reaching out for a branch to scramble down there, I saw that the branch was occupied by a sizable black snake. I was taking students out individually and teaching site survey, so I wasn't there very much. (personal communication, 2012)

Mocas and Engelbrecht also remember the tall dense brambles at Corey that made mapping and general orientation difficult.

White's student Brian Shero conducted an early experiment in water flotation to recover plant remains that included two samples from the Corey test excavations. His primary work was based on White's excavations at the nearby Underwood, Weir, and Mahaney sites. A small collection of plant remains was recovered from Corey: one corn kernel, ten bedstraw (*Galium* sp.) seeds, and eight blackberry/raspberry (*Rubus* sp.) seeds (Shero 1970).

The limited excavations conducted by White at the Corey site from 1968 to 1970 established the presence of a village with both areas of midden with heavy artifact densities and sparser areas with only topsoil and subsoil. No features like hearths or post molds were recorded. Diagnostic ceramics and one Madison projectile point suggested a late prehistoric date (ca. fourteenth to sixteenth century). One important observation was the recording of midden deposits somewhere in the ravine or gorge below the site proper, which supports the 1901 statement of William Beauchamp.

Unfortunately, Marian White's untimely passing in 1975 prevented her research at sites in Cayuga County, including Corey, from being fully realized (Milisauskas 1977). None of her students or colleagues continued her research.

Revisiting the Corey Site

My original introduction to the Corey site was in 2001, when it was mentioned to me by area residents. The site had local fame because of its double earthen embankment and ditch that runs along the western edge of the site for 50 meters along the steep cliff line (figure 1.3). This area is about one-sixth of the site perimeter. Because of the protected site location and embankment, the site has long been locally referred to as "the fort." The enigma of this interpretation is that the embankment is located along the most naturally protected and unapproachable edge of the site, while the level eastern site edge is open. Site excavation and test excavations determined that this settlement is small, with an area of 2.2 acres. Only two short longhouses, or "shorthouses," are present. (The term *shorthouse* was used by Kurt Jordan [2003] to describe the shorter version of longhouses that retain the formal attributes of longhouse construction such as paired posts and aligned hearths.) Archaeologists have used midline hearths, family compartments, and pit-feature density to estimate village population sizes (Funk and Kuhn 2003). This calculation would presume a site population of eight to twelve families, or between forty and sixty people. This population estimate is based on the presence of five or six compartments (midline hearths) in the excavated Corey longhouse and a presumed equal size of the unexcavated longhouse, along with a "family" size of five to six. The site also contains an open-air ground stone workshop. A relatively deep midden accumulation (up to 1.3 meters deep) is present along the site's west side, above the steep gorge but inside the village proper within the earthen embankments.

Alongside the southern edge of the site is a path to the gorge bottom below. It is the only way down to Paines Creek and appears to be an ancient path. At the bottom of the path is a sheltered area with what the Haudenosaunee view as an unusual variety of women's medicinal herbs, including

1.3. Midden deposits. (Courtesy of Jack Rossen)

endangered species. This area was examined as part of a regional study of medicinal herbs in gullies and gorges (Keemer and Williams 2003). The concentration of herbs led the investigators to believe that this area was an herb-collecting area if not an actual herb-garden remnant.

The 2003 excavations focused on the western site edge with its midden accumulation. During this field season, the center of the site was in active agriculture, restricting work to the field edges. Block and test excavations along the site perimeter showed a shallow (horse-drawn) plowzone. Beneath the plowzone were complex stratified midden deposits with excellent faunal bone preservation (figure 1.4). Thirteen square meters were excavated (Units 1–9). No features were encountered within the midden zone.

On returning to the site in 2005, farmer Wayne Bowman graciously left the site fallow for our investigations. During this field season, we examined surface artifact concentrations through shovel testing, and Michael "Bodhi" Rogers of the Physics Department at Ithaca College

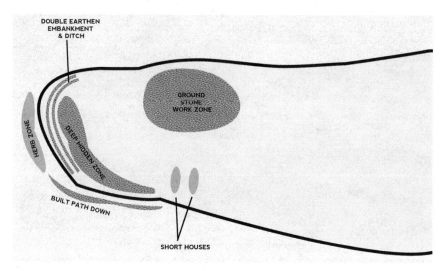

1.4. Village layout and activity areas. (Courtesy of Matt Gorney and Ithaca College Digital Media Resources)

conducted a magnetometer survey with his students (see chapter 2). Units 15 to 41, or 48 square meters, were excavated, for a two-season total of 61 square meters.

Village Layout

The village layout contains distinctive zones and activity areas (figures 1.5 and 1.6). Along the village western end is the double earthen embankment and ditch and deep midden disposal zone. Side-by-side short longhouses, or "shorthouses," were located along the southern periphery, while an open-air ground stone work area occupied the northern sector. A built path led down to an herb zone, either a garden or collecting area.

Shorthouse Area

During the 2005 field season, an excavation block of 28 square meters developed as hearth and post features were revealed. At the base of the plowzone in this block are five to seven aligned hearths (Features 1, 2, 3, 11, 12a, 12b, 12c). The exact number depends on the interpretation of Features 12b and 12c, which are either smaller hearths overlapping with

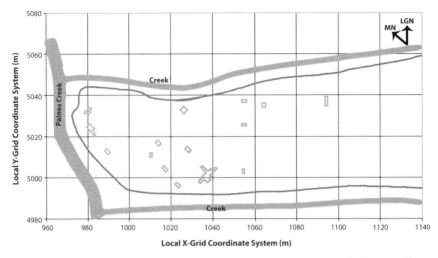

1.5. Location of site excavations. (Courtesy of Matt Gorney and Ithaca College Digital Media Resources)

Feature 12a or large posts alongside it. Based on the contents and basin shapes of those two features, along with the great concentrations of faunal remains present (see chapter 9), I tend to view them as hearths (figures 1.7 to 1.12). Block excavations revealed nearly an entire shorthouse with formal paired post construction and the aforementioned row of fire hearths. Just outside the shorthouse is an elongated pit containing ashes and no artifacts, probably representing cleaning activities.

The hearths are aligned to almost true north-south (note that units were excavated on magnetic north). They range in length from 34 to 88 centimeters and in shape from perfectly circular (Features 1 and 2) and slightly ovate (Features 3, 12a, and 12c) to elliptical and elongated (Features 11 and 12a). Depths below subsoil range from 18 to 35 centimeters. Feature 2 is a tailed or ventilated hearth. These hearths are known in several regions and were used for efficient wood burning (Makowski 2008; T. Pozorski and S. Pozorski 1996; S. Pozorski and T. Pozorski 2008).

Nine post molds show the extent of the shorthouse. Post diameters range from 5 to 18 centimeters. Depths below subsoil are 17 to 34 centimeters. These shallow depths suggest that the posts and features were truncated by plowing. The arrangement of posts indicates a house width

Fire Pits and Post Holes in House Units

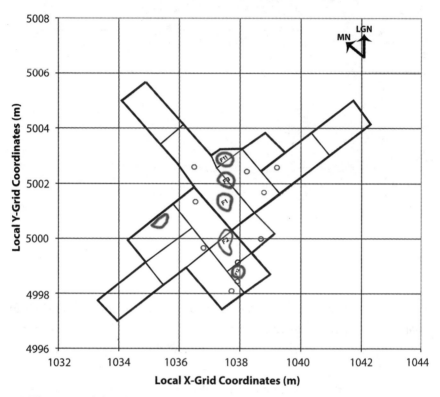

1.6. Plan view of shorthouse excavation block, showing hearths and posts. (Courtesy of Matt Gorney and Ithaca College Digital Media Resources)

of 2.2 meters and a length of about 7 meters. A light scatter of daub inside the shorthouse area suggests a light use of the material in construction, perhaps as a roof lining to protect against fire (Brennan 2007, 78). The Corey shorthouse length is similar to that of a seventeenth-century Seneca short longhouse at the Townley-Read site, near Geneva, New York, but the Corey structure is less than half the width, at 2.2 versus 5.3 meters for the later Seneca structure (Jordan 2003). Another structure roughly contemporary to Corey that could be classified as a shorthouse (7.9 by 5.5 m) was excavated at the sixteenth-century Atwell Fort site, an Onondaga site in Madison County, New York (Jordan 2008, 63; Ricklis 1967).

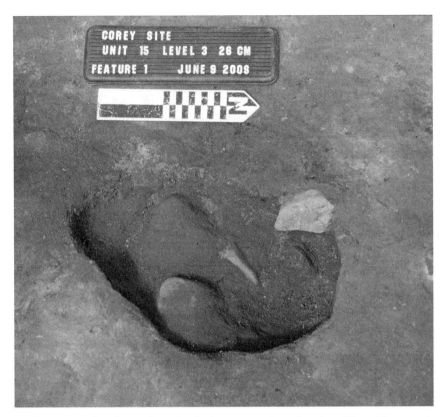

1.7. Feature 1, shorthouse hearth, during excavation, showing fill and bone awl. (Courtesy of Jack Rossen)

There has been a renewed emphasis in eastern US archaeology on examining posthole patterns in detail to understand the aboveground structure (Lacquement 2007). This interest has revived the decades-old debate of where and when flexed-pole versus rigid-pole construction techniques were used. The Haudenosaunee are long assumed to have used flexed-pole, curved-roof construction for their longhouses (Reed 2007), although reconstructions like the longhouse at the Seneca site of Ganondagan, utilizing postholes defined archaeologically (although from a different site), used rigid-pole and gabled-roof techniques (Underhill 2001). Flexed-pole construction is marked by many smaller posts.

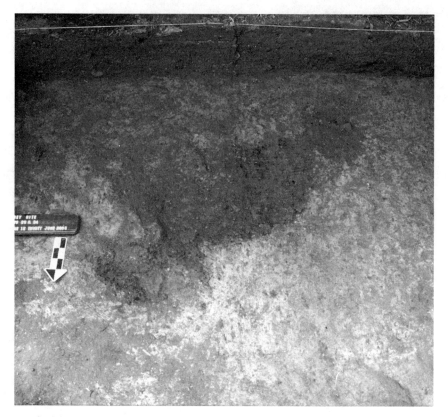

1.8. Overlapping shorthouse hearths, Feature 12 a, b, c, before excavation. (Courtesy of Jack Rossen)

Estimates of the largest diameter of posts that can be used for flexed-pole, curved-roof construction range from 7.5 to 10 centimeters (Brennan 2007, 82; Reed 2007, 21). The Corey site posts are burned in place, and thus there are no issues with differences between post and posthole size. All but two posts are between 15 and 18 centimeters in diameter, too large for flexed-pole construction. This evidence suggests a form of rigid-pole construction at the excavated Corey shorthouse, particularly a "pi-frame" form resembling the Greek letter (Beauchamp 1905, 206–7; Engelbrecht 2003, 74–75; Wright 1995).

Archaeogeophysical surveys and an area with a high-density surface artifact concentration revealed the presence of a second row of fire

1.9. Shorthouse post excavation, showing profile. (Courtesy of Jack Rossen)

hearths and thus a second shorthouse 5 meters west and parallel to the excavated shorthouse. If, as in my opinion, the Haudenosaunee Confederacy and clan system was long in place by the time of the Corey occupation, two parallel shorthouses representing a moiety or clan system would be a logical small village organization.

Double Earthen Embankment and Ditch

This conspicuous feature running for 50 meters along the western edge of the site probably accounts for the discovery and early mentions of the site discussed above. The embankments are presently 1 meter high. Local residents remember the embankment and ditch system being as deep as 3 meters early in the twentieth century. Test excavations on top of the

1.10. Double earthen embankment and ditch. (Courtesy of Jack Rossen)

embankments did not reveal post molds or features, but they may have been removed by erosion.

Midden Area

The midden area was excavated in 1-square-meter horizontal units and 10-centimeter levels. Below the plowzone, the midden contained strata and lenses to a depth of 1.3 meters below surface. No features were encountered in this midden zone. Excavation units placed around the site periphery during the 2003 season showed that a ring or strip of midden extends around the site perimeter inside the double earthen embankment and ditch for at least 100 meters. The midden is deepest along the western site edge and becomes gradually more shallow toward the north and south.

1.11. Pathway from site to gorge. (Courtesy of Jack Rossen)

Workshop Area

The northeast area of the site did not reveal features, but instead contained a number of small ground stone pallets and unfinished grooved ax and celts. All six possible gaming pieces, small mahjong-tile-size cut and smooth stones, were recovered from these excavation units. This area appears to have been an open-air workshop zone for producing ground stone implements and articles.

Herb Area

A path leading down from the southern edge of the site to the gorge bottom is an area with an unusual amount and variety of medicinal herbs.

1.12. Ernie Olson, Wells College, examining herb area located in the gorge below the site. (Courtesy of Jack Rossen)

A regional survey of gorges found that many similar areas have some herbs, but this area is the most concentrated and varied herbal zone encountered. Table 1.1 is a list of fifteen native herbs documented during this study and selected medicinal uses (Keemer and Williams 2003). Together, these herbs include preventative and curative medicinal properties. The same area contains Eurasian-introduced herbs. These plants were adapted easily to traditional herb areas and were incorporated by the Haudenosaunee soon after European contact (table 1.1). Readers are reminded that the use of medicinal herbs should be conducted only by trained specialists. There is also a source of pure clay nearby in the creek bank.

TABLE 1.1. Inventory from herb area adjacent to site

Bloodroot (*Sanguinaria canadensis*)
    Emetic, respiratory aid.
Blue cohosh (*Caulophyllum thalictroides* (L.) (Michx.)
    Febrifuge, analgesic, labor regulator, abortifacient, contraceptive.
Boneset (*Eupatorium perfoliatum* L.)
    Anti-inflammatory, febrifuge.
Catnip (*Nepeta cataria* L.)
    Sleep inducer, stress reducer/relaxant, insect repellant, culinary herb.
False Solomon's seal (*Smilacina racemes*)
    Expectorant, constipation, fish poison.
Fleabane (*Erigeron philadelphicus* L.)
    Protects cuts from infection, promotes healing, insect repellent.
Goldenrod (*Solidago* sp.)
    Kidney tonic to counter inflammation and irritation caused by bacterial
    infections or kidney stones. Leaves chewed to relieve sore throats and roots
    chewed to relieve toothaches.
Horsetail (*Equisetum* sp.)
    Vulnerary, diuretic, astringent.
Jack-in-the-pulpit (*Impatiens* sp.)
    Treatment for sore eyes. Preparations treat rheumatism, bronchitis, and
    snakebites, as well as induce sterility.
Jewelweed (*Impatiens capensis*)
    Treatment for poison ivy, rashes.
Joe-pye weed (*Eupatorium purpureum*)
    Tonic for urinary system, bladder, and kidneys. Treats chills, febrifuge.
Mayapple (*Podophyllum peltatum*)
    Emetic, cathartic, and anthelmintic agent. Poisonous root boiled, with water
    used to cure stomachaches. Used topically for warts.
Stinging nettle (*Urtica dioica*)
    Clinically proven adjuvant remedy in the treatment of arthritis.
Trillium (*Trillium* sp.)
    Astringent tonic from the root useful in controlling bleeding and diarrhea.
Wild ginger (*Asarum canadense*)
    Bitter, carminative, diaphoretic/sudorific, diuretic, expectorant, stimulant.

Sources: Herrick 1995; Keemer and Williams 2003; Moerman 1998.
Note: The same area contains Eurasian-introduced herbs adapted easily to traditional herb areas and were incorporated by the Haudenosaunee soon after European contact. These plants are angelica (*Angelica archangelica*), coltsfoot (*Tussilago* sp.), lady's thumb (*Polygonum persicaria*), motherwort (*Leonurus cardiaca*), mullein (*Verbascum thapsus*), sweet woodruff (*Galium odoratum*), and yellow dock (*Rumex crispus*).

Both William Beauchamp's (1901) and Marian White's (1971) field notes mentioned midden zones in the ravine below the site proper, but they could not be relocated. It is noteworthy that the deepest midden area is directly above the possible herb zone. This point raised the question of why trash was not disposed over the cliff edge but was deposited on site. An herbal collecting area or garden beneath the cliff would explain the midden accumulation at the site edge, as people would not dispose of trash into an active herb-growing or -collecting zone.

Radiocarbon Dates

Two radiocarbon samples, one each from a hearth and post of the short-house, produced mid- to late-sixteenth-century dates. The sixteenth century is difficult to precisely radiocarbon date because the multiple intercepts of the radiocarbon curve often span a century or more, as is the case with both Corey site dates. The agreement of these calibrated dates with each other (1558+/-62 Feature 12B hearth BETA298934 and 1573+/-48 Feature 17 post ILLINOIS STATE A2590) and the artifact assemblages leads to a general acceptance of the core dates. Only the absence of European trade items at the site leaves some colleagues wondering if the site is slightly earlier in the sixteenth century (Kurt Jordan, personal communication, 2013).

Notes on Excavation and Analysis

Excavations were undertaken with the understanding that the Corey site is not endangered. It is under a farmer's stewardship, and most of the site is a standard plowed field. The site was excavated by archaeological field school students from Ithaca College, Wells College, and Colgate University. Almost all excavations were undertaken with trowels, although a few midden levels were skimmed with flat shovels near the end of the 2003 season. The entire shorthouse block was excavated exclusively by trowel in 10-centimeter levels and 1-square-meter horizontal units. Excavation was supplemented by a magnetometer survey (chapter 2). Because of the research orientation of the project and the continued preservation of the site, the second shorthouse directly west of the excavated house was left intact. During excavation, emphasis was placed on recovery of large samples for water flotation. All fill from hearths and posts was collected and floated, and systematic column samples were taken from the short-house and midden units. Flotation aided not only in collecting archaeobotanical remains but also in recovering fine remains for the faunal analysis.

Artifact analysis emphasized aspects of the site assemblages that are not often given attention in this region. Ceramics have traditionally been the focal point of Haudenosaunee artifact studies (MacNeish 1952), and the analysis by David Pollack adds an important assemblage to this literature (chapter 3). Pollack has conducted extensive studies of Mississippian and Fort Ancient ceramic collections of the Ohio Valley, and this analysis brings a fresh perspective to Haudenosaunee studies. A petrographic study by Wesley D. Stoner also adds a new dimension, including an identification of the ceramic tempering material (chapter 4). A study of area quarries and geology by Joseph Winiarz was able to place lithic procurement into a regional framework (chapter 5). Lithic analysis by Martin Smith included non-projectile-point tools such as scrapers and explored the gendered nature of stone tool manufacture and use (chapter 6).

Ground stone is a good example of materials that are not often carefully analyzed, but the unusual small ground pallets of Corey merited the study by Macy O'Hearn (chapter 7). Faunal analysis by April M. Beisaw (chapter 8) and my archaeobotanical work (chapter 9) examined plant and animal inventories, as well as the activity-area implications of spatial distinctions between the shorthouse and midden areas. Minor assemblages (smoking pipes, calcite, temper, daub), analyzed by Macy O'Hearn and Sarah Ward, are presented here in the hope that they add depth to our understanding of site activities and connections beyond Cayuga territory (chapter 10). The ultimate goal of all the analyses was to together achieve an understanding of the layout, atmosphere, circulations, and connections of a small sixteenth-century Cayuga village. This objective may be achieved only by integrating the analyses and special studies into a cohesive narrative (chapter 11).

Finally, the epilogue addresses a broader and perhaps more abstract and pressing issue in Haudenosaunee archaeology. Dominant narratives have long been established and maintained despite relatively little field archaeology in recent decades. These narratives, both scientific and popular, have become important reference points as the Haudenosaunee and other Native peoples throughout the world undergo cultural revitalization. The Corey excavations and analyses occurred within the political context of the Cayuga Land Claim (1980–2006) and during ongoing controversies surrounding attempts at repatriating human remains to the Haudenosaunee from state institutions through the 1990 federal law of the Native American Graves Protection and Repatriation Act (Beisaw 2010). Within this multidimensionally charged context, dominant narratives may erase, revise, or fabricate history to continue the disenfranchisement of the Haudenosaunee. It is time to examine the narratives in light of the most recent archaeological research.

2

Archaeogeophysical Surveys

Michael Rogers

Magnetic gradiometer surveys were conducted from May 16 to May 27, 2005, using a Geometrics G858 cesium magnetometer system configured in 0.50-meter vertical gradient mode. A Sokkia SET6 total station was used to set out sixteen 20-by-20-meter contiguous archaeogeophysical survey units oriented on the northern tree line. Additional smaller units were established to cover more of the site while avoiding the trees that bound the site. The magnetometer surveys intended to identify features associated with houses (for example, fire pits and post molds), extramural features, and general village layout.

Cesium Magnetometry

A cesium magnetometer was selected for this project owing to its availability at no cost to the project and its likelihood for identifying features of interest. A cesium magnetometer uses optical pumping of cesium vapor to measure near-surface variations in the magnitude of the earth's local magnetic field, which ranges from 30,000 nT in the equatorial regions to 60,000 nT near the poles. (The Tesla is a unit of magnetic flux density in the International Systems of Units and named in honor of Nikola Tesla. A nanoTesla [nT] is 10^{-9} Tesla.) Readings are taken every tenth of a second to an accuracy of 0.1 nT (Scollar et al. 1990). To put this sensitivity in a common context, the magnetometer operator cannot wear metal-rimmed glasses, pants with a zipper, or shoes with metal eyelets because of the magnetic field of these objects disturbing the measurements. Local magnetic field variability can be generated by soil disturbance from human activity at the site and human-created fires on the soil surface.

Nonmagnetic fiberglass survey tapes were stretched to mark the meridian line (north-south running line at the western extent of the sub-unit) and a parallel control line (at the eastern extent of the subunit). In the east-west direction, forty-one blaze-orange, 0.95-gauge plastic "weed-whacker" lines served as transect lines stretching from the meridian line to the parallel control line at half-meter intervals. These lines are used to keep the magnetometer operator walking in a straight line.

The magnetic surveys used a bidirectional survey method. When the eastern end of the first transect was reached, the gradiometer operator moved northward 0.25 meter and surveyed from east to west along transect 2. Transects were spaced 0.25 meter apart, with every other transect marked using a weed-whacker line. The position of the unmarked transects is estimated by looking at the marked transects. Marking only every other transect introduces a small amount of error that is outweighed by the time saved when moving transect lines. Upon completing the survey of the first subunit, the data file is saved, the transect lines are moved to the next survey subunit, and the second subunit is surveyed. Approximately six of these subunits can be surveyed each day based upon the number of obstacles and difficulty in putting in the transect lines.

Analysis

A sequence of steps must occur before magnetic data can be plotted and interpreted. For the Corey site data, these steps were:

1. Check coordinates
2. Remove dropouts
3. Despike
4. Destagger
5. Grid
6. Edge match
7. Create mosaic

Check Coordinates

The data files for each unit were opened in a program called MagMap. Upon inspection only a few minor errors were found and corrected.

Remove Dropouts

While conducting the survey, the magnetometer will occasionally lose its ability to record the magnetic field. This loss of data is referred to as a dropout. The Remove Dropout feature in MagMap examines the data for missing values and removes the X and Y coordinates for these missing values to ensure that the missing information is not treated as a zero value.

Despike

Magnetic data often contain very high magnetic signals that are very spatially local. These local "spikes" are often just one or two points that have values much larger than the surrounding signals. Archaeogeophysical surveys are often looking for small changes in the magnetic field that become masked by these magnetic spikes that are often created by contamination on the ground surface. Only one unit had significant spikes, and they were removed using MagMap's Range Despike filter, where the person processing the data selects the range of the magnetic data to keep and which to discard.

Destagger

The Geometrics G858 control unit records a reading every tenth of a second, and the operator programs the start and end points of the grid into the control unit. The system assumes that the operator is walking at a constant speed and uses the location of the start and end of each line to evenly distribute the data points. This assumption creates positional errors if the operator speeds up or slows down while surveying a transect. These positional errors are magnified owing to the bidirectional survey method. This error is often referred to as staggering, zigzag, or zipper because of linear features being distorted by slight shifts in every other line. Essentially, a straight feature takes on the appearance of a zipper's teeth.

The processed data in MagMap are exported into a format that MS Excel can open. MS Excel is used to shift every other line to ensure that linear features look more like a line and less like a zipper. The amount of correction needed is identified through a guess-and-check method. An estimated correction is applied, the data are plotted, the success of the correction is visually examined, and a new correction is tried.

Grid

The number of points for each transect is different owing to variation in operator walking speeds. This difference creates an uneven data set that is difficult to process and plot. Golden Software's Surfer is used to take the unevenly spaced data and employ a statistical method called Kriging to create a file of uniformly spaced data. This process also interpolates across lines to add additional points between the 0.25-meter spaced transects, resulting in a high-resolution image.

Edge Match

Earth's magnetic field changes throughout the day and from day to day owing to the earth's rotation about its axis, its revolution around the sun, and solar activity. Because the magnetic data at the Corey site were gathered over several days, the baseline of the earth's magnetic field is different for each unit surveyed. To facilitate a comparison of all units, they need to be on the same baseline. MS Excel was used to process the gridded files by selecting points every 0.25 meter along the western edge of one unit and the corresponding points along the eastern edge of the adjacent unit. An error-correction amount results from subtracting these two values. This process requires us to start with a reference unit and work sequentially through each survey unit. The error-correction factors are gridded in Surfer to create a file that has the same number of points as the unit being corrected. The error-correction file is then subtracted from the unit being corrected. Doing so aligns the unit being corrected with the reference unit. The next unit in sequence is then aligned to the unit that was just corrected.

Create Mosaic

When all of the units have the same baseline, they are combined using Surfer's Grid Mosaic feature that takes each individual grid file and puts them into a single site file. The site file is then plotted as an image plot or shaded relief plot, using 256 gray or color scale.

Discussion

The magnetic data have larger variability in the magnetic field in the southern portion of the site, with regions of less variability to the west and north (figure 2.1). The linear features at right angles to each other in the northern part of the site (1080 m, 5035 m) turned out to be deep plow scarring. Excavations identified that the southern region contains at least one house, which accounts for the greater magnetic variability. Figure 2.2 shows the magnetic data in the region of the main excavation. Post molds and fire pits appear as magnetic monopoles both within the excavation zone and in a nearby unexcavated area.

Acknowledgments

The 2005 survey team was composed of two Ithaca College undergraduate physics majors, Kevin Faehndrich and Kris Georgiev. The processing and images were done by Ithaca College undergraduate physics major Charlie Woodward.

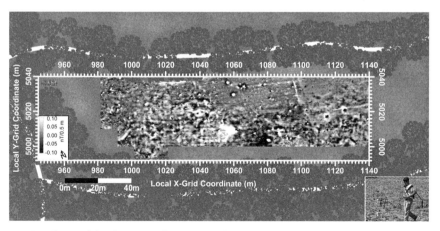

2.1. Air photo of the Corey site location with a magnetometer data overlay showing the location of the archaeogeophysics survey grid. (Courtesy of Michael Rogers)

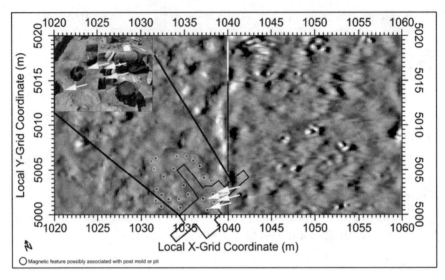

2.2. View of the magnetic data in comparison to the excavation features. The arrows point toward magnetic monopoles that appear spatially located with excavated fire pits and post molds. The arrows identify similar magnetic features in an unexcavated region. (Courtesy of Michael Rogers)

3

Ceramic Artifacts

DAVID POLLACK

The analysis of the Corey site ceramic assemblage was guided by three primary goals. The first was to describe the salient characteristics of the ceramics recovered from the site, the second was to characterize the ceramic assemblage, and the third was to contextualize these materials relative to other Cayuga sites.

In discussing regional interactions, this analysis utilizes ceramic types of Haudenosaunee territory to approximate ethnicities. It is a complex debate among archaeologists, some of whom maintain that "pots are not people" (Cruz 2011). In Haudenosaunee archaeology, the trend is to recognize that differences between ceramic assemblages represent regional and community differences that "reflect expressions of ethnicity" (Birch and Williamson 2013, 129). Even Hart and Engelbrecht's (2011) rhizotic model, developed to describe how ceramic design motifs do not match Haudenosaunee ethnic areas, attaches those motifs to groups of people within a social network analysis. Ethnoarchaeological studies tend to confirm that ceramic styles are "past choice(s), made at some time in the past by a social, though not necessarily an 'ethnic' group [that] is reaffirmed and inculcated through apprenticeship" (David and Kramer 2001, 148–49). In this sense, ceramics and existing ceramic typologies suggest social connections and interactions within regions that are traditionally associated with the various Haudenosaunee peoples.

Including nonvessel ceramic objects, 1,124 ceramics (1,122 sherds, with mended sherds considered to represent a single specimen, and 2 nonvessel objects) were analyzed (table 3.1). This chapter begins with a discussion of the methods used in this analysis. Descriptions of the salient

41

TABLE 3.1. Corey site ceramic assemblage

Ceramic type/group	Frequency	Percentage
Richmond Incised	54	12.6
Cayuga Horizontal	36	8.4
Richmond Incised/Cayuga Horizontal	129	30.2
Dutch Hollow Notched	14	3.3
Otstungo Notched	2	0.5
Otstungo Incised	1	0.2
Seneca Notched	1	0.2
Ontario Horizontal	2	0.5
Untyped Plain rim, Interior Decorated	1	0.2
Untyped Decorated, trailed lines below collar	1	0.2
Untyped Plain rim with deep lip notches	1	0.2
Untyped Plain (includes four plain rims)	82	19.2
Untyped Cordmarked	103	24.1
Total	427	100.0
Untyped Plain and Untyped Cordmarked less than 4 cm²	695	
Nonvessel ceramic objects		
Cylinder	1	
Fired clay	1	
Grand Total	1,124	

characteristics of the ceramic collection and the nonvessel clay objects (clay cylinder and fired clay) are presented next. This chapter concludes with a summary and contextualization of the Corey site ceramic assemblage.

Methodology

All rims, decorated collars, and plain and cordmarked body sherds were analyzed (n=427). The analyzed sample included 273 sherds greater than 4 cm² in size and 154 rims and decorated collars less than 4 cm² in size. The remaining 695 body sherds (less than 4 cm² in size) were counted, but no additional analysis was conducted on these specimens. In addition, to the typological and attribute analysis presented in this report, a detailed petrographic analysis was conducted on 27 rims, collars, and body sherds (see chapter 4).

Basic attributes were recorded for analyzed specimens: cordage twist, vessel form, vessel fragment (that is, whether body, collar, lip, or rim), lip shape, rim orientation and modification, rim orifice diameter and percentage of rim orifice represented, decoration type and location, sherd thickness, sherd size, and incised/trailed-line width. Details relating to how these data were recorded and to particular data-recording exceptions are outlined below.

Cordmarked and plain surface treatments reflect a continuum in smoothing (ranging from poorly smoothed to burnished). For the former, this continuum was divided into cordmarked and smoothed-over cordmarked, with smoothed-over cordmarked sherds displaying evidence of some obliteration of impressions. For the latter, the continuum was divided into poorly smoothed, smoothed, well smoothed to very well smoothed, and burnished. Poorly smoothed surfaces were lumpy and irregular (some exhibited finger depressions). Well smoothed to very well smoothed surfaces were clear and even, as if more care had been taken in finishing the surface. Burnished surfaces appeared almost shiny or polished. Specimens with weathered or worn areas on their exteriors, but that otherwise had identifiable surfaces, were considered eroded cordmarked, eroded plain, and so forth. Sherd surfaces were considered eroded in cases where the surface had been damaged beyond conclusive identification.

In order to investigate twist, impressions from exterior surfaces of all cordmarked sherds were taken with Sculpey (a modeling clay that can be reused repeatedly and hardened by baking in an oven). Twist was determined from the cast. Digital calipers were used to measure sherd thickness. For all bodies and necks, thickness was taken at the thickest spot.

Orifice diameter and percentage of orifice diameter represented was measured for all rim sherds large enough for reliable measurements to be taken. No measurements were attempted for very small rims, for larger rims broken in such a way that the curve was too small for reliable measurement, or if vessel form and rim orientation could not be determined.

A concentric-circle chart graduated in two-centimeter increments (see Rice 1987, 223) was used. If orifice diameter could not be measured, specimens were assigned an arbitrary value of 5 percent of orifice diameter represented. Thickness measurements on rims were taken at the thickest spot at the lip (lip thickness) and one centimeter below the lip (rim or collar thickness). The collar/neck-juncture thickness was also measured. Photographs and profiles were made of representative specimens.

Additional information about decoration was collected. It included incised/trailed-line width, depth of incised/trailed lines (shallow, medium deep, deep), shape of punctations, and location of notching on lips and collars. Decoration was classified as incising if the lines were V-shaped and trailing if the lines were U-shaped.

Artifact Descriptions

As a result of this analysis, eight ceramic types and five ceramic groups were identified on the basis of exterior surface treatment and decoration. Of the ceramic types, seven correspond to previously defined ceramic types, and one is a combination of two types. With respect to the ceramic groups, one consists of plain body sherds, with very small rims, necks, and collars, and another cordmarked body sherds, necks, and collars. The remaining three groups consist of single examples of decorated rims or collars that could not be assigned to a previously defined type. Nor did they warrant the creation of a new ceramic type. All of the ceramic types and groups are described in the following section. Before each of the ceramic types/groups are described, the results of a petrographic study are summarized.

Based on a visual inspection of the Corey site ceramic assemblage, it was clear that most of the ceramic vessels were moderately tempered with granite-like rocks, though a few were lightly tempered and others were more heavily tempered with similar materials. Because the visual inspection of the ceramic sample led to the conclusion that all of the ceramic vessels were tempered with similar materials, it was thought that a petrographic analysis would be a good way to characterize the paste and temper of the Corey site ceramic assemblage. With this thought in mind, twenty-seven sherds were subjected to a detailed petrographic analysis (see chapter 4).

The petrographic analysis determined that virtually all of the sherds were manufactured from locally available clays. These clays were fairly clean, as they lack large numbers of inclusions, and most sherds contained less than 10 percent natural inclusions. When present, inclusions consisted primarily of silt-size quartz fragments. With the exception of a Cayuga Horizontal rim, which contained significantly more quartz inclusions and thus may not have been manufactured at Corey, all appear to have been manufactured from the same clay source.

All of the sherds were tempered with granite-like rocks obtained from nearby glacial tills. The diversity of the raw materials present in these tills is reflected in the heterogeneity of the composition of the temper documented within the Corey site ceramic assemblage. However, while diversity was observed between sherds and vessels, the temper within each sherd or vessel was rather homogenous, suggesting that a single crushed granitic rock was used to temper each vessel or batch of vessels (see chapter 4).

Rims and Decorated Collars

Richmond Incised (n=54; 34 rims, 20 collars)

This ceramic type accounts for 22 percent of the Corey site assemblage (not counting the plain and cordmarked body sherds) and 42 percent of the rims (tables 3.2 and 3.3). Richmond Incised is characterized by collars that have a series of vertical or oblique lines, with the latter often forming line-filled triangles (figure 3.1). Sometimes one or two horizontal lines form the upper border of this motif (S. Clark 1998, 59–66; MacNeish 1952, 51) (figure 3.1c). When present, these lines occur just below the lip. Trailed lines are associated with forty-nine sherds and incised lines with five sherds. The former range from narrow and deep to broad and shallow. This variation is reflected in the width of the trailed lines, which range from 1.26 to 3.77 mm, with a mean of 2.08 mm. Incised lines range in width from 0.75 to 2.47 mm, with a mean of 1.47 mm.

3.1. Richmond Incised ceramics. (Courtesy of Hayward Wilkerson)

All of the rims that could be oriented are direct, and all have flat lips (figure 3.2c, e). Most lips have a well-defined juncture with the rim, but a few have rounded edges. Only two are clearly associated with a castellation. Rim orifice diameter, which could be determined for six rims, ranges from 14 to 20 cm, with a mean of 15.33 cm. Four of the six rims have diameters of 14 cm. The one complete collar had a height of 3.52 cm.

Lips range in thickness from 3.57 to 10.17 mm, with a mean of 7.70 mm. Collar thickness, measured 1 cm below the lip, ranges in thickness from 4.61 to 9.25 mm, with a mean of 7.22 mm. Basal collar thickness ranges from 6.54 to 10 mm, with a mean of 8.43 mm. Vessel neck thickness taken directly below the collar ranges from 4.02 to 6.62 mm, with a mean of 5.41 mm. These data illustrate that jars are thickest at the neck/collar juncture. The collar then thins slightly toward the lip, before thickening again at the lip.

TABLE 3.2. Corey site rims and decorated collars

Ceramic type	Frequency	Percentage
Richmond Incised	54	22.0
Cayuga Horizontal	36	14.6
Richmond Incised/Cayuga Horizontal	129	52.4
Dutch Hollow Notched	14	5.7
Otstungo Notched	2	0.8
Otstungo Incised	1	0.4
Seneca Notched	1	0.4
Ontario Horizontal	2	0.8
Untyped Plain	4	1.6
Untyped Plain rim, Interior Decorated	1	0.4
Untyped Decorated, trailed lines below collar	1	0.4
Untyped Plain rim with deep lip notches	1	0.4
Total	246	100.0

TABLE 3.3. Corey site ceramic rims

Ceramic type	Frequency	Percentage
Richmond Incised	34	42.0
Cayuga Horizontal	23	28.4
Dutch Hollow Notched	14	17.3
Otstungo Notched	2	2.5
Ontario Horizontal	1	1.2
Seneca Notched	1	1.2
Untyped Plain	4	4.9
Untyped Plain rim, Interior Decorated	1	1.2
Untyped Plain rim with deep lip notches	1	1.2
Total	81	100.0

Lip decoration was associated with eighteen of the thirty-four rims. It takes the form of exterior notching (n=5) (figure 3.1c, d) or linear perpendicular or oblique notches that extend across the lip (n=13). One of the former also has interior lip notching.

Notching (n=14) or punctations (n=1) are associated with collar bases (figure 3.1b, c and figure 3.2e, j, l), with one rim exhibiting notching above and below the collar (figure 3.1c). Notching consists of width oblong indentations probably made with a stick (n=10) and more narrow examples made with a fingernail (n=2). One sherd exhibits shallow oval punctations.

A few rims deserve special mention. One is a direct rim with a flat lip and an orifice diameter of 14 cm. It exhibits both exterior and interior notches. A series of oblique trailed lines with a width of 2.23 mm extend from the lip toward the base of the collar.

Another has one of the few complete collars recovered from the site. It exhibits deep exterior lip notches as well as notches at the base of a collar 3.66 cm wide (figure 3.1c and figure 3.2e). The basal thickness of this collar is 9.67 mm. The collar exhibits slight thinning (8.29 mm) toward the lip, which has a thickness of 8.67 mm. The motif associated with this rim consists of broad line-filled triangles bordered by three horizontal lines. Trailed lines associated with this direct rim have a width of 2.78 mm. The lip is flat, and this vessel has an orifice diameter of 14 cm.

A third direct rim has an associated vertical applied notched strip (orifice could not be determined) (figure 3.1a and figure 3.2c). This strip may be part of an effigy (Hayes 1980; figure 3.2a). It is bounded on one side by three vertical incised lines (the motif on the other side is not present). Two parallel incised lines are situated just below a notched flat lip (that is, they extend across the lip). The vertical and horizontal lines bound a series of oblique lines (number could not be determined).

A thin rim (4.68 mm) exhibits shallow lip notching (lip thickness is 3.57 mm) and parallel oblique trailed lines on what is presumed to be a high collar.

Finally, one of the decorated collars has an incised motif and notches that are similar to an Otstungo Incised sherd illustrated by MacNeish (1952, plate XXXI6). Unfortunately, the sherd from Corey lacks its rim, so it could not be determined if the parallel horizontal lines were located

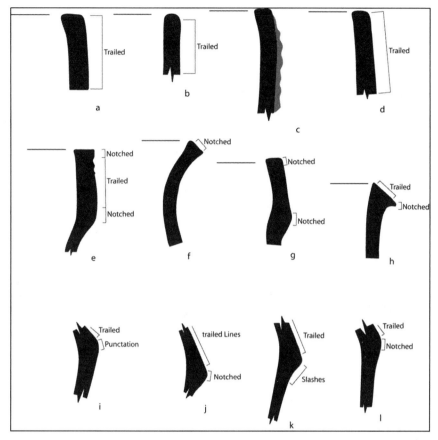

3.2. Profiles: c, e, j, l, Richmond Incised; a, b, d, i, k, Cayuga Horizontal; f, Dutch Hollow Notched; g, Seneca Notched; h, Otstungo Notched. (Courtesy of David Pollack)

directly below the lip. Because Richmond Incised and Otstungo Incised can both have line-filled triangular motifs associated with notched collars, this sherd was assigned to the former type. That this specimen is one of the few incised sherds recovered from Corey, however, could be used to argue that it should be classified as Otstungo Incised.

Cayuga Horizontal (n=36; 23 rims, 13 collars)

This ceramic type accounts for 14.6 percent of the Corey site assemblage (not counting the plain and cordmarked body sherds) and 28.4 percent of the rims (see tables 3.2 and 3.3). It is characterized by high collars that have a series of horizontal lines bounded by vertical or oblique lines (S. Clark 1998, 66; Hayes 1980, figure 2a; MacNeish 1952, 52) (figure 3.3). Collars that met these criteria and collars that were decorated with horizontal lines bounded by notching or punctations, or where a series of horizontal lines was found directly below the lip, were assigned to this type.

Niemczycki (1984, 133) believed that because the horizontal motif was not frequent in the site assemblages she examined, it did not merit a separate classification. In her study, she combined Cayuga Horizontal with Richmond Incised, although she did use the presence of horizontal lines to classify some sherds as Ontario Horizontal (see below). Because the use of horizontal lines as a decorative treatment is quite common in the Corey site assemblage, following Sara Clark (1998; see also Abel 2000), I attempted to distinguish between Richmond Incised and Cayuga Horizontal.

Trailed lines are associated with all of the sherds assigned to this type. All of the motifs are characterized by multiple horizontal lines. Ten examples are clearly bound by oblique or vertical lines (figure 3.3c). Trailed lines range in width from 0.84 to 3.18 mm, with a mean of 2.07 mm. They range from narrow and deep to broad and shallow. Incised lines were not associated with any of the Cayuga Horizontal sherds.

All of the rims that could be oriented are direct, and all of the rims have flat lips (figure 3.2a, b, d). Only two are clearly associated with a castellation. Rim orifice diameter, which could be determined for five rims, ranges from 4 to 22 cm, with a mean of 14 cm. The smallest orifice was derived from a miniature vessel.

Lips range in thickness from 5.97 to 10.33 mm, with a mean of 7.64 mm. Collars, measured 1 cm below the lip, range in thickness from 4.42 to 10.24 mm, with a mean of 7.2 mm. Basal collar thickness ranges from 7.27 to 10.49 mm, with a mean of 9.59 mm. Vessel neck thickness taken directly below the collar ranges from 4.02 to 6.62 mm, with a mean of 5.36 mm. As with Richmond Incised, these data point to thickening of the vessel at the neck/collar juncture, with some thinning of the collar toward the lip.

Decoration was associated with the sixteen of the twenty-three lips (figure 3.3a). It takes the form of exterior notching (n=1), linear perpendicular or oblique notches that extend across the lip (n=14), or oblong notches

3.3. Cayuga Horizontal ceramics. (Courtesy of Hayward Wilkerson)

(n=1) in the center of the lip that do not extend to either edge. In comparison to Richmond Incised, exterior lip notching is not as common.

Notching (n=10) is also associated with collar bases (figures 3.2i, k and 3c). They tend to be deep and oblong in shape. One in particular is very wide, deep, and square. Vertical dashes (ca. 16 mm in length) (figures 3.2k and 3.3b) extend from the bottom of another collar.

Richmond Incised/Cayuga Horizontal (n=129; 129 collars)

This ceramic type accounts for 52.4 percent of the Corey site assemblage (not counting the cordmarked and plain body sherds). It is primarily characterized by collar fragments that exhibit decoration in the form of trailed (n=116) and occasionally incised (n=2) lines. None of the trailed or incised motifs on their collars were of sufficient size to assign them to Richmond Incised or Cayuga Horizontal. Following Sara Clark (1998, 67), they were classified as Richmond Incised/Cayuga Horizontal. Also assigned to this group were twelve sherds that exhibit notching at the base of the collar. Unfortunately, these sherds were not of sufficient size to determine if the notches were associated with plain or decorated collars. Because these notches are consistent with the ones associated with Richmond Incised or Cayuga Horizontal, they were assigned to this group, though the possibility that they are derived from Seneca Notched vessels cannot be totally ruled out.

Trailed line width ranges from 1.12 to 3.50 mm, with a mean of 2.04 mm. Line width for the two incised sherds ranges from 0.71 to 1.63 mm, with a mean of 1.17 mm. Most of the trailed lines consisted of one or more parallel (n=76) or intersecting (n=27) lines that could not be oriented. Thirteen small sherds exhibited a single trailed line. One of the incised sherds consisted of a fragment of a motif with intersecting lines and the other two parallel lines.

Notching was associated with the base of eleven collars, with the remainder of the collar missing. Most notches were oblong, but on one specimen they were similar to the dashes associated with one of the Richmond Incised collars. Basal collar thickness ranges from 6.27 to 9.83 mm, with a mean of 7.90 mm. Vessel neck thickness, measured 1 cm below the collar, ranges from 4.12 to 9.85 mm, with a mean of 7.03 mm.

Dutch Hollow Notched (n=14; 14 rims)

This ceramic type accounts for 5.6 percent of the Corey site assemblage (not counting the cordmarked and plain body sherds) and 17.3 percent of the rims (figures 3.2f, 3.4, and 3.5b, c) (see tables 3.2 and 3.3). Dutch Hollow Notched is one of three collarless ceramic types recovered from the Corey site. The presence of lip notching distinguishes this type and Otstungo Notched from Untyped Plain (rims assigned to this group lack any form of decoration). On Dutch Hollow vessels, notching may occur on the exterior of the lip (n=8) (figure 3.5b, c) or across the lip (n=6) (figure 3.4).

3.4. Dutch Hollow Notched ceramic. (Courtesy of Hayward Wilkerson)

Lip thickness ranges from 4.63 to 10.86 mm, with a mean of 7.60 mm. Rim thickness, measured 1 cm below the rim, ranges from 4.69 to 10.05 mm, with a mean of 6.76 mm. Neck thickness could be determined for only one sherd. It has a thickness of 5.80 mm.

Though it lacks a collar, one of the rims has an associated rimfold and castellation. The rimfold has a width of 8.24 mm and a thickness of 10.52 mm. Shallow exterior notching is present.

Of the remaining thirteen rims, ten are unmodified and three are wedge shaped (that is, they exhibit thickening of the rim). Five of the unmodified rims exhibit exterior lip notching, and five have notching that extends across the lip. Two of the former exhibit wide, very shallow notches; two are much narrower and somewhat deeper; and the fifth exhibits notches that are much deeper and are associated with a castellation. These five rims could not be oriented.

Three unmodified rims exhibit wide and very shallow notches that extend across the lip. These rims could not be oriented. Another specimen exhibits wide and very deep notches that also extend across the lip, creating an almost crenulated lip. This rim is direct, with an orifice diameter of 8 cm.

The last of the unmodified rims exhibits closely spaced deep notches that extend across a castellated lip (figure 3.2f and figure 3.4). About 50 percent of this vessel was recovered. Its rim is slightly outflaring, with an orifice diameter of 12 cm, and the vessel has a conoidal shape.

Of the wedge-shaped rims, two have a rounded exterior wedges and a direct orientation, while the third has a sharply angled wedge and a slightly outflaring orientation. The rounded wedges have well-defined exterior lip notches, while the angled wedge has long oblique notches.

Otstungo Notched (n=2; 2 rims)

This ceramic type accounts for 0.8 percent of the Corey site assemblage (not counting the cordmarked and plain body sherds) and 2.5 percent of the rims. Like Dutch Hollow Notched, this collarless ceramic type is characterized by wedged-shaped rims with notched lips (figures 3.2h and 3.5a). It is distinguished from Dutch Hollow Notched by the presence of shallow trailed lines on the lip that encircle the entire vessel (figures 3.2h and 3.5a) (MacNeish 1952, 75–76).

Both of the rims assigned to this type have well-defined exterior lip notches. One has a rounded wedge with a single trailed line (line width is 1.17 mm). This rim is slightly outflaring, with an orifice diameter of 18 cm. The other rim has an angled wedge and two parallel trailed lines (line width is 2.90 mm) (figures 3.2h and 3.5a). The orifice diameter of the this rim could not be determined.

Otstungo Incised (n=1; 1 collar)

This ceramic type accounts for 0.4 percent of the Corey site assemblage (not counting the cordmarked and plain body sherds) (see table 3.2). It is characterized by a series of notches bounded by oblique lines (MacNeish 1952; Niemczycki 1984). The Corey site collar is small, measuring less than 4 cm^2 in size. It consists of two trailed lines (line width is 2.42 mm) on either side of a series of notches.

3.5. Otstungo Notched (a) and Dutch Hollow Notched (b, c). (Courtesy of Hayward Wilkerson)

Seneca Notched (n=1; 1 rim)

This type accounts for 0.4 percent of the Corey site assemblage (not counting the cordmarked and plain body sherds) and 1.7 percent of the rims (see tables 3.2 and 3.3). Seneca Notched is characterized by jars with exterior lip notching and notching of the bottom of an otherwise plain collar (figure 3.6). Only one rim assignable to this type was recovered from the Corey site. Notches on the exterior of the lip and the base of the collar are broad and wide. This rim is direct in profile with an orifice diameter of 16 cm (figure 3.2g). It has a flat lip with a thickness of 7.14 mm. The collar has a thickness of 6.86 mm (1 cm below the lip). The base of the collar has a thickness of 9.40 mm. The collar has a height of 3.18 cm.

Ontario Horizontal (n=2; 1 rim, 1 collar)

This ceramic type accounts for 0.8 percent of the Corey site assemblage (not counting the cordmarked and plain body sherds) and 1.2 percent of the rims (see tables 3.2 and 3.3). As with Cayuga Horizontal, this type is

3.6. Seneca Notched ceramic. (Courtesy of Hayward Wilkerson)

characterized by horizontal lines often bordered by notching or puncta-tions at the base of the collar. It is primarily distinguished from Cayuga Horizontal by a shorter collar and fewer horizontal lines (often only two or three lines are present).

The rim is associated with a complete collar that exhibits two trailed horizontal lines (line width is 1.93 mm) bordered by oblong notches. The collar has a height of 1.55 cm. The collar fragment has a least three hori-zontal incised lines (line width is 1.96 mm) bordered by a vertical row of small circular punctations adjacent to an applied strip and a series of triangular punctations at the base of the collar.

Untyped Plain Rims (n=4; 4 rims)

This ceramic group accounts for 1.6 percent of the Corey site assemblage (not counting the cordmarked and plain body sherds) and 4.9 percent of the rims (see tables 3.2 and 3.3). (For comparative and descriptive purposes, these rims are described separately from the Untyped Plain body sherds.) Plain jars along with Dutch Hollow Notched and Otstungo Notched jars lack collars. All of the rims assigned to this group were less than 4 cm² in size. Given the small size of these rims, it is possible that they are derived from Dutch Hollow Notched vessels, but they are not of sufficient size to exhibit the lip notching that is the hallmark of this type.

All four rims have flat lips. Two are wedge shaped, one is rounded, and one is sharply angled. One of the wedge-shaped rims has a lip thickness of 9.90 mm and a thickness of 4.73 mm 1 cm below the lip. The lip thickness of the other wedged-shaped rims could not be determined. The third rim has a lip thickness of 9.40 mm, and the fourth rim has a lip thickness of 9.90 mm and is castellated.

Untyped Plain Rim, Interior Decoration (n=1; 1 rim)

This type accounts for 0.3 percent of the Corey site assemblage (not counting the cordmarked and plain body sherds) and 1.7 percent of the rims (see tables 3.2 and 3.3). The shape of this rim is similar to that of the sharply angled wedge-shaped rims associated with Dutch Hollow Notched and Untyped Plain. It is distinguished from both, however, by shallow oblique parallel trailed lines on the interior. These lines have a width of 2.26 mm. The flat lip has a thickness of 9.25 mm and the rim a thickness of 6.79 mm. The rim could not be oriented.

Untyped Plain Rim with Deep Lip Notches (n=1; 1 rim)

This type accounts for 0.3 percent of the Corey site assemblage (not counting the cordmarked and plain body sherds) and 1.2 percent of the rims (see tables 3.2 and 3.3). This small rim has a rounded lip (lip thickness is 8.45 mm), with deep, wide notches on either side of the lip. Both notches extend across the lip. The width and deepness of the two notches distinguish this specimen from Dutch Hollow Notched.

Untyped Decorated with Trailed Lines below Collar (n=1; 1 collar)

This type accounts for 0.4 percent of the Corey site assemblage (not counting the cordmarked and plain body sherds) (see table 3.2). It is

3.7. Trailed lines below collar. (Courtesy of Hayward Wilkerson)

characterized by two wide, shallow trailed lines located on the neck just below where the collar starts to thicken (figure 3.7). The presence of similar decoration was noted on a sherd from the Indian Fort Road site, across Cayuga Lake from Corey, near Perry City (S. Clark 1998, 70–71). On the Indian Fort Road specimen, however, the trailed lines are clearly located just below a notched wedge-shaped rim. The trailed lines associated with the Corey site specimen have a width of 2.58 mm. The neck below the decoration has a thickness of 5.08 mm.

Plain and Cordmarked Bodies, Necks, and Collars

Untyped Plain (n=78; 72 bodies, 5 necks; 1 collar)

These sherds account for 18.3 percent of the Corey site assemblage. (For intersite comparative purposes, the four rims assigned to this group are described above.) Most exhibit well-smoothed exterior surfaces, but a few are poorly smoothed. Body sherd thickness ranges from 4.12 to 9.06 mm, with a mean of 6.14 mm. Neck thickness ranges from 4.01 to 7.39 mm, with a mean of 5.67 mm. The one collar is from a section of a small vessel that is lacking a rim. It has a thickness of 7.73 mm at the collar-neck juncture. The collar thins to 2.67 mm just below the rim, and the neck has a thickness of 6.25 mm.

Untyped Cordmarked (n=103; 102 bodies, 1 collar)

These sherds account for 24.1 percent of the Corey site assemblage (see table 3.1). Twist was determined for fifty-eight specimens, with twenty-one (36.2 percent) being S-twist and thirty-seven (63.8 percent) being Z-twist.

With the exception of one collar, all of the specimens are body sherds. The collar is derived from a jar with a cordmarked body and a plain collar. Unfortunately, not enough of the collar was recovered to determine if it had also been decorated. The collar has a thickness of 6.32 mm. Body sherd thickness ranges from 4.02 to 8.77 mm, with a mean of 6.28 mm.

Nonvessel Clay Objects

Two nonvessel ceramics objects were recovered from the Corey site. One consists of an untempered clay cylinder, and one is a fragment of fired clay.

Clay Cylinder (n=1)

The clay cylinder has a diameter of 9.33 mm. It is broken on both ends, with the remaining section having a length of 2.1 cm. This cylinder is light brown to tan in color and does not appear to contain any temper. Its function could not be determined.

Fired Clay (n=1)

One large fragment of fired clay was recovered from the Corey site. It measures 1.88 mm by 17.58 mm, with a thickness of 11.44 mm. The clay does not appear to contain any temper. That it is well fired suggests that it may have originally been associated with a hearth.

Summary and Discussion

Untyped Cordmarked and Untyped Plain sherds account for slightly more than 40 percent of the analyzed ceramic sample, and when considered with the unanalyzed plain and cordmarked body sherds, they account for almost 80 percent of the ceramics recovered from the Corey site. That Untyped Cordmarked (24.1 percent) sherds account for slightly more of the assemblage than Untyped Plain (19.2 percent) (see table 3.1) suggests that a large number of vessels had cordmarked bodies. Vessel necks, however, are predominantly plain. As a group, Untyped Cordmarked and Untyped Plain body sherds have a mean thickness of 6.22 mm, necks a mean thickness of 5.67 mm, the one plain collar a thickness of 6.32 mm, and the one cordmarked collar base a thickness of 6.25 mm.

Most of the eighty-one rims are direct, though a few are slightly flaring. Based on the size and orientation of these rims, all appear to be derived from jars. Jar vessel orifice diameter could be determined for fifteen rims. It ranges from 4 to 22 cm, with a mean diameter of 14.40 cm. Five of the rims have an orifice diameter of 14 cm. Of the remaining rims, four have diameters of 12 cm or less, and six have diameters 16 cm or greater. The rim with a 4 cm diameter is associated with a miniature Cayuga Horizontal vessel.

Though jar shape could not be determined for most of the rims, one fairly complete vessel has a conoidal shape. Based on comparisons with other site assemblages, it can be suggested that it was the dominant jar shape at Corey.

When present collars tend to be thicker than vessel necks. Collars are thickest at the vessel/collar juncture (mean is 8.44 mm). They thin slightly toward the lip (mean is 7.02 mm, 1 cm below the lip), before thickening again at the lip (mean is 7.90 mm). Lips are primarily flat and slightly thicker than the collar. Collarless rims recovered from Corey have a lip thickness of 7.75 mm and 6.08 mm (1 cm below the lip). Wedge-shaped lips have a width of 11.12 mm and 7.30 mm (1 cm below the lip).

Vessel orifice diameter could be determined for fifteen rims. It ranges from 4 to 22 cm, with a mean diameter of 14.40 cm. Of the fifteen rims for which orifice diameter could be determined, a third have an orifice diameter of 14 cm. Of the remaining rims, four have diameters of 12 cm or less, and six have diameters 16 cm or greater. The rim with a 4 cm diameter is associated with a miniature Cayuga Horizontal vessel.

With respect to decorated ceramic types, the Corey site ceramic assemblage is dominated by Richmond Incised, Cayuga Horizontal, and Richmond Incised/Cayuga Horizontal. The most common motifs are line-filled triangles and horizontal bands bounded by diagonal or vertical lines. Most of the motifs were made with trailed lines; only seven incised sherds are present. Trailed lines have an average width of 2.04 mm and incised lines an average width of 1.38 mm. The former tend to be wider and shallower than the latter, though the width of these lines is, in part, related to vessel size. In general, the larger the vessel, the wider the trailed line.

Lip notching is associated with fifty-one of the eighty-one rims recovered from the Corey site. Not surprisingly, notching is associated with all of the Dutch Hollow Notched, Otstungo Notched, and Seneca Notched rims, because, as their name implies, notching is the primary decoration associated with these types. The two Otstungo Notched rims and the one Seneca Notched rim exhibit exterior lip notching, as do 58.3 percent of the Dutch Hollow Notched rims. The remaining Dutch Hollow rims exhibit notches that extend across the lip.

Notched lips are associated with 69.6 percent of the Cayuga Horizontal and 52.3 percent of the Richmond Incised rims. When present, notching on Cayuga Horizontal rims (87.5 percent) almost always extends across the entire lip. This decorative motif stands in contrast to Richmond Incised, where 72.2 percent exhibit this form of notching, with the remaining 27.8 percent exhibiting exterior lip notching. That lip notching is more common on Seneca ceramic types than traditional Cayuga types suggests that it is more of a Seneca than a Cayuga ceramic trait.

Niemczycki (1984, 42, table 8) assigned Corey to the early Iroquois period (AD 1350 to 1450). It is not entirely evident from her report what this assignment was based on, as materials from Corey were not included in her analyses. That the Corey site assemblage lacks corded collars, however, is indicative of a post–AD 1350 occupation (Niemczycki 1984, 33). The predominance of Richmond Incised and Cayuga Horizontal, some with high collars, coupled with a respectable amount of Dutch Hollow Notched and the presence of a Seneca Notched rim is suggestive of a post–AD 1450 occupation (Niemczycki 1984, 32, table 3; 35, table 4). On the other hand, the absence of Genoa Frilled and Seneca Bared is suggestive of a pre–AD 1550 occupation. As will be discussed later in this chapter in comparison to nearby sites included in Niemczycki's study, Corey has most in common with Nolan, which she suggested dated from AD 1500 to 1600.

Context

At Corey ceramics were recovered from surface, unit, and feature contexts (tables 3.4–3.6). All levels represent an identical depth across the site and are considered contemporary. Because only a few sherds were recovered from surface contexts, the following discussion focuses on the ones recovered from levels within units and from features.

Ceramics were recovered from Levels 1 through 7, with most being recovered from Levels 1 through 5 (see table 3.4). Only eight analyzable sherds were recovered from Levels 6 and 7. Untyped Cordmarked sherds account for 57.1 percent of the sherds from Level 5, but for only 20 percent of the sherds from Level 4. They peak again in Level 2, but for the most part after Level 5, they account for only about one-quarter of the sherds. Untyped Plain sherds have a somewhat different distribution, accounting for only 5 percent of the ceramics from Levels 4 and 5, but about 30 percent of the sherds in Levels 1 and 3, with a slight decline in Level 2. Overall, these trends suggest a decrease in cordmarked vessels through time.

By Level 5 Richmond Incised accounts for 14.3 percent of the sherds, and after that level it never accounts for more than 25 percent of the assemblage. In comparison, Cayuga Horizontal is not present until Level 4, when it accounts for 15 percent of the assemblage. Though it dips in popularity in Level 3 to 5.8 percent, by Levels 1 and 2 it again accounts for about 15 percent of the assemblage. Richmond Incised/Cayuga Horizontal is present in all levels, accounting for as much as 35 percent of the sherds in Level 4 to as little as 2.9 percent of the sherds in Level 2.

TABLE 3.4. Distribution of ceramics by level

		Level							Total
		1	2	3	4	5	6	7	
Richmond Incised	Frequency	6	7	13	3	3	2	0	34
	Percentage	15.4	20.0	25.0	15.0	14.3	28.6	.0	19.4
Cayuga Horizontal	Frequency	6	5	3	3	0	0	0	17
	Percentage	15.4	14.3	5.8	15.0	.0	.0	.0	9.7
Richmond/Cayuga	Frequency	5	1	4	7	2	2	1	22
	Percentage	12.8	2.9	7.7	35.0	9.5	28.6	100.0	12.6
Dutch Hollow Notched	Frequency	2	3	2	1	3	0	0	11
	Percentage	5.1	8.6	3.8	5.0	14.3	.0	.0	6.3
Otstungo Notched	Frequency	0	0	0	1	0	0	0	1
	Percentage	.0	.0	.0	5.0	.0	.0	.0	.6
Ontario Horizontal	Frequency	0	1	0	0	0	0	0	1
	Percentage	.0	2.9	.0	.0	.0	.0	.0	.6
Untyped Plain	Frequency	12	5	16	1	1	1	0	36
	Percentage	30.8	14.3	30.8	5.0	4.8	14.3	.0	20.6
Untyped Cordmarked	Frequency	8	13	13	4	12	2	0	52
	Percentage	20.5	37.1	25.0	20.0	57.1	28.6	.0	29.7
Plain rim with possible effigy	Frequency	0	0	1	0	0	0	0	1
	Percentage	.0	.0	1.9	.0	.0	.0	.0	.6
Total	Frequency	39	35	52	20	21	7	1	175
	Percentage	100.0	100.0	100.0	100.0	100.0	100.0	100.0	100.0

TABLE 3·5 · Ceramics recovered from features

					Feature Number					
		Units/Surface	*1*	*11*	*12b*	*15*	*2*	*3*	Total
Richmond Incised	Frequency	36	2	1	1	0	1	4	45
	Percentage	19.6	5.4	50.0	3.3	.0	11.1	7.4	14.2
Cayuga Horizontal	Frequency	20	4	0	2	0	0	8	34
	Percentage	10.9	10.8	.0	6.7	.0	.0	14.8	10.7
Ontario Horizontal	Frequency	2	0	0	0	0	0	0	2
	Percentage	1.1	.0	.0	.0	.0	.0	.0	.6
Richmond/Cayuga	Frequency	23	2	0	2	0	0	4	31
	Percentage	12.5	5.4	.0	6.7	.0	.0	7.4	9.8
Dutch Hollow Notched	Frequency	11	1	1	0	0	0	1	14
	Percentage	6.0	2.7	50.0	.0	.0	.0	1.9	4.4
Otstungo Notched	Frequency	1	0	0	0	0	0	1	2
	Percentage	.5	.0	.0	.0	.0	.0	1.9	.6

									Total
Plain	Frequency	36	19	0	9	0	5	13	82
	Percentage	19.6	51.4	.0	30.0	.0	55.6	24.1	25.9
Cordmarked	Frequency	54	7	0	15	1	3	23	103
	Percentage	29.3	18.9	.0	50.0	100.0	33.3	42.6	32.5
Seneca Notched	Frequency	0	1	0	0	0	0	0	1
	Percentage	.0	2.7	.0	.0	.0	.0	.0	.3
Untyped Interior dec	Frequency	0	1	0	0	0	0	0	1
	Percentage	.0	2.7	.0	.0	.0	.0	.0	.3
Decoration below collar	Frequency	0	0	0	1	0	0	0	1
	Percentage	.0	.0	.0	3.3	.0	.0	.0	.3
Plain rim with possible effigy	Frequency	1	0	0	0	0	0	0	1
	Percentage	.5	.0	.0	.0	.0	.0	.0	.3
Total	Frequency	184	37	2	30	1	9	54	317
	Percentage	100.0	100.0	100.0	100.0	100.0	100.0	100.0	100.0

TABLE 3.6. Comparison of Corey and Indian Fort Road site decorated rims and collars

Ceramic type	Corey		Indian Fort Road	
	Frequency	Percentage	Frequency	Percentage
Richmond Incised	54	22.3	16	20.5
Cayuga Horizontal	36	14.9	5	6.4
Richmond Incised/ Cayuga Horizontal	129	53.3	42*	53.8
Ontario Horizontal	2	0.8	0	0.0
Dutch Hollow Notched/ Otstungo Notched	16	6.6	4	5.1
Otstungo Incised	1	0.4	1	1.3
Seneca Notched	1	0.4	0	0.0
Untyped Trailed below collar/rim	1	0.4	1	1.3
Rice Diagonal	0	0.0	3	3.8
Warminster Crossed	0	0.0	1	1.3
Ripley Triangular	0	0.0	1	1.3
Unidentifiable	2	0.8	4	20.5
Total	242	100.0	78	100.0

* Includes collar fragments where only the basal notching was present, which were classified by Clark as unidentified. Plain rims not included.

As a group, Dutch Hollow Notched and Otstungo Notched exhibit a distributional pattern similar to that of Untyped Cordmarked vessels. They peak in Levels 5 and 2 and have similar percentages in Levels 1, 3, and 4. These patterns are suggestive of a decline in the popularity of decorated uncollared vessels relative to decorated collared vessels.

Ceramics were recovered from six features, three of which yielded fewer than ten analyzable sherds (see table 3.5). Of the three features that yielded larger amounts of ceramics (Features 1, 3, and 12b), Untyped Cordmarked specimens account for 50 and 42.6 percent, respectively, of the ceramic recovered from Features 12b and 3, but only 18.9 percent of the sherds from Feature 1. In comparison, Untyped Plain sherds account for 51.4 percent of the ceramics from Feature 1, but only 24.1 percent of the sherds from Feature 3 and 30 percent from Feature 12b.

Richmond Incised accounts for 3.3 to 7.4 percent of the sherds from Features 1, 3, and 12b. In comparison, Cayuga Horizontal accounts for 6.7 to 14.8 percent of the ceramics from these features. These lower percentages stand in sharp contrast to the level data, where Richmond Incised is more prevalent than Cayuga Horizontal. The combination of uncollared Dutch Hollow Notched/Otstungo Notched was recovered from Features 1 and 3, and Seneca Notched was recovered only from Feature 1.

Among the three features that yielded a large amount of ceramics, Feature 1 may postdate the other two. This suggestion is based on the high percentage of Untyped Plain, Richmond Incised, and Cayuga Horizontal ceramics recovered from this feature relative to the other two.

Intersite Comparisons

That the Corey site assemblage is dominated by Richmond Incised, Cayuga Horizontal, and Richmond Incised/Cayuga Horizontal is consistent with what has been observed at other Cayuga sites (S. Clark 1998; MacNeish 1952; Niemczycki 1984) (see tables 3.6 and 3.7). For instance, these types constitute 90 percent of the decorated ceramics from Corey and 80 percent of the ceramics from the (west Cayuga Lake) Indian Fort Road site (S. Clark 1998), whose primary occupation dates from AD 1520–1560, contemporary or just earlier than Corey (Sanft 2013; see table 3.6). As a group, Dutch Hollow Notched and Otstungo Notched collarless vessels are the third most common ceramic type, accounting for a similar percentage of the ceramics at these two sites.

With respect to other decorated types, the primary differences between Corey and Indian Fort Road are reflected by a much higher percentage of Cayuga Horizontal at Corey than at Indian Fort Road, the presence of a wider range of minor types at Indian Fort Road than Corey, and the almost exclusive use of incising at Indian Fort Road versus trailing at Corey (see table 3.6). The latter difference is primarily related to how the Indian Fort Road researchers distinguish between incised and trailed ceramics. At Indian Fort Road, only one trailed sherd was identified. It was classified as such based on the width and shallowness of the lines (S. Clark 1998, 71). Yet many of the illustrated ceramics in Clark's report exhibit the U-shaped appearance that was used in this analysis to classify the decoration as trailing. Thus, the observed differences in incising versus trailing probably have more to do with analytical definitions than intersite cultural differences.

Corey is also distinguished from the Indian Fort Road site by a much greater quantity of cordmarked specimens. In fact, very few cordmarked specimens were recovered from the Indian Fort Road site. But at Corey they account for almost a quarter of the sherds (see table 3.1). The larger amount of cordmarked ceramics at Corey relative to Indian Fort Road coupled with the decline in the use of cordmarking as a surface treatment after AD 1400 (Snow 1994, 36, as cited in S. Clark 1998, 72) would normally suggest that Corey was occupied somewhat earlier than the Indian Fort Road site (S. Clark 1998), although radiocarbon dates do not support this idea (Sanft 2013). That in other respects these two site assemblages are extremely similar, however, suggests some degree of contemporaneity, which is more in line with the radiocarbon dates. In this regard it is worth noting that none of the decorated ceramic types are associated with cordmarked bodies. Nor were any rims assigned to this ceramic group.

The Corey site ceramic assemblage was also compared to select sites included in Niemczycki's 1984 study (see table 3.5). The focus of this comparison was those sites that had thirty or more decorated rims or collars, were located in close proximity to Corey or on the west site of the Cayuga Lake, and were occupied between AD 1400 and 1600. At all of these sites Richmond Incised/Cayuga Horizontal accounts for at least 40 percent of the rims and collars, with Dutch Hollow Notched/Otstungo Notched being the next most common type. Of the two sites located in close proximity to Corey, it has more in common with Nolan, which was occupied sometime between AD 1500 and 1600, than Weir, which was occupied sometime between AD 1400 and 1550 (table 3.7). The primary difference between Corey and Nolan is the higher percentage of Ontario Horizontal at the latter and the higher percentage of Dutch Hollow Notched/Otstungo Notched at the former. Based on this comparison, it would appear that Corey was occupied toward the end of the 1400s and perhaps into the 1500s.

TABLE 3.7. Comparison of Corey with select nearby sites

| | Corey | | Located near Corey | | | | Located West Cayuga Lake, south of Corey | | | |
| | | | Weir* | | Nolan (Landon)** | | Parker Farm** | | Klinko* | |
	No.	%	No.	%	No.	%	No.	%	No.	%
Richmond Incised/Cayuga Horizontal	57	74.0	50	43.0	90	79.0	22	51.0	73	47.0
Ontario Horizontal	1	1.3	2	2.0	10	9.0	2	5.0		
Dutch Hollow Notched/Otstungo Notched	16	20.8	38	33.0	15	13.0	10	23.0	51	33.0
Seneca Notched	1	1.3					3	7.0		
Other	2	2.6	26	22.4	2	2.0	6	14.3	30	19.2
Total	77	100.0	116	100.8	117	102.9	43	100.3	154	100.0

* Niemczycki 1984, 35 (AD 1400-1550); ** Niemczycki 1984, 38 (AD 1500-1660);

Seneca ceramic types, such as Dutch Hollow Notched and Seneca Notched, and the Mohawk type, Otstungo Notched, account for 22.1 percent of the rims from Corey. Several of the Dutch Hollow and the two Otstungo Notched rims at Corey also exhibit the wedge-shaped collarless profile associated with many of these vessels at Seneca sites (Hayes 1980, figure 2a; Wray et al. 1987; Wray, Sempowski, and Saunders 1991). As with other Cayuga sites, the presence of these types as well as their lip shape reflects some level of interaction between Cayuga and Seneca groups.

Conclusion

The Corey site assemblage is dominated by Richmond Incised, Cayuga Horizontal, and Dutch Hollow Notched/Otstungo Notched. Most vessels have collars, and most collars are decorated with trailed lines and notches. Lip notching is also common. Overall, the assemblage is consistent with a village that was occupied between AD 1450 and 1550. The high percentage of cordmarked sherds relative to the Indian Fort Road suggests that Corey was occupied somewhat earlier in the Cayuga sequence than this village or that it contains more than one component. The presence of Dutch Hollow Notched and Seneca Notched reflects some level of interaction between residents of the Cayuga and Seneca sites.

4

Petrographic Analysis of Ceramics

Wesley D. Stoner

Petrographic point counting is a very useful technique for characterizing ancient pottery. At a basic level, petrographic analysis is used to identify mineral and textural variation within a ceramic assemblage. This variation is introduced into a ceramic vessel through two major means: the use of different raw material sources and different paste recipes for production.

The first source of variation provides the means to associate a ceramic sherd with different raw material sources on the landscape. Knowledge of the geological availability and distribution of clay outcrops and temper has in many cases proven useful for characterizing raw material procurement strategies employed by ancient potters (Arnold 1985).

The second source of compositional variation is also interesting and culturally relevant. Ancient potters chose different materials to produce their ceramics, processed those materials in different ways, and combined clays and temper in different proportions. The particular method for doing so is referred to as a *paste recipe*. Paste recipes can vary from one ceramic-producing community to another (Arnold, Bishop, and Neff 1991; Stoner et al. 2003). Paste recipes may also be constrained by cultural norms, as they are passed down from one generation to another. They therefore represent a particularly durable aspect of social identity that may indicate real differences between social groups (Gosselain 2000; Sillar and Tite 2000).

Before describing the petrographic methods in more detail, it should be mentioned that precise results require a regional comparative database of pottery and raw materials. This analysis is the first attempt to characterize Cayuga pottery in this way, so little can be said about interaction between sites. By initiating such a study, it is hoped that others will follow suit and conduct additional compositional characterizations of Cayuga pottery to develop a regional comparative database.

Petrographic point-counting analysis was undertaken on twenty-seven sherds recovered from the Corey site in order to characterize textural and mineral variation within this assemblage. For comparative purposes, two sherds from the nearby Great Gully Farm site were also examined. Among the ceramic types sampled from Corey were Richmond Incised, Cayuga Horizontal, Dutch Hollow Notched, Otstungo Notched, and Seneca Notched. Also sampled were plain and cordmarked body sherds.

This petrographic analysis attempted to address the following questions:

1. Is there textural or mineralogical variation (or both) among the ceramic types/groups sampled?

    a. Were the clays of a fine texture, or did they contain large amounts of natural aplastic inclusions?

    b. What kind of temper was used?

    c. What is the likely source of this temper?

2. What is the likelihood that some of the ceramics recovered from the Corey site represent extraregional procurement or exchange?

Methods

The petrographic techniques employed in this research combine qualitative mineral identification and quantitative point counting (Betts 1991; Day et al. 1999; Stoltman 1989, 1991; Stoner 2002). Initially, a 0.667-meter grid was used to count the grains, but this method proved to be impractical, as on average the temper grains measured from one to two millimeters in size. The grid was thus increased to one millimeter. In addition to identifying all of the minerals, the size of the grain was measured and categorized using the Wentworth Scale (silt, very fine sand, fine sand, medium sand, coarse sand, very coarse sand, or granule). Also characterized was the angularity of the grain, which permits, in part, the differentiation of temper (often crushed and thus angular) versus natural inclusions in the clay (most often displaying a more rounded shape) to be identified.

Early in the point-counting phase of analysis, it was determined that three separate measures would be useful in this analysis. First, clays used to manufacture the ceramic were characterized according to their texture, percentage of natural aplastic inclusions, and type of mineral inclusions. This measure is useful to characterize the type of clays used to manufacture the pots in question. Variation would potentially indicate the use of different clay sources to manufacture the sample.

The second measure was specifically designed to determine what type of rock was used to temper the ceramics. In almost all cases, a granite-like igneous rock was used as temper. To determine the type of rock used, qualitative mineral information on the composition of each temper grain was collected. Different types of granite-like rocks are characterized based on the relative proportion of plagioclase feldspar, K-feldspar, and quartz.

The third measure specifically targeted the size and frequency of the temper grains. This measure is more sensitive to the cultural behavior of crushing the temper before mixing it into the paste. It is particularly useful to compare temper size and amount to the proportion of clay and nontemper, natural aplastic inclusions in the raw clays. The value of each measure, and the statistical techniques used to assess each, will be discussed further below.

Results

In general, all specimens sampled were made of fine-textured clays with few aplastic inclusions. There was, however, a significant textural difference between the clays used at the Corey site and the clay used to make the two specimens from the Great Gully Farm site. Clays used to manufacture the Great Gully Farm ceramics contained many more natural aplastic inclusions than with the Corey ceramics. Most of the natural inclusions in the Great Gully Farm ceramics were silt-size quartz grains, but individual muscovite minerals that were visible at 10x magnification were also observed in the paste of these ceramics. While silt-size quartz inclusions also were observed in the paste of the Corey site ceramics, the muscovite in the paste of these sherds was so small that individual grains could not be identified. This observation suggests that the ceramics from these two nearby sites were produced using distinct clay sources.

Among the Corey site sample, a Cayuga Horizontal rim (JR24) contained significantly more quartz inclusions than the other sherds recovered from this site. This difference does not necessarily indicate that it represents a nonlocal trade sherd, but it does suggest that a different clay source was used to manufacture this vessel. The remainder of the Corey ceramics appear to have been produced using a single clay source.

All of the specimens were tempered with some type of granite-like rock such as granitic feldspar. The minerals in this rock sometimes displayed alteration, in the case of K-feldspar and plagioclase, and stressing was rarely identified in the case of quartz. Stressed quartz is typically found in granite gneiss, which is a metamorphic rock that altered directly from granite. (It should be noted that the temper grains observed in the paste were often very small, which made it difficult to differentiate granitic gneiss from granite, but I am confident that the overwhelming majority of the temper identified was from igneous rock.)

The igneous rocks used to temper ceramic vessels at Corey and Great Gully Farm might be expected to have been obtained from glacial tills that can be found throughout the region. Glacial tills consist of many different types of rock. It may thus be significant that the potters at Corey and Great Gully Farm specifically targeted granite-like rock to temper their vessels.

There may be properties of this rock that are particularly advantageous for use as temper (for example, crushability, angularity of crushed grains, and thermal shock resistance). Alternatively, cultural preferences may have dictated the selection of granitic rock.

An interesting tempering pattern was observed at both sites. While the composition of the granitic rock used as temper varied from one sherd to the next, the overall composition of temper within each specimen was rather homogeneous. This observation suggests that the temper used to produce each vessel was derived from a single crushed rock, rather than several different rocks. It also suggests that potters did not produce and stockpile a large amount of temper in advance of ceramic production. Creation of a stockpile would have required the crushing of several rocks, which would have resulted in a more heterogeneous temper, though such a temper would appear to be more homogenous, as many sherds would have a similar temper composition. It is also possible that stockpiled temper may have been crushed gradually during the process of pottery manufacturing. (Editor's note: the presence of nonlocal temper chunks throughout the site suggests the latter scenario.) The possibility that river sediment or gravel was used as temper can be ruled out. Such a source for temper would be much more heterogeneous (but more homogenous within the sample). Therefore, it seems that potters selected a single granitic rock and crushed it for temper as needed.

To determine the specific type of rock used to temper each specimen, the sample was plotted on a QAPF diagram (Streckeisen 1974). (A QAPF diagram is a double triangle diagram that is used to classify igneous rocks based on mineralogical composition. QAPF stands for quartz, alkali feldspar, plagioclase, and feldspathoid [foid], the mineral groups used for classification in a QAPF diagram. Q, A, P, and F percentages are normalized, that is, recalculated so that their sum is 100 percent.) Because no feldspathoid minerals were identified, only the top triangle of this diamond-shaped diagram was used (figure 4.1). The majority of tempering rocks were quartz monzonite (n=8) or quartz monzodiorite (n=8). Quartz monzonite contains about equal proportions of alkali feldspars (orthoclase, sanidine, microcline) and plagioclase minerals with significant amounts of quartz (5–20 percent).[1] It is often confused with granite; the only difference is that granite has greater than 20 percent quartz. Quartz monzodiorite contains somewhat higher proportions of plagioclase than alkali feldspars but similar amounts of quartz as quartz monzonite. The next most frequently occurring temper type was granite (n=7). Granite contains relatively equal proportions of alkali feldspar (35–90 percent), plagioclase (10–65 percent), and quartz (20–60 percent), but alkali feldspar may be more prevalent. Three other types of rock occurred in equal proportions. Granodiorite (n=2) contains more plagioclase than alkali feldspar but similar proportions of quartz as granite. Monzodiorite (n=2)

---

1. Alkali feldspars identified in this study were limited to orthoclase and microcline.

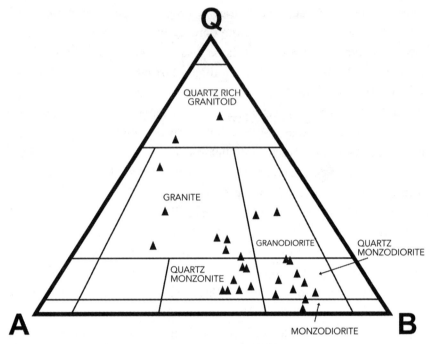

4.1. QAP (F omitted) diagram of igneous rock composition showing how the temper for each specimen plots. (Prepared by Wesley D. Stoner)

contains higher levels of plagioclase than alkali feldspar and very few quartz grains (<5 percent). Finally, quartz-rich granitoid (n=2) contains greater than 60 percent quartz.

Many of the specimens contained significant amounts of auxiliary minerals (hornblende, biotite, augite, and opaque minerals) in the temper grains. To include these minerals in the analysis, a hierarchical cluster analysis using percentages of plagioclase, alkali feldspar, quartz, hornblende, biotite, augite, and opaque minerals that occurred within temper as the input variables was undertaken. Three main groups were identified through this statistical technique.

All but one specimen in the first group was characterized by quartz monzodiorite; the exception was monzodiorite. The Group 1 cluster contained a high proportion of plagioclase, a moderate to low proportion of alkali feldspar, and a very low proportion of quartz. The temper associated with the sherds assigned to this group also had only a very low proportion of other minerals, including biotite, hornblende, and augite.

Group 2 contained more equal proportions of the three main constituents, but plagioclase still occurred in higher frequencies, followed by alkali feldspar and then quartz. Within Group 2, several specimens were observed to have rather high frequencies of auxiliary minerals. For instance, a Richmond Incised/Cayuga Horizontal collar fragment (JR5), a cordmarked body sherd (JR14), and a Dutch Hollow Notched rim (JR28) had relatively high percentages of augite. They were given the subgroup label Group 2a. A Richmond Incised rim (JR18) and a Richmond Incised/ Cayuga Horizontal collar fragment (JR26) were given the subgroup label of Group 2b because they contained relatively high proportions of biotite.

Group 3 was separated based on high proportions of alkali feldspar and quartz and low quantities of plagioclase. The two sherds from the Great Gully Farm site were assigned to this group, along with three specimens from the Corey site: a Seneca Notch rim (Jr22) and two Richmond Incised/Cayuga Horizontal collar fragments (JR7 and JR12). One Richmond Incised/Cayuga Horizontal collar fragment (JR12) was given the subgroup label Group 3h because it contained unusually high quantities of hornblende.

Texture

The final measure considered in this study is the overall texture of the ceramics. This measure considers the relative proportions of clay, temper, and natural aplastic inclusions and therefore reflects the cultural behavior of crushing the temper and mixing it with clays to form a paste recipe. Figure 4.2 depicts the distribution of specimens along the three axes of percentage of clay, natural inclusions, and temper.[2] Visual inspection of this figure led to the identification of four groups that represent significant variation in the paste recipe.

---

2. No temper grain was counted more than once regardless of size. For example, even a grain with a 4 mm diameter counted as one. Considering the recounts of large temper grains would elevate the temper fraction considerably.

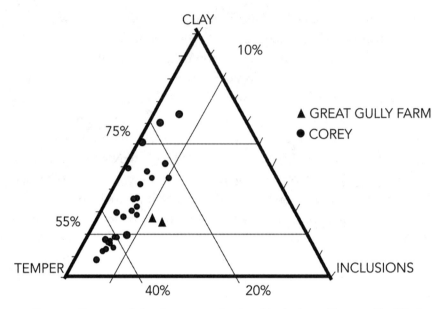

4.2. Ternary diagram of clay, temper, and natural inclusions. (Prepared by Wesley D. Stoner)

The majority of specimens fell into two groups. The largest group (n=12; blue) contained between 55 and 75 percent clay, less than 10 percent natural inclusions, and between 20 and 40 percent temper. The temper grains were of average size in relation to the remainder of the sample. Most of the temper grains measured between medium sand and very coarse sand (0.25–2 mm).

The second largest group (n=10; red) contained greater than 40 percent temper, less than 55 percent clay, and less than 10 percent natural inclusions. The temper of the red group was also average in relation to the remainder of the sample, but there was a slightly higher proportion of coarse sand and very coarse sand.

A third group consisted of just two specimens (clear). They were characterized by greater than 75 percent clay, less than 20 percent temper, and less than 10 percent natural inclusions. These two specimens were the finest-textured ceramics in the sample. They contained among the lowest frequencies of temper in every grain size category, except granule-size

(2–4 mm) temper grains. Although they were among the lightest-tempered specimens, the temper that was present was very coarsely ground.

Three specimens (green) contained greater than 10 percent natural inclusions. Two of them were from the Great Gully Farm site and were already discussed above with regard to the texture of their clays. The third was the Cayuga Horizontal rim that contained a large amount of more quartz inclusions. All three specimens contained smaller than average temper grain sizes, with a modal temper grain size of medium sand.

Conclusion

The goal of this study was to characterize the paste and temper of the Corey site ceramic assemblage through a petrographic analysis. The paste of the Corey site ceramics was relatively clean, with most sherds containing less than 10 percent natural inclusions, primarily consisting of silt-size quartz. All of the sherds were tempered with granitic rock, obtained from nearby glacial tills. Variation, however, was identified in the mineral composition of individual granitic rocks used to temper specific ceramic vessels. Many different types of granitic rocks are available in these glacial tills, which undoubtedly contributed to the heterogeneity observed in the materials used to temper the Corey site ceramics. Although comparison of temper profiles between sherds documented a great deal of diversity, temper grains associated with a particular sherd tended to be rather homogeneous. This pattern suggests that a single rock was selected to temper each vessel or batch of vessels. In addition, that all of the sherds were tempered with granite-like rocks suggests that potters did exercise some selection parameters when procuring temper.

In comparison to the Corey site, the two sherds from the Great Gully Farm site were produced from clays that had a higher portion of natural aplastic inclusions. This notion is evidenced by silt-size quartz inclusions and individual muscovite minerals that were visible at 10x magnification in the paste of the Great Gully Farm site ceramics. Although the latter was present in the paste of the Corey site ceramics, the muscovite in the paste of these sherds was so small that individual grains could not be identified. These differences in paste composition indicate that the potters at these two sites used different local clay sources. In addition to utilizing different clays, the rock used by Great Gully Farm potters to temper their vessels was qualitatively different from the rock used to temper Corey site ceramics.

Though the paste and temper composition of most of the Corey site ceramics was very similar, one sherd, a Cayuga Horizontal collar (JR24), contained more natural aplastics and less temper than the average Corey site sherd. The temper itself was not very different, but it was one of only four specimens from the Corey site that contained hornblende. This sherd is the best candidate for a ceramic vessel in the Corey site sample that was not produced at this site. There is nothing, however, about its paste or temper composition to suggest that it was manufactured outside the Cayuga region.

Finally, although this study was not successful in documenting the presence of nonlocal ceramics in the Corey site ceramic collection, it was able to characterize the composition of the paste and temper of the Corey site ceramics in much greater detail than a more traditional examination. That all of the sherds appear to have been manufactured at or in the vicinity of the Corey site suggests that the widespread distribution of certain ceramic types, such as Seneca Notched or Dutch Hollow Notched, throughout the Cayuga and Seneca regions may reflect information exchange and intermarriage and not the movement of ceramic vessels throughout these regions. If different groups of people were responsible for producing the decorated types recovered from Corey, one would expect at least some correlation between ceramic types and paste recipes.

This analysis is the first attempt to characterize the composition of Cayuga ceramics, and one of the problems encountered was a lack of comparative data. In order for technological and composition studies to be most successful, additional research aimed at identifying and characterizing the composition of site ceramic assemblages is needed. A technological approach to ceramics is necessary to understand many aspects of ancient pottery production and exchange, and it should be attempted whenever possible. Compositional studies, in particular, reveal more significant information as regional comparative databases grow. Future research should continue to utilize petrography, but should also incorporate other approaches, such as point chemical analyses (SEM, laser ablation ICP) of the clay fraction of ceramics coupled with a systematic geological survey of clay outcrops in the region. Such studies have the potential to source the ceramic vessels to clay outcrops on the landscape.

5

Lithic Raw Material Sources

JOSEPH F. WINIARZ

During the investigations of the Corey site, it was decided that a non-destructive and inexpensive method of comparing artifacts to raw lithic sources was needed. In order to fully assess the natural variations in the region's geology, and to aid in identifying the origin of artifact material recovered, raw material samples were collected from areas that were suspected local source sites, in addition to more distant localities that were possible candidates. These locales are situated along the Onondaga Escarpment, a ridge of sedimentary limestones and dolostones of Devonian age. The escarpment outcrop can be traced from the Hudson River valley along the southern rim of the Mohawk River valley, passing just south of Syracuse and along the northern heads of the major Finger Lakes to Buffalo, New York (figure 5.1). The Corey site is located fourteen miles south of the escarpment.

Because the appropriate analytical mode is dependent on the question asked, and because the question can often be constrained by the resources available, the goal of this work was to establish a microscopographic database of local raw lithic materials so that an initial visual comparison could be made to help determine the origin of recovered lithic artifacts (chapter 6). The database is meant to supplement more technically accurate methods by providing a cost-effective and nondestructive method of comparing lithic sources. This raw material database and the comparative lithic analysis experiment is a pilot study that should be expanded by adding additional quarry-site sample information as well as geological testing data.

5.1. The Onondaga escarpment, where prehistoric quarries of high-quality chert were located. (Courtesy of Matt Gorney and Ithaca College Digital Media Resources)

Background

When Jack Rossen of Ithaca College began excavating the Corey site in central New York, the subject of lithic material origins came into question. Rossen understood that by determining the origin of the lithic material used, it was possible to make certain ecological and cultural inferences. Sixty years ago, Alex Krieger and John Witthoft faced the same question: "The presence or absence of indigenous materials at a site can infer cultural selection" (Krieger 1954, 275). "If manufacturing materials not indigenous to a region are found in a site, trade or migration can be inferred" (Witthoft 1952, 470–73).

There are several different methodological approaches used in the systematic examination of lithic artifacts. Each of these methods has varying benefits and limitations, including cost, ease of application, and sensitivity to particular elements. Among these methods are visual and microscopic petrology, optical emission spectrography, atomic absorption spectrometry, X-ray fluorescence (XRF), and instrumental neutron activation analysis (INAA) (Jarvis 1988, 5). For this project, the appropriate analytical mode would have to be one that was nondestructive, inexpensive, and readily available for use both in the field and in the laboratory. Using the fingerprint analysis database that law enforcement agencies have as a model, a similar photomicroscopic database of locally obtained raw lithic material was created to provide preliminary identifying characteristics such as color, grain size, composition, fracture planes, inclusions, and luster.

Although specialists have repeatedly stressed that visual lithic analysis is both unreliable and inaccurate (Jarvis 1988, 5), the statement was made in reference to "eyeballing artifacts" and not to matching materials using a microscopic database. In New York State, the only major chert resource is one that is not only visually similar but also chemically homogenous. Because some Onondaga cherts are accessible across much of the state, it is very difficult to determine where any artifact may have specifically originated (Jarvis 1988, 1). A basic assumption of this study is that if the cherts are similar but not identical, individual samples could reveal differences. Thus, I began the collection and categorization of raw lithic materials from various quarry sites located along the Onondaga Escarpment in order to establish a database as a reference point for material origin. Within the Onondaga cherts, it has proven possible to distinguish high-quality Onondaga Escarpment quarry cherts from lower-quality streambed cherts.

Data on northeastern US chert sources was described by Barbara Luedtke as chaotic (1992, 1993). Although there are voluminous amounts of information pertaining to morphology and typology, there is limited geological cross-referencing on the origin of materials. Access to this type of data would be a boon to New York State archaeology (Jarvis 1988, 2). Although there are partial compilations of chert sources in New England, there is no single publication that draws together all information available about lithic sources in the greater Northeast, including New York (Luedtke 1992, 1993). Lithic sources expert Jack Holland stated that he has more information in his head than he does on paper and that it was a growing concern of his as he reached his eighties (personal communication, 2006). Holland has assembled a collection of more than twenty-two thousand samples of chert and other workable lithic material from throughout the world. He has identified eighty-five types of lithic material in New York State and an additional eighty-seven types in Pennsylvania.

I began by contacting James Sorauf of SUNY-Binghamton's Geology Department. After showing a sampling of lithic artifacts, he visually identified the pieces as chert, possibly from the Onondaga Formation. Chert (silica, SiO_2) is a hard, compact, fine-grained biochemical sedimentary rock formed almost entirely of chalcedonic or opaline silica. It occurs in two principal forms—as irregular, lumpy nodules within other rocks and as layered deposits like other sedimentary rocks. The nodules, which are often found in limestone, probably formed from inorganic precipitation as underground water replaced part of the original rock with water.

Sorauf directed me to the primary sources of chert in New York State, the Onondaga Limestone (Devonian) Formation that runs from Albany to Buffalo and the Bertie (Silurian) Formation of the Hudson River valley. A US Geological Survey chart of New York State confirms Sorauf's information by showing the physiographic province boundary of the Devonian/Silurian Formations running parallel to Interstate 90 from Albany to Buffalo through central New York's Finger Lakes region (Van Diver 1985, viii; figure 5.1).

The US Geological Survey chart confirms that a source of flint was available to inhabitants of the Corey site area both from bedrock outcroppings just north of Great Gully, near Union Springs, New York, and from glacially deposited cobbles south of the escarpment. Because an acceptable source of local material was available, Jarvis believes there was no reason to import large quantities of unreduced chert from any great distance (Jarvis 1988, 31). Furthermore, this study revealed that the decision to use quarried materials as opposed to glacially deposited materials infers cultural selection. Because men were traditionally travelers within the gender-differentiated Haudenosaunee Woods and Clearing Model (Hertzberg 1970, 23–34; Green 1997, 14; Richter 1992, 23), the apparent use of high-quality quarry material for projectile points is logical, as men were mobile and had access to quarry sites and trade. In contrast, women were traditionally less mobile (but see Green 1997, 14), and their use of readily available glacially deposited (Seneca member formation) material for their scrapers and tools is logical (see chapter 6). The decision of whether to use glacially deposited material thus depended not only on accessibility but also on fracturability. Weathering renders glacially deposited material coarse, and fracturability becomes more difficult owing to pressure flaws from glacial activity (Jarvis 1988, 23).

Methodology

The chert samples collected for this study are from Onondaga Escarpment locales at Phelps and Canoga, west of Cayuga Lake, and from Union Springs and Skaneateles Falls, east of the lake. Quarry samples were found in both pockets or nodules and in layered deposits throughout the blue-gray limestone. Field chert and streambed chert were also collected south of the Onondaga Escarpment, in areas where chert was most likely glacially deposited and not transported by humans.

When collecting raw samples, consideration must be given to the differences between exposed and unexposed materials. Luedtke discusses the effects of chemical weathering on artifacts. Flakes are especially vulnerable owing to their small size and extreme thinness. Jarvis notes that the majority (62 percent) of Luedtke's archaeological samples had mean elemental concentrations that were below the recorded levels of their probable sources and that iron and sodium levels were especially low (Jarvis 1988, 46), probably because chert will tripolize (turn chalky) when exposed to solar bleaching and acid rain precipitation (Holland 2003). This result was evident while collecting samples at New York State Thruway and Central New York Railroad rock cuts. Exposed pieces lying on the ground did not have the surface luster, rich black shine, or "greasy" texture of the subsurface samples, but instead were flat or matte, like charcoal (F. Cowan 1987, 2). Furthermore, heat treating of lithic material by prehistoric knappers could produce some subtle color changes in Onondaga chert, although the resulting color changes were still within the natural range of variation for this material (F. Cowan 1987, 1). Heat-treated artifacts may be found alongside untreated artifacts, which while appearing slightly different in color could in fact be from the same source.

The collection area extended from Phelps in the West to Skaneateles Falls in the East. Collection points along the Onondaga Escarpment were devised in consultation with John Holland. Geological charts and topographic maps mark the Onondaga Limestone Formation between the neighboring northern Silurian shales and southern Hamilton shales, which were cross-referenced with public access points. More detailed topographic analysis was done using Maptech Topography (http://www .maptech.com) and with US Geological Survey satellite imagery (http:// terraserver-usa.com). Raw chert samples were collected from six sites both along and south of the Onondaga Escarpment. Sampling was done from both the exposed and the unexposed parent matrix, so that weathering degeneration could be compared. Material was also collected from streambed "grab" samples. As this project is a pilot study, it was produced with the intention of later adding more quarry-site locations.

Phelps and the surrounding hamlets of Phelps Junction and Unionville provide ample natural and man-made collection sites. Carl Peake of the Village of Phelps Water Department provided valuable local knowledge and access to collection sites. The confluence area of Flint Creek and the Canandaigua River, just north of the village, provided one sampling site. Additional sampling was done at the New York State Thruway and Central New York Railroad rock cuts, along with modern-day limestone quarries surrounding the location, most of which offered access to the exposed stratified geological levels.

Heading east from Phelps, along the northwestern shore of Cayuga Lake from Bridgeport south to Canoga, a number of collection sites were uncovered. Most notable were the exposed stratified layers in Canoga Creek near the Red Jacket Cemetery and the exposed limestone beds along the lakeside a few miles north of the Canoga Creek outlet. One particular sample, collected from an outcropping on the bank of Cayuga Lake just north of Canoga, was a six-to-eight-inch band of chert stratified within the blue-gray limestone.

On the eastern side of Cayuga Lake, the Onondaga Formation band narrows considerably to about one-third (two miles) the width of the western side of the lake. Between Union Springs and Farley's Point, the band moves in a northeasterly direction toward Auburn. In the Skaneateles Falls area along Skaneateles Creek, locating quarry sites was much more difficult than at Phelps or Canoga, owing to the narrow band of the formation and private-property access restrictions. South of the Onondaga Escarpment, glacially deposited material was found in both the Great Gully streambed and on the Cayuga-SHARE Farm in Springport.

Samples were photographed and analyzed for microscopic characteristics, including color, composition, fracture traits, and inclusions. The
photomicrographic methods used in this study are similar to the ones
designed, practiced, and taught by John Gustav Delly, senior research
microscopist of the Eastman Kodak Company (Delly 1988, 1). All pho-
tographic work was performed with a Canon EOS D60 camera, and all
microscopic work was performed with a National 160 series compound
biological microscope at 40x and 100x magnification.

Results

The study demonstrated that cherts along the escarpment could be differ-
entiated and that these same differences are observable in an archaeological site collection. Attributes were revealed that could be used to identify
members of the Onondaga Formation cherts, just as previous preliminary
works suggested (Jarvis 1988; Ritchie 1980 [1965], 26–30). Raw materials
collected from the escarpment and artifacts recovered at the Corey site
can be visually compared to establish material origins.

The Onondaga Limestone Formation of central New York can be
divided into five members. These members are in the following descend-
ing stratigraphic order: Seneca, Moorehouse, Clarence, Nedrow, and
Edgecliff.

Seneca: Dark to Black, Fine Grained, Fossiliferous

Most of this material was lost to erosion (now available as stream cobbles),
but a few meters of bedrock material can still be found in some areas
(figure 5.2).

• Black lustrous chert with brown patches and white quartz
marbleizing/banding

• Generally smooth, minimal quartz inclusions

• At 40x magnification siliceous dark brown to charcoal, numerous
white and clear quartz crystals and marbleizing; red or rust, light and
dark brown, mustard or gold flecking

• Cobbles generally exhibit a cross-hatched fracturing pattern owing
to pressure flaws from glacial activity and stream tumbling

• Flakes are nontranslucent

5.2. Seneca chert at 40x magnification. (Courtesy of Joseph Winiarz)

- Exhibits poor flaking characteristics
- Primary use as scrapers and other domestic tools

Moorehouse: Medium Gray, Fine Grained, Fossiliferous

This material is found at a depth of eight meters in central New York to about sixteen meters near Buffalo (figure 5.3).

- Predominantly gray bedrock chert, found in natural and man-made quarry sites
- Medium blue-gray chert with white, black, blue, and brown flecking, brown patches, some marbleizing
- Generally smooth with conchoidal fractures, minimal quartz inclusions
- At 40x magnification siliceous light to medium brown with white and clear quartz crystals; black and brown and blue flecking
- Exhibits good flaking characteristics
- Flakes are nontranslucent
- Primary use as points and scrapers

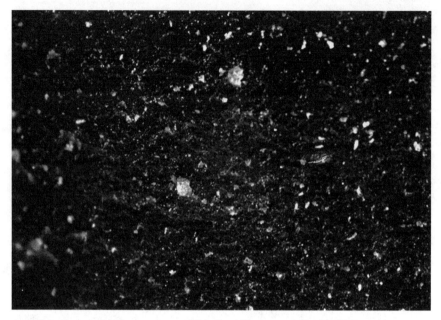

5.3. Moorehouse chert at 40x magnification. (Courtesy of Joseph Winiarz)

Clarence: Dark Blue and Black, Fine Grained

This material is found at a depth of five meters in central New York to about fourteen meters near Buffalo.

- Predominantly dark-blue and black bedrock chert with and without striations, found in natural and man-made quarry sites
- At 40x magnification dark brown with white and clear quartz crystal flecking and black, brown, red, mustard particulates; minimal quartz inclusions
- Exhibits good flaking characteristics
- Generally smooth to fine-grit texture
- Flakes are nontranslucent
- Primary use as points

Nedrow: Very Dark, Grayish Black

This material is rare and has been previously grouped with the Clarence member owing to its similarity in color (figure 5.4).

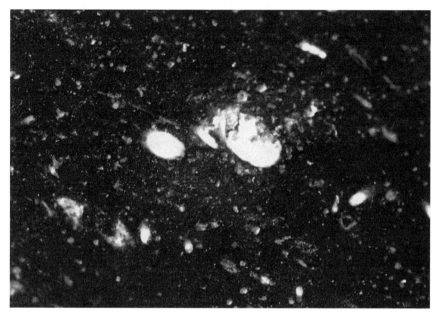

5.4. Nedrow chert at 40x magnification. (Courtesy of Joseph Winiarz)

Edgecliff: Light to Medium Gray, Medium Grained, Fossiliferous

- Five to ten meters across New York, dominated by corals (figure 5.5)
- Medium to dark-gray chert with white quartz crystals
- Generally coarse grained with inclusions, poor conchoidal fracture
- Exhibits poor flaking characteristics
- Flakes are nontranslucent

Comparison of Collected Cherts with Corey Site Materials

A preliminary comparison was made of the collected chert samples with projectile points, tools, and debitage from the Corey site. These comparisons are elaborated in chapter 6. Virtually all debitage examined was similar to the samples collected at Great Gully. Most specimens did not exhibit the traditional manufacturing characteristics such as bulb of percussion, compression waves, arris, or eraillure scars. This debris was cubicle in form and matched the cross-hatched fracturing pattern found in cobbles resulting from pressure flaws. These traits are commonly found in the

5.5. Edgecliff chert at 40x magnification. (Courtesy of Joseph Winiarz)

Seneca member material, indicating the material was glacially transported. These materials probably represent chert cobbles from the creeks
adjacent to the Corey site.

Because an acceptable (but not outstanding in terms of quality) source
of lithic material was locally available to the inhabitants of the Corey site,
there was no reason to import large quantities of unreduced chert from a
great distance. A preliminary analysis of the Corey artifacts and the microscopic comparison with collected raw material revealed that scrapers and
other unifacial tools were made from the poorer-quality Onondaga chert,
specifically the glacially deposited Seneca member material. In contrast,
projectile points are of higher-quality Onondaga material, specifically the
quarried Moorehouse and Clarence cherts. In addition, a few points and
flakes are of exotic origin. The preliminary analysis supports the working
hypothesis of gendered division of raw material use, perhaps related to
the types of demands of manufactured tools and mobility differences (see
chapter 6).

6

Chipped Lithic Artifacts

MARTIN J. SMITH

One pervasive aspect of Haudenosaunee archeology is the emphasis on the analysis of ceramics (Niemczycki 1984; Hayes 1980; MacNeish 1952). In contrast, other assemblages including chipped lithics (beyond projectile points) have been relatively neglected. By examining all lithic tools recovered from the Corey site, it is possible to discern a more complete range of domestic activities that occurred at the site.

The goals of this analysis were to understand the relationships between raw materials and tool types and to explore possible connections between the manufacture and use of stone tools and gender (Gero and Conkey 1991). The analysis suggests that most lithic tools recovered from the site were manufactured and used by women, with the likely exception of the six projectile points, which statistically represent only 6 percent of the recovered tools.

The Corey site primarily exhibits an "expedient" lithic technology. Most implements are flake tools struck from cores of different shapes. These tools were used briefly and discarded. This type of lithic industry is opposed to more "curated" industries in which tools were more carefully fashioned and were utilized for longer periods of time (Binford 1973, 1980). Expedient lithic industries have been associated with an abundance of raw lithic material (Binford 1977), decreased mobility or sedentism (Parry and Kelly 1987), and the adoption of the bow and arrow (Railey 2010).

Analysis Description

A total of ninety-three lithic tools were recovered from the Corey site. Flake tools were sorted into types based on morphology and the relative

93

location of use edge in relation to striking platform. Spatial distributions of tools were examined in terms of presence in the midden area. Projectile points were analyzed by type and breakage pattern. Raw material types of tools were analyzed to separate the use of locally available streambed versus more distant quarry cherts (see chapter 5).

The analysis of raw material types dovetails with the study by Joseph Winiarz, who sampled quarry sites along the Onondaga Escarpment. This geological formation is orientated in an east-west direction along the northern edge of the Finger Lakes, near the route of Interstate 90. The study was useful in identifying many of the lithic materials found at the Corey site and their likely origins. A total of fifteen material types were identified in the Corey assemblage, including four unknown types.

Within the lithic assemblage, there are several types of Onondaga cherts discussed by Winiarz. The first is the Seneca type, which is characterized as being dark to black in color, fine grained, and fossiliferous. Most Seneca-type chert was removed by glaciers and deposited as nodules in streambeds south of the Onondaga Escarpment, including Paines Creek, below the Corey site.

Moorehouse, the second type of Onondaga chert, is medium gray in color and fine grained. It is found in stratified layers of up to eight meters deep in central New York to up to sixteen meters deep near Buffalo. Clarence chert is characterized by being dark blue and black as well as fine grained, and it is found in stratified layers of five meters or so in central New York to fourteen meters near Buffalo. Nedrow is a very dark to grayish black chert with high shale content; Nedrow is generally courser in texture, likely owing to the increased erosion of the uplifting landforms to the east. The last of the Onondaga cherts is Edgecliff, which is light to medium gray in color, medium grained, and also fossiliferous. Edgecliff can be found in stratified layers of five to ten meters deep, dominated by corals (see chapter 5).

In addition to the Onondaga cherts, there are several samples of Mohawk Valley cherts, which are characterized by a very dark blue to black color with lighter-blue to light-colored mottling. Other lithic artifacts are made of slate, shale, limestone, sandstone, and mudstone. Unidentified raw materials include a dark-brown chert.

One issue is whether there was gendered use of lithic raw materials, based on availability and relative mobility of men and women living at the site. There has been a growing realization among archaeologists that both women and men were active in the collection of raw materials and the manufacture of lithic tools (Gero and Conkey 1991). In the case of the Corey materials, the working hypothesis was that lower-quality local materials such as streambed nodules (Seneca chert) would have been primarily used by women. Presumed to have been generally less mobile than men, women would have made and used lithic tools for tasks like food processing in the village. In contrast, more mobile men would have access to higher-quality cherts from the Onondaga Escarpment quarries for tasks such as hunting (projectile points). Based on these presumed differences in mobility patterns, men probably had access to more nonlocal materials owing to their higher percentage of time spent away from the village or town (Green 1997). In order to address the working hypothesis, tool-type frequencies were analyzed in terms of comparing and contrasting local streambed cobble cherts to higher-quality quarry cherts available only from the Onondaga Escarpment, at least fourteen miles north of the Corey site.

Typological Analysis

Twelve lithic tool types were classified, including utilized flakes, modified flakes, side scrapers, end scrapers, blades, hafted blades, hoe blade, hafted tools, core tools, projectile points, and lithic eccentrics.

For the purpose of this analysis, a utilized flake is defined as any flake that has evidence of use, either edge damage or use wear. An edge-modified flake is a flake with evidence of deliberate modification along one or more edges. Both types generally have acute edge angles. Side scrapers are defined as multidirectionally worked specimens having use on a lateral edge, perpendicular to the striking platform. End scrapers, in contrast, have a use edge parallel to the striking platform, generally either the proximal or the distal end of the specimen (Kooyman 2000, 102). Blades are characterized as being thin and chipped or having been likely separated from a blade core. Hafted blades are similarly characterized, except by having noticeable haft wear marks or haft notches. There is one tool that is likely a hoe blade; it is a large flat piece of stone with one ventrally removed flake likely used for a haft. Core tools are tools that have flakes removed, along with chipped use edges. Projectile points are bifacially worked artifacts either with or without haft marks, in this collection represented by the Madison and Levanna types (Ritchie 1971). Finally, there are two lithic eccentrics; artifacts with obvious and apparently patterned flake removal, but for unknown purposes.

Analysis Results

Projectile Points

Six projectile points were recovered at the site, including four of the Levanna type and two of the Madison type (figure 6.1). Levanna points are broad and triangular, almost equilateral with a one-to-one length-to-width ratio. Levanna points appeared around AD 700 and became common by AD 900 (Ritchie 1971, 31). Recent reexcavation of the Levanna site, with its tenth- to twelfth-century radiocarbon dates, locally confirms

6.1. Projectile points. (Courtesy of Jack Rossen)

these projectile-point dates. According to traditional typologies, Levanna points began to be replaced by Madison points around AD 1350 (Ritchie 1971). Madison points, which are finer and slimmer triangular points than Levanna specimens with at least a two-to-one length-to-width ratio, may be technologically associated with the adoption of or development of a more refined version of the bow and arrow (Blitz 1988; Engelbrecht 2003, 8). The presence of Levanna points at the Corey site suggests that this type retained regional importance into the fifteenth century and that there was not a simple stylistic replacement in Cayuga territory.

All six recovered points are finished specimens with broken tips, and all four points with barbs have at least one broken barb. Two points were recovered from Unit 2, while Units 1, 4, 6, and 7 each contained one point. There were two projectile points in Level 2 and Level 6, one point each in Levels 1 and 3, and no points in Levels 4 and 5 (table 6.1). In terms of material, there are three made of Edgecliff chert and one each made of Moorehouse, Clarence, and Nedrow (table 6.2).

The distribution of projectile points at Corey suggests they appear as only occasional broken discards. They are widely scattered in the deep midden at the site edge and are absent from the sheet midden of the short-house zone. The scarcity of points supports the woods-clearing model in which villages were female-dominated locales, while men spent considerably more time in the woods and less in the village (Hertzberg 1970, 23–34; Green 1997, 14; Richter 1992, 23; see chapter 11).

TABLE 6.1. **Location of lithic tool types by midden unit**

	Unit 1	Unit 2	Unit 3	Unit 4	Unit 5	Unit 6	Unit 7	Unit 8	Unit 9
Projectile Points/ preforms	1	2	0	1	0	1	1	0	0
Side scrapers	0	2	0	4	0	5	0	1	1
End scrapers	0	2	1	4	0	2	0	2	1
Modified flakes	0	4	2	8	0	2	1	0	3
Utilized flakes	0	6	0	7	0	5	2	0	1

Side Scrapers

There were twelve side scrapers recovered from the site. These specimens were widely scattered in six midden units throughout Levels 1 to 6 (tables 6.3 and 6.4). Most side scrapers are made of Seneca (n=6), the locally available streambed chert. One side scraper each was fashioned from Moorehouse, Clarence, and Edgecliff, the quarry cherts, plus one was made of an unidentified brown chert. Two were made of a local limestone (table 6.3).

End Scrapers

There are thirteen end scrapers in the Corey assemblage, recovered only from four midden units (tables 6.4 and 6.5). The material frequencies that were observed in relation to the set of end scrapers were as follows: three Seneca, three Moorehouse, four Edgecliff, one slate, one sandstone, and one exotic chert (see table 6.2).

TABLE **6.2. Lithic tool types and raw material types**

	Seneca	Moorehouse	Clarence	Nedrow	Edgecliff	"Other"
Projectile Points/ preforms	0	1	1	1	3	0
Side scrapers	6	1	1	1	1	2
End scrapers	3	3	4	0	0	2
Modified flakes	18	1	1	0	1	1
Utilized flakes	12	4	0	0	1	4

TABLE **6.3. Location of lithic tool types by midden level**

	Level 1	Level 2	Level 3	Level 4	Level 5	Level 6
Projectile Points/ preforms	1	2	1	0	0	2
Side scrapers	4	2	3	0	3	1
End scrapers	0	2	4	4	1	1
Modified flakes	4	4	8	4	1	0
Utilized flakes	4	7	6	3	2	0

TABLE 6.4. Lithic tool distribution in midden zone

	Artifacts per unit	Percentage
Unit 1	4	4.4
Unit 2	21	22.6
Unit 3	3	3.3
Unit 4	34	36.6
Unit 5	0	0
Unit 6	17	18.2
Unit 7	6	6.4
Unit 8	2	2.1
Unit 9	6	6.4
Total	93	100

TABLE 6.5. Raw material types of unifacial scraping and cutting tools

Material type	Frequency	Percentage of total
Seneca	46	49.5
Moorehouse	13	13.9
Clarence	1	1.1
Nedrow	2	2.2
Edgecliff	11	11.8
Other	20	21.5
Total	93	100

Modified Flakes

The modified flakes (n=22) were made from a variety of material with Seneca chert predominant (see table 6.1).

Utilized Flakes

There are twenty-one utilized flakes in the collection, and they are made primarily of the Seneca chert type (see table 6.1). There is also one translucent black obsidian flake of unknown origin. Most flakes were recovered from the northern sector of the midden are (Units 2 and 4; see table 6.3).

Distribution and Material-Type Analysis

Spatial analysis was conducted for the four most common tool types, the modified flakes, utilized flakes, side scrapers, and end scrapers, along with the rare projectile points.

The six projectiles were widely scattered in the northern portion of the midden (Units 1, 2, 4, 6, and 7). In terms of vertical distribution, projectile points were relatively evenly distributed, with the absence of specimens in Levels 4 and 5. Of the two points that were recovered from Level 6, one is a Madison and the other a Levanna type, made of Clarence and Nedrow, respectively. The second Madison type point that was recovered was from Level 2, and the rest of the Levanna points were distributed in Levels 1, 2, and 3, indicating that there is no vertical separation between the types of projectile points. The pattern is an indicator of rapid midden accumulation in the village. All six points are made of quarry cherts and not locally available streambed cobbles.

The highest percentages of side scrapers were in Units 4 and 6, at 30.7 percent and 38.4 percent, respectively. Units 2, 8, and 9 displayed much lower side-scraper densities, at 15.4 percent and 7.6 percent (for both Units 8 and 9), respectively. Side scrapers were predominately manufactured from the local Seneca-type chert, with much lower frequencies of the Onondaga Escarpment cherts, including single specimens each of Moorehouse, Clarence, Nedrow, and Edgecliff, with two of exotic material.

Discussion

The Corey site is an expedient lithic assemblage containing a variety of flake tools, with the collection dominated by side scrapers and end scrapers that are not often examined by archaeologists, along with a low frequency of projectile points. All these tools were exclusively found in the midden area at the western site edge and primarily in Units 2 and 4 in the northern portion of the midden. Shorthouses were possibly swept clean of lithic material, or flintknapping and tool-equipping activities took place outside the houses.

Projectile-Point Breakage

All projectile points from the Corey site exhibit impact fractures, probably from use in the field. I am a bow hunter, and although modern bows and arrows and projectile points are different from the ones used by the inhabitants of the Corey site, some mechanical and technological similarities exist.

The fracturing of chert projectile points exhibits similarities to the types of deformation and breakage that occur in modern steel broadhead points when the archer misses the target and strikes a rock or other hard material or when the archer scores a hit and strikes the internal bone structures of game animals, such as deer, elk, or bear. A modern broad head made of steel will often deform rather than break, but even high tensile steel breaks or cracks, and these points must be discarded. In such a case, the archer detaches the broken point, whether fastened by a screw in arrangement or adhesives, and replaces it with a fresh point. This system allows the reuse of arrow shafts, regardless of the condition of the original broad head. In my experience, broken point shoulders or tangs tend to result from animal hits when the point strikes an internal bone. Broken tips tend to result from misses when the point strikes a hard surface. Bases are damaged more often in hits but are often left intact in misses as tips break. These two breakage patterns are present in the Corey points. I hypothesize that the Corey points were broken in the field through both hits and misses, and arrows were brought to the village where broken points were removed and discarded in what became the trash midden. A new projectile point was then manufactured or taken from a supply of premade points and fastened in place of the broken point.

Raw Material Use, Tool Types, and Gender

One focus of this lithic analysis was to examine material usage patterns at the Corey site. In considering raw material frequencies, by far the most utilized material is Seneca chert, the streambed cobbles available in the gorges below the site. The next most common types are Moorehouse and Edgecliff, available at quarry sites fourteen to thirty miles north, northwest, and northeast of Corey (see table 6.5). Locally available Seneca chert, though lower in quality owing to fracture plains associated with battering and rolling in streambeds, was suitable for most flake tool-cutting and scraping purposes. Seneca chert, however, was not the most desirable material for projectile points.

One goal of the lithic analysis was to explore the potential to discern gender patterns among prehistoric lithic tools. Feminist archaeological writings have been concerned with bringing awareness and visibility to previously neglected women's activities in the archaeological record (Gero and Conkey 1991). The work of Joan Gero is concerned with recognizing how the production of lithic tools was undertaken by both men and women in prehistory. From ethnographic literature, there is general understanding of both symbolic and practical gender separations of activities and responsibilities among the Haudenosaunee that are embodied in the woods and clearing model. According to this model, at a small village like Corey, women would have been primarily responsible for horticultural activities except for initial clearing of land that was conducted by men. Ceramics were produced, broken, and discarded by women through various domestic activities, including cooking and food storage. Furthermore, women were responsible for the utilization and care of hides for clothing. In contrast, men were primarily responsible for hunting, trading, procurement, and diplomatic activities that would take them far from the village (Hertzberg 1970, 23–34; Green 1997, 14; Richter 1992, 23; Venables 2000, 93–98).

Given the general model, and recognizing that there were exceptions such as examples of women's long-distance travel and cooperation in fishing (Green 1997; Parmenter 2010, xxxix–xl), it can be suggested that the majority of the Corey lithic assemblage consists of female tools used in daily domestic activities. Most expedient flake tools are made of lower-quality but locally available Seneca chert. This evidence suggests that women were procuring chert near the site and manufacturing and using the cutting and scraping tools. The working hypothesis of gendered division of the collection, manufacture, and use of lithic material and tools is generally supported. There are also low percentages of flake tools and utilized flakes made of quarry cherts and exotic materials, suggesting either that there were some expedient tools made by men or that women had some access to quarry and exotic raw material. Projectile points were apparently manufactured by men, although changing and discard of broken points may have sometimes been a women's activity.

7

Ground Stone Artifacts

MACY O'HEARN

Ground stone is considered to be any stone artifact that is not flaked during the course of manufacture, and includes non-chert artifacts produced by battering, grinding, abrading, smoothing, or polishing. In total, 167 ground stone artifacts were recovered over the two field seasons at the Corey site (table 7.1). Ground stone artifacts are not often included in detailed formal artifact analysis and interpretation in the Northeast. However, a consideration of the ground stone assemblage is essential to understanding the possibility of occupational specialization at Corey.

Miniature Pallets (n=51)

One unique aspect of the ground stone assemblage from the Corey site is the large number of small grinding pallets (figure 7.1). These are characterized by a smooth, slightly concave grinding surface. An additional characteristic of the pallet assemblage is the reddish-brown or black discolorations that are evident on the grinding surface of at least five pallets. Excluding broken specimens, the pallets range in length between 3.75 and 12.25 centimeters, 2.75 and 8.25 centimeters in width, and 0.75 and 7.25 centimeters in depth, and they weigh between 3 and 745 grams. The average length is 7.16 centimeters, width is 5.59 centimeters, depth is 2.72 centimeters, and weight is 166.43 grams. The average grinding surface area of this miniature pallet assemblage is 28.3 square centimeters.

A typology based on the general shape and appearance of small pallets places them into four categories. The pallets that are primarily rounded were classified as "ovate or rounded" (n=26), and the ones with straighter edges were classified as "angular or rectangular" (n=4). Each

TABLE 7.1. Frequency of ground stone artifacts

Ground stone artifact type	Frequency
Miniature pallet	51
Hand grinder (mano)	46
Pestle	32
Hammer stone	20
Abrader	7
Nutting stone	2
Grooved axhead	1
Unfinished celt	1
Large metate	1
Net sinker	1
Polisher	1

7.1. Miniature pallets. (Courtesy of Jack Rossen)

of these two types may be separated into small, medium, and large sub-types. An "irregular" type (n=12) is for specimens that possess elements of both rounded and angular pallets or are otherwise unclassifiable. Last, pallets that were broken prior to excavation are designated simply as "unknown broken" (n=9).

Pallets were also sorted based on thickness, as either "shallow" pallets (less than or equal to 2 cm in depth), "medium" (between 2.1 and 4 cm in depth), or "thick" (greater than or equal to 4.1 cm in depth). Of the fifty-one pallets in the sample, seventeen are shallow, twenty-five are medium, and nine are thick. It is unknown whether the differentiation in shape or size within this sample of small pallets bears any significance to the type of material being processed.

Hand Grinders (n=46)

A total of forty-six hand grinders (manos) was recovered at the Corey site. Length (3.5–15.5 cm, average 8.5 cm), width (3.3–12 cm, average 5.8 cm), depth (2–8 cm, average 4.5 cm), and weight (26–3,020 gm, average 310 gm) vary substantially. The average area of the grinding surface is 24 square centimeters. The average surface grinding area of manos is larger than for pestles (see below), and it is possible that the differences are related to the specific plant material being processed.

Pestles (n=32)

Ground stone pestles found at the Corey site are characterized by an elongated handle and small grinding area on one end. They are distinguished from hand grinders because they are generally smaller and longer in relation to the small grinding surface. Like hand grinders, pestles show variability in handle length (2.5–8.3 cm, average 5 cm), width (1–3.5 cm, average 2.8 cm), depth (2–6.3 cm, average 4.3 cm), and especially weight (7–239 gm, average 80 gm). Grinding surfaces of pestles range from 1.5 to 12.5 square centimeters with an average 6.3 square centimeters.

Three pestles have evidence of such heavy use that they have developed a glassy sheen, and twelve others have sustained dark-gray, black, reddish-brown, or reddish-purple discoloration, possibly from pigments or plant materials. One pestle possesses both a glassy sheen and a reddish-brown discoloration on the grinding surface. At least three "erratic" pestles were manufactured from chert, which is highly unusual among ground stone artifacts. They have been chipped in a similar fashion to other chert artifacts, yet also show the clear evidence of grinding found on other pestles.

Hammer Stones (n=26)

Hammer stones from the Corey site are characterized by considerable pitting and evidence of battering. Many hammer stones have multiple use areas, making it difficult to distinguish one area for measurement. These artifacts range from 4 to 8.5 centimeters in length, with an average of 6 centimeters. They weigh between 32 to 320 grams, with an average of 165 grams. They were crafted from granitic stone or quartzite.

Abraders (n=7)

Abraders in this assemblage are small artifacts that average 100 grams in weight and are characterized by a rough surface, generally on a single side. They are manufactured exclusively of granite or conglomerate limestone. Deposits of the latter are found in the gorges of the surrounding region. Some possess evidence of heavy wear, with much of the surface worn to a smooth finish, but there is still a rough surface along the edges. Two specimens show evidence of reddish discoloration from use. It is unknown what was being abraded with these objects, but they are similar in texture to coarse-grained sandpaper. Based on materials recovered at the site, possible abraded materials were bone, pigment, feldspar (ceramic temper), antler tine, and calcite.

Metates (n=2)

Two metates (large grinding slabs) were recovered, which average 2,536.5 grams in weight. The average length and width are, respectively, 23.5 centimeters and 13.5 centimeters. The metates are characterized by a large, flat, or slightly concave grinding surface and a bottom surface that is roughly parallel.

Nutting Stones (n=2)

Two nutting stones average 144 grams in weight. The average length and width are, respectively, 6.75 centimeters and 5.25 centimeters. Both show evidence of much localized battering; each contains a single round depression, likely from the processing of nuts. This depression averages 2.5 centimeters in diameter.

Other Ground Stone Artifacts (n=7)

A number of other miscellaneous ground stone artifacts are present. These include two unfinished celts, one small hoe blade, one grooved ax, one small net sinker with shallow grooves, and two small, round polishing stones. The latter may have been used for smoothing clay during the ceramic-making process, as they are similar in size and appearance to a tool used by contemporary Onondaga potters.

Discussion

The basic types of ground stone artifacts that are commonly found on northeastern US sites, such as metates, nutting stones, celts, and a grooved ax, were recovered in only low frequencies at Corey. These artifacts were utilized primarily in activities such as grinding corn, preparing temper for ceramic manufacture, and cracking nuts. The low frequencies indicate the curated nature, durability, and stability of this type of tool use.

In contrast, the high frequencies of miniature pallets and pestles are striking. Forty-four of the pallets are from units with shallow midden in the northern site sector. Also included in the artifacts from this area are those specimens involved in the manufacturing process, such as the unfinished celts and grooved ax. The remaining seven pallets from the assemblage were recovered from the shorthouse area in the southern sector of the site. This distribution indicates that there was an outdoor ground stone production area in the northern site sector, where very few ceramics and other artifact types were recovered.

The miniaturization of the ground stone pallets and pestles at Corey suggests that they were not being used in the processing of food, specifically corn, but that they served a more specialized use. For example, the average weight of the large corn-grinding metates is more than twenty times the average miniature pallet weight of 166.4 grams. It appears that the small pallets were used to grind small amounts of plant or animal material for their pigments or medicinal uses. Other aspects of the site, including the ground antler tines (see chapter 8), worn pathway from the site down to the gorge below, and high-concentration area of medicinal herbs (see chapter 9), support this interpretation of the pallets.

8

Faunal Remains

APRIL M. BEISAW

This chapter describes and discusses the evidence of broad-spectrum animal exploitation at the Corey site, ranging in size from chipmunk to black bear. This analysis includes all recovered materials from both the 2003 excavation of the site midden and the 2005 excavation of a shorthouse and row of hearth/pit features. The hearths from the shorthouse were completely floated, and small faunal materials that are often lost during excavation were recovered and analyzed.

A wide range of faunal remains, including mammals, birds, fish, mollusks, amphibians, and reptiles, was identified. This collection undermines existing stereotypes of Cayuga hunters as heavily focused on deer (Hertzberg 1970, 68), perhaps because of emphasis on collection of faunal materials from soil-flotation samples. Even with this caveat, analysis of the Engelbert site (Tioga County, New York) also found that Iroquoian diets were more diverse than expected (Beisaw 2006) and that collection did not include flotation samples. Contextual analyses of the Corey fauna revealed specific activities related to some shorthouse hearths such as Feature 12A (processing elk hide), Feature 12B (mammal cooking), and Feature 12C (fish cooking). As expected, a higher diversity of faunal remains was found in the midden trash area than in the shorthouse area.

Analysis Results

Taxonomic Identification

Thirty-four taxonomic categories were used to describe the Corey faunal assemblage (table 8.1). Material that was not taxonomically identifiable

TABLE 8.1. Taxons identified in the Corey faunal assemblage
including the Minimum Number of Individuals calculated for the site

Taxonomic name	Common name	Site MNI
Castor canadensis	Beaver	1
Ursus americanus	Black bear	1
Micropterus salmoides	Bigmouth bass	1
Cyprinidae	Carp/minnow	1
Siluriformes	Catfish	1
Tamias striatus	Chipmunk	2
Canis familiaris	Domestic dog	1
Cervus elaphus	Elk	1
Fish, unidentified	Fish	
Anura	Frog/toad	
Sciurus carolinensis	Gray squirrel	3
Rana clamitans	Green frog	2
Leporidae	Hare/rabbit	1
Large mammal	Large mammal	
Medium bird	Medium bird	
Medium mammal	Medium mammal	
Mollusc	Mollusk	
Ondatra zibethicus	Muskrat	1
Passeriforme	Perching bird	
Columba livia	Pigeon	6
Procyon lotor	Raccoon	1
Cricetidae	Rat/mouse	1
Lutra canadensis	River otter	1
Salmonidae	Salmon/trout	1
Small bird	Small bird	
Small mammal	Small mammal	
Catostomidae	Sucker	1
Centrarchidae	Sunfish	
Bufonidae	Toad	1

TABLE 8.1. Taxons identified in the Corey faunal assemblage including the Minimum Number of Individuals calculated for the site (Continued)

Taxonomic name	Common name	Site MNI
Testudines	Tortoise/turtle	1
Phasianidae	Turkey/pheasant	1
Odocoileus virginianus	White-tailed deer	2
Marmota monax	Woodchuck	1
Peromyscus leucopus	White-footed mouse	3
Total		36

beyond class (mammal, fish, bird, and so on) was cataloged using approximate size groupings. Material identifiable to the genus or species level was classified using seven distinct mammal categories.

The distribution of species was quantified using both Number of Identified Specimens (NISP) and Minimum Number of Individuals (MNI). Research has shown that differences in bone fragmentation can result in misleading NISP calculations. To minimize this source of bias, bone fragments with recent breaks were temporarily mended during analysis. Also, the single-component nature of the site suggests that portions of one animal could be found in multiple contexts across the site, so both NISP and MNI were calculated on the assemblage as a whole. MNIs were also calculated such that they would be mutually exclusive from other categories. Therefore, no MNI is listed for the unidentified fish, as most of these specimens are likely components of those fish that were identified to order, family, or genus. Similarly, no MNI is listed for Centrarchidae (sunfish), as the identified *Micropterus salmoides* belongs to the Centrarchidae family.

Once the faunal remains were identified to the lowest taxonomic group possible and quantified by NISP and MNI, the University of Michigan Animal Diversity Web was consulted for information on habitat and abundance of each taxonomic group. This information allows for visualization of the environments occupied and used by the site inhabitants. The taxonomic groups described below are organized alphabetically, by common name, within each taxonomic class. Zoological classification follows the basic hierarchy: kingdom, phylum, class, order, family, genus, and species. Zooarchaeology deals exclusively with the kingdom Animalia. Class identification sorts a faunal assemblage into mammal, fish, bird, reptile, and amphibian remains.

Mammals

American Beaver (*Castor canadensis*)
>The American beaver is found throughout North America, in the vicinity of lakes, ponds, rivers, and streams. These aquatic rodents are commonly sought for their waterproof pelts.

Black Bear (*Ursus americanus*)
>The black bear is found throughout North America's forests, usually in areas with changing topography. Although they are carnivores, the black bear diet consists mainly of vegetable matter. This species hibernates in the winter months.

Domestic Dog (*Canis familiaris*)
>The domestic dog is found at archaeological sites throughout North America. This species has been used as hunting aides, pack animals, pets, a food source, and, in the Haudenosaunee case, ritual sacrifice.

Eastern Chipmunk (*Tamias striatus*)
>The eastern chipmunk is found throughout North America, mainly living in burrows of lightly forested areas. Because they are a burrowing species, they may be intrusive to archaeological sites, especially in areas of rock piles.

Eastern Gray Squirrel (*Sciurus carolinensis*)
>This species of squirrel is common throughout the woodlands of eastern North America. They are most active in the spring, summer, and autumn months. These rodents live in trees, not burrows, and therefore are more likely to represent a food source than an intrusive species in archaeological sites.

Elk (*Cervus elaphus*)
>Elk were once common throughout North America but are now found only in western regions. This species prefers open woodlands.

Hares and Rabbits (Leporidae)
> The hares and rabbits family includes fifty-four species. Hares differ from rabbits in having longer legs and ears and preferring areas of open vegetation.

Muskrat (*Ondatra zibethicus*)
> The muskrat is found throughout North America, in marshes, swamps, and bogs associated with lakes, ponds, river, and streams. Muskrats have been sought for their pelts.

New World Rats, Mice, Voles, and Hamsters (Cricetidae)
> The Cricetidae family of rodents is very diverse and includes the subfamilies of North American rats and mice (Neotominae) to which the white-footed mouse (*Peromyscus leucopus*) belongs.

Northern Raccoon (*Procyon lotor*)
> The northern raccoon is common throughout North America. This species is not habitat specific. Raccoons have been sought for their pelts.

Northern River Otter (*Lutra canadensis*)
> This species was once common throughout North America. Semi-aquatic, this species lives near lakes, ponds, river, streams, and even along the coast. It has been hunted for its pelts.

White-Footed Mouse (*Peromyscus leucopus*)
> The white-footed mouse is common throughout eastern North America.

White-Tailed Deer (*Odocoileus virginianus*)
> The white-tailed deer is common throughout eastern North America. Although deer can inhabit a variety of ecosystems, they prefer areas that include both thick vegetation and open edges to provide protection and food.

Woodchuck (*Marmota monax*)
> The woodchuck is common throughout eastern North America. This species prefers the forest edges and grassy pastures. As a burrowing species, woodchuck remains may be intrusive to archaeological sites.

Birds

Perching Birds (Passeriformes)
> The order Passeriformes includes perching birds of the world.

Pigeon (*Columba livia*)

    The specimens identified as pigeon within this assemblage are likely the now-extinct passenger pigeon (*Ectopistes migratorius*). However, owing to the difficulty in obtaining comparative specimens of extinct species, these specimens could be compared only to the common pigeon, which is not native to North America. The passenger pigeon was a migratory species, moving north in March and south in the late autumn or early winter. The birds were most easily captured during their spring nesting period (Orlandini 1996).

Turkeys, Grouse, Pheasants, and Partridges (Phasianidae)

    This family includes the turkey and other wild pheasants.

Fish

Bigmouth Bass (*Micropterus salmoides*)

    The bigmouth bass is native to eastern North America's lakes, ponds, rivers, and streams. They prefer quiet shallow waters with ample vegetation. This species is considered an important game fish.

Carps and Minnows (Cyprinidae)

    This family includes fifty-three species that occur in northeastern North America. Some species are small stream dwellers, while others are large riverine inhabitants (Daniels 1996).

Catfish (Siluriformes)

    This order includes many species of catfish that inhabit freshwater of every continent except Antarctica. Catfish do not have scales.

Salmons, Salmonids, and Trouts (Salmonidae)

    This family is composed of relatively large fish that were important food sources to Native Americans (Daniels 1996).

Suckers (Catostomidae)

    This family of freshwater fish is common in the lakes and rivers of the Northeast. These relatively large fish were important food sources to Native Americans (Daniels 1996).

Sunfish (Centrarchidae)

    This family of fish includes species of sunfish, perch, bass, and crappie. The species of bigmouth bass (*Micropterus salmoides*) identified in this assemblage is a member of this family.

Amphibians

Frogs and Toads (Anura)
  This order includes the frogs and toads of the world.
Green Frog (*Rana clamitans*)
  The green frog is common around inland waters of the East Coast of North America. Lakes, ponds, river, streams, marshes, swamps, and bogs are the primary habitats of this species. Green frogs spend the winter buried in the substrate below shallow water.
Toads (Bufonidae)
  This family is made up of the true toads, which have thick and warty skins and tend to be terrestrial.

Reptiles

Tortoises and Turtles (Testudines)
  This order includes the tortoises and turtles of the world.

Taphonomic Analysis

The analysis of animal bones from archaeological sites, at its empirical core, provides information regarding the diet of a site's occupants and their immediate habitat. However, quantification of animal remains to produce rank-ordered lists of food or habitat preference can generate misleading results. Cultural and environmental processes, such as differential methods of food preparation and disposal or differential destruction of bone through decompositional processes, can affect quantities of identifiable bone. The adoption of taphonomy, originally a paleontological field, into faunal analysis provides a means of recovering information lost owing to biasing factors. Taphonomy also provides a framework for data analysis and interpretation that has moved faunal analysis well past the standard dietary and habitat assessments (Beisaw 2012).

  Taphonomy is, in general terms, a study of the postmortem, preburial, and postburial histories of faunal remains (Lyman 1994). Taphonomic analysis attempts to reconstruct the chronology of a variety of postmortem processes that have produced a faunal assemblage or a subset of the assemblage. Many of these processes leave signatures on the surface of bone, which, if properly identified, provide a powerful method of assessing natural and cultural formation processes.

Weathering, Sun Bleaching, and Root Etching

The slow decomposition of bone results in a somewhat predictable alteration of the bone surface. Cracking of the surface, parallel to fiber structure, results in surface exfoliation. The loss of the outermost surface causes the bone to have a fibrous appearance, which increases in coarseness with exposure until the bone loses integrity (Behrensmeyer 1978). In areas of root activity, chemicals secreted by roots etch the bone surface and accelerate this weathering process. Bone that remains unburied for extended periods of time can also become bleached white by the sun. This bleaching also accelerates the weathering process of a bone.

Weathering of bone was not common in this collection, but was noted within the shorthouse units. Sun bleaching was somewhat more common in the midden units, and root etching was absent. Overall, the taphonomic signatures suggest that faunal material was quickly buried and therefore is well preserved. There is also evidence of carnivore activity at the site that likely destroyed some bone.

Carnivore and Rodent Gnawing and Digestive Damage

Unburied and near-surface bone is often subject to alteration by scavenging carnivores. In their attempts to remove meat from the bone, and even transport the bone itself, carnivore teeth leave characteristic markings on the bone surface, which can often be identified with the naked eye or minor magnification. While carnivores tend to prefer fresh bone for flesh and marrow procurement, rodents tend to gnaw at dry bone to obtain minerals and to sharpen and shorten their ever-growing incisors. Rodent gnawing leaves a predictable pattern of markings on bone surfaces, which are easily identified by the naked eye. Documentation of carnivore and rodent modification of bone reveals important information regarding disposal practices as well as environmental conditions.

When carnivores swallow bone, the acidic digestive environment etches the bone in an attempt to digest it. Only the smallest consumed bone can be digested, while larger fragments are regurgitated or passed through the digestive system. These bones show distinctive patterns of damage, often a smooth polish with pock-marked surface texture. Digestively damaged bones suggest the activity of carnivores on site that would be contemporaneous with human occupation. Very high rates of digestive damage suggest that some of the site's faunal assemblage may be the result of carnivore kills.

Rodent gnawing of bone was very rare, but when present it was in the midden. Carnivore gnawing was found in the shorthouse units and several features. This distinction suggests that dogs were not picking over the midden areas, possibly because they had access to sufficient bones within the main living areas of the site. This interpretation is supported by digestive damage evident on bones within both features and midden. Dogs may have kept rodent activity at a minimum, although some rodents were tolerated around the midden area.

Burning

When in contact with heat or fire for a relatively short duration of time, bone becomes charred or blackened. Bone that is in contact with heat for long periods of time or is repeatedly heated and cooled attains the white appearance of calcined bone. The effect of burning on the resiliency of bone varies with animal class, skeletal element, and intensity of the burning (Beisaw 2000). Documentation of burned and calcined bone signatures allows for analysis of cooking and disposal practices. Charred and calcined bone was common throughout the collection, with the exception of Feature 17, which has few faunal remains. Patterns of burning vary and therefore will be discussed in more detail in the contextual analysis section.

Butchery Cut Marks

In addition to the size and shape of faunal remains allowing for identification of those cuts of meat obtained from a carcass, taphonomic analysis provides information regarding the types of tools used to obtain these cuts. Sawed, chopped, and fractured bones retain signatures of skinning, evisceration, disarticulation, and marrow extraction. Cut marks were identified on medium and large mammal bone in one feature and in the midden. One deer antler was hacked.

Working and Polish

Bone can be used as a raw material for the construction of formal or expedient tools, ornaments, and even musical instruments. The identification of working on a bone can be expected both on the resulting object and on the refuse from the construction of the object. The most common worked bones recovered from North American sites are awls, tubes, and beads. Bone that has been utilized often develops a shine or polish from the rubbing of the bone on the hands of the user or on the object it is being used on, such as animal hides. The identification of worked and polished bone is therefore important to the understanding of the role of this raw material within a site.

Worked bone was identified in a feature and in the midden. The production and use of bone awls are evident. Polished bone was identified in two features, the midden, and the shorthouse units. These specimens are interpreted as remnants of an oil-producing activity such as hide tanning.

Recent Breaks and Surface Marks

As archaeological excavation is part of the taphonomic history of an assemblage, the effects of excavation and recovery are an integral part of taphonomic analysis. Surface marks and breaks that occur during and after excavation are easily identified. Together with an assessment of the recovery techniques used (screen aperture size, excavation tools used, and so forth), an analysis of the excavation impact on the representativeness of the assemblage can proceed. The thorough recovery techniques used at Corey maximized recovery of small animal bones. During this analysis, all recent breaks were temporarily mended to increase bone identifiability. The biasing effects of the excavation process were minimal.

Contextual Analysis

Quantification of bone taphonomy can reveal the formation processes that created site features. The contextual analysis that follows combines taxonomic and taphonomic data to help characterize the cultural and natural processes at work across the site. After the contents of features, middens, and shorthouse units are quantified, comparisons of these contexts provide an overall view of the site based on zooarchaeology and taphonomy.

Feature 1

This shorthouse hearth contains 263 mammal, bird, fish, and amphibian remains, totaling 109.5 grams in weight (table 8.2). Twenty-eight percent of the feature's specimens are burned, gnawed, worked, or show digestive damage. Forty-two specimens are calcined (21.1 grams), 10 are charred (21.8 grams), and 1 appears to have had some exposure to heat (0.3 grams). All of the burned bones are fragments of unidentified medium to large mammal bone with the exception of 4 deer-foot bones (navicular, metatarsal, phalange) and 2 green-frog leg bones. Nineteen unburned specimens (9.4 grams) show evidence of digestive damage, including unidentified medium to large mammal bone and 2 fragments of deer phalange.

TABLE 8.2. Taxons identified in Feature 1

ID	Name	Count	Weight	MNI
Cyprinidae	Carp/minnow	7	0.4	1
Tamias striatus	Chipmunk	3	0.3	1
Fish, unidentified	Fish	36	1.8	
Sciurus carolinensis	Gray squirrel	5	0.9	1
Rana clamitans	Green frog	4	0.5	1
Large mammal	Large mammal	65	40.2	
Medium mammal	Medium mammal	60	9.0	
Columba livia	Pigeon	6	1.0	2
Lutra canadensis	River otter	1	0.5	1
Salmonidae	Salmon/trout	2	0.5	1
Small bird	Small bird	40	1.6	
Small mammal	Small mammal	22	1.4	
Odocoileus virginianus	White-tailed deer	11	50.9	1
Marmota monax	Woodchuck	1	0.5	1
Total		263	109.5	10

Carnivore gnawing was evident on 1 woodchuck tibia (0.5 grams) and rodent gnawing on 1 medium mammal long bone (0.2 grams). One large mammal long bone (3.1 grams) shows evidence of working and was probably used as an awl or needle.

A total of 189 specimens (53.1 grams) appear unmodified and include carp/minnow (n=7), chipmunk (n=3), unidentified fish (n=36), gray squirrel (n=5), green frog (n=2), large mammal (n=11), medium mammal (n=49), pigeon (n=6), river otter (n=1), salmon/trout (n=2), small bird (n=40), small mammal (n=22), and deer (n=5).

Feature 2

This shorthouse hearth contains 17 mammal, bird, and fish remains, totaling 22.9 grams in weight (table 8.3). Forty-seven percent of the feature specimens are burned, gnawed, worked, or show digestive damage. Four specimens are calcined (1.5 grams), and 1 is charred (3.9 grams). All of the burned bones are fragments of unidentified medium to large mammal bone with the exception of the calcined deer-pelvis fragment. One unburned specimen (0.4 grams), a large mammal bone, shows evidence of digestive damage. Carnivore gnawing is evident on 1 large mammal long bone (1.1 grams). One medium mammal long bone (3 grams) shows evidence of working and was possibly part of an awl. Nine specimens (13 grams) appear unmodified and include unidentified fish (n=2) and gray squirrel (n=1).

TABLE 8.3. Taxons identified in Feature 2

ID	Name	Count	Weight	MNI
Fish, unidentified	Fish	2	0.1	1
Sciurus carolinensis	Gray squirrel	1	0.2	1
Large mammal	Large mammal	8	10.6	
Medium mammal	Medium mammal	2	3.2	
Columba livia	Pigeon	2	4.2	1
Odocoileus virginianus	White-tailed deer	2	4.6	1
Total		17	22.9	4

Feature 3

This shorthouse hearth contains 693 mammal, bird, fish, amphibian, and mollusk remains, totaling 255.7 grams in weight (table 8.4). Twenty-seven percent of the feature's specimens are burned, gnawed, polished, cut marked, or show digestive damage. One hundred and thirty specimens are calcined (30.2 grams), and 17 are charred (12.7 grams). All of the burned bones are fragments of unidentified small, medium, and large mammal bone with the exception of 4 deer-foot bones (metatarsals and phalanges), 1 gray squirrel tibia, 1 pigeon coracoid and small bird humerus, and 1 mouse metatarsal.

Thirty-four unburned specimens (10.3 grams) show evidence of digestive damage, including unidentified medium and large mammal bone, a

TABLE 8.4. Taxons identified in Feature 3

ID	Name	Count	Weight	MNI
Canis familiaris	Domestic dog	1	5.5	1
Cervus elaphus	Elk	2	28.0	1
Fish, unidentified	Fish	183	4.4	
Sciurus carolinensis	Gray squirrel	9	1.4	1
Rana clamitans	Green frog	4	0.3	1
Large mammal	Large mammal	93	146.1	
Medium mammal	Medium mammal	195	24.7	
Mollusc	Mollusk	20	8.4	1
Columba livia	Pigeon	6	1.1	1
Cricetidae	Rat/mouse	6	0.5	
Salmonidae	Salmon/trout	8	0.6	1
Small bird	Small bird	63	2.8	
Small mammal	Small mammal	85	4.6	
Odocoileus virginianus	White-tailed deer	10	26.6	1
Peromyscus leucopus	White-footed Mouse	8	0.7	3
Total		693	255.7	11

charred deer phalange, and a gray squirrel calcaneus. Carnivore gnawing is evident on an elk carpal (12 grams), a deer metatarsal (3.6 grams), and a large mammal vertebra (3 grams). Cut marks were identified on 5 specimens (80.8 grams) of medium and large mammal long bone. One large mammal long bone (0.6 grams) shows evidence of a polish.

A total of 504 specimens (104.7 grams) appear unmodified and include domestic dog (n=1), elk (n=1), unidentified fish (n=183), gray squirrel (n=7), green frog (n=4), large mammal (n=26), medium mammal (n=111), mollusk (n=20), pigeon (n=5), rat/mouse (n=5), salmon/trout (n=8), small bird (n=62), small mammal (n=58), deer (n=5), and white-footed mouse (n=8).

Feature 12a

This shorthouse hearth contains 57 mammal, bird, fish, and mollusk remains, totaling 37.5 grams in weight (table 8.5). Thirty percent of the feature specimens are burned or polished. Fourteen specimens are calcined (2.8 grams), and 2 are charred (2.2 grams). All burned bones are fragments of medium to large mammal ribs and long bones. One medium mammal long bone (2.1 grams) shows evidence of a polish.

Forty-five specimens (30.4 grams) appear unmodified and include catfish (n=1), unidentified fish (n=5), large mammal (n=12), medium mammal

TABLE 8.5. Taxons identified in Feature 12a

ID	Name	Count	Weight	MNI
Siluriformes	Catfish	1	0.1	1
Fish unidentified	Fish	5	0.3	
Large mammal	Large mammal	26	18.2	1
Medium mammal	Medium mammal	6	2.9	
Mollusc	Mollusk	12	15.2	1
Small mammal	Small mammal	6	0.3	1
Phasianidae	Turkey/pheasant	1	0.5	1
Total		57	37.5	5

(n=3), mollusk (n=12), small mammal (n=6), deer (n=5), and turkey/pheasant (n=1).

Feature 12b

This feature, probably a small shorthouse hearth, contains 1,739 mammal, bird, fish, amphibian, and mollusk remains, totaling 386.2 grams in weight (table 8.6). Thirty-three percent of the feature specimens are burned, gnawed, worked, or show digestive damage. A total of 394 specimens are calcined (39.5 grams), 194 are charred (86.3 grams), and 2 have been exposed to some heat (5.6 grams). All of the burned bones are fragments of unidentified small, medium, and large mammal bone with the exception of a chipmunk femur, a dog phalange, 1 carp and one catfish vertebra, and 28 additional fish bones, 1 frog leg bone, a squirrel tarsal and tooth, 9 pigeon bones, a mouse metatarsal, 16 small and medium bird bones, 9 deer-foot bones, and a deer mandible and humerus. Fifty-nine unburned specimens (17.4 grams) show evidence of digestive damage, including fragments of unidentified medium and large mammal rib, crania, and tarsals; a deer phalange; and a pigeon coracoid. Carnivore gnawing was evident on 1 medium mammal long bone (0.6 grams) and a large mammal rib (4.4 grams). One medium mammal long bone (0.5 grams) appears to have been worked into a bone tube.

A total of 1,157 specimens (231.9 grams) appear unmodified and include bigmouth bass (n=1), carp/minnow (n=24), catfish (n=16), chipmunk (n=2), dog (n=1), unidentified fish (n=202), frog/toad (n=7), gray squirrel (n=12), green frog (n=1), large mammal (n=96), medium mammal (n=117), mollusk (n=6), pigeon (n=23), rat/mouse (n=6), salmon/trout (n=6), small bird (n=71), small mammal (n=556), toad (n=1), and deer (n=9).

Feature 12c

This probable shorthouse hearth contains 616 mammal, bird, fish, and amphibian remains, totaling 34.7 grams in weight (table 8.7). Eleven percent of the feature specimens are burned, gnawed, or show digestive damage. Forty-four specimens are calcined (3.2 grams), and 16 are charred (9.6 grams). All of the burned bones are fragments of unidentified small,

TABLE 8.6. Taxons identified in Feature 12b

ID	Name	Count	Weight	MNI
Micropterus salmoides	Bigmouth bass	1	0.1	1
Cyprinidae	Carp/minnow	25	1.0	1
Siluriformes	Catfish	17	0.7	1
Tamias striatus	Chipmunk	3	0.3	1
Canis familiaris	Domestic dog	2	1.6	1
Fish, unidentified	Fish	228	10.3	
Anura	Frog/toad	8	0.7	
Sciurus carolinensis	Gray squirrel	15	0.7	1
Rana clamitans	Green frog	1	0.1	1
Large mammal	Large mammal	253	187.5	
Medium bird	Medium bird	1	0.7	
Medium mammal	Medium mammal	263	32.7	
Mollusc	Mollusk	8	1.0	1
Columba livia	Pigeon	33	2.6	5
Cricetidae	Rat/mouse	7	0.6	1
Salmonidae	Salmon/trout	6	0.6	1
Small bird	Small bird	86	2.8	
Small mammal	Small mammal	760	23.3	
Bufonidae	Toad	1	0.1	1
Odocoileus virginianus	White-tailed deer	21	118.8	1
Total		1,739	386.2	17

medium, and large mammal ribs and long bone with the exception of 14 fragments of deer metatarsal, 2 large mammal teeth, and 11 small bird bones. Seven unburned specimens (1 grams) show evidence of digestive damage, including fragments of unidentified medium and large mammal long bone.

A total of 549 specimens (20.9 grams) appear unmodified and include catfish (n=11), chipmunk (n=5), dog (n=1), unidentified fish (n=360), frog/toad (n=2), gray squirrel (n=1), large mammal (n=1), medium mammal

TABLE 8.7. Taxons identified in Feature 12c

ID	Name	Count	Weight	MNI
Siluriformes	Catfish	11	0.6	1
Tamias striatus	Chipmunk	5	0.5	1
Canis familiaris	Domestic dog	2	0.1	1
Fish, unidentified	Fish	360	9.9	
Anura	Frog/toad	2	0.2	1
Sciurus carolinensis	Gray squirrel	1	0.1	1
Large mammal	Large mammal	16	3.5	
Medium mammal	Medium mammal	42	5.5	
Columba livia	Pigeon	10	1	1
Small bird	Small bird	79	1.6	
Small mammal	Small mammal	72	2.3	
Catostomidae	Sucker	2	0.1	1
Centrarchidae	Sunfish	1	0.1	1
Odocoileus virginianus	White-tailed deer	14	9.1	1
Total		617	34.6	9

(n=29), pigeon (n=10), small bird (n=68), small mammal (n=58), sucker (n=2), and sunfish (n=1).

Feature 17

This pit feature located just outside the shorthouse provides a stark contrast with the high frequencies of fauna in the shorthouse hearths. It contains only 8 mammal remains, totaling 1.3 grams in weight (table 8.8). All specimens appear unmodified and include both long bone (n=4) and cranial elements (n=4).

Midden Units

The 2003 excavation of units within the site midden yielded 2,401 fragments of mammal, fish, bird, amphibian, reptile, and mollusk remains,

TABLE **8.8. Taxons identified in Feature 17**

ID	Name	Count	Weight	MNI
Medium mammal	Medium mammal	8	1.3	1
Total		8	1.3	1

totaling 1,003.8 grams (table 8.9). Forty-five percent of the feature specimens are burned, gnawed, sun bleached, cut marked, polished, worked,
or show digestive damage. A total of 1,204 specimens are calcined (389.7
grams), 191 are charred (124.4 grams), and 10 have been exposed to some
heat (6 grams). All of the burned bones are fragments of unidentified
small, medium, and large mammal bone with the exception of deer
humerus, ulna, radius, antler, tooth, and many foot bones; a black bear
phalange; dog lumbar vertebra; and a fragment of turtle carapace. Twenty-
three unburned specimens (7.5 grams) show evidence of digestive damage, including fragments of unidentified medium and large mammal long
bones, squirrel femur and tarsal, a deer tarsal, and a large mammal mandible fragment. Rodent gnawing was evident on 1 medium mammal long
bone (0.2 grams), and sun bleaching was recorded on 6 specimens (3.5
grams) including small, medium, and large mammal crania, vertebra, rib,
and long bone fragments and a fragment of fish crania.

Cut marks were recorded on two calcined fragments of deer antler
and a fragment of charred large mammal long bone. Larger cut marks or
hack marks were noted on 1 deer antler. In all 4 specimens showed these
cut marks (4.7 grams). A clear polish was noted on 14 specimens (7.6
grams), all medium and large mammal long bone, deer antler, and deer
metacarpal. Two of these specimens were calcined, 6 were charred, and
1 was heat treated. Eleven additional specimens (9.6 grams) showed a
lighter polish, including large mammal long bone fragments, a vertebra
fragment, and a section of deer metatarsal. These polished specimens
occurred in seven of the nine midden units and mostly in Levels 3 and
4. Two additional specimens appear to be both polished and worked.
These are charred and calcined large mammal long bone fragments

TABLE 8.9. Taxons identified in midden units

ID	Name	Count	Weight	MNI
Castor Canadensis	Beaver	1	0.2	1
Ursus americanus	Black bear	7	8.3	1
Siluriformes	Catfish	5	0.6	1
Tamias striatus	Chipmunk	1	0.1	1
Canis familiaris	Domestic dog	9	6.2	1
Fish, unidentified	Fish	6	0.7	
Anura	Frog/toad	1	0.1	1
Sciurus carolinensis	Gray squirrel	22	5.7	2
Leporidae	Hare/rabbit	2	0.4	1
Large mammal	Large mammal	1,556	699.9	
Medium bird	Medium bird	4	1.2	
Medium mammal	Medium mammal	557	99.8	
Mollusc	Mollusk	11	1.3	1
Ondatra zibethicus	Muskrat	2	0.5	1
Passeriforme	Perching bird	2	0.2	
Columba livia	Pigeon	4	0.5	1
Procyon lotor	Raccoon	4	1.8	1
Salmonidae	Salmon/trout	2	0.3	1
Small bird	Small bird	3	0.2	
Small mammal	Small mammal	63	7.7	
Testudines	Tortoise/turtle	3	0.7	1
Phasianidae	Turkey/pheasant	1	0.7	1
Odocoileus virginianus	White-tailed deer	129	164.5	2
Marmota monax	Woodchuck	7	2.7	1
Total		2,402	1,004.3	19

from Level 4. Five additional specimens (1.3 grams) may have evidence of working. These specimens are charred medium and large mammal long bone fragments and an unburned deer metatarsal from Levels 3 and 4. Clear working was evident on 6 specimens (3.4 grams) of medium and large mammal long bone. Three of them are charred, and 1 is calcined. These worked specimens occur in Levels 3, 4, and 5 of Units 1, 4, 6, and 9, or four of the nine midden units. One artifact is clearly an awl (Unit 1W, Level 4), while another may also be an awl (Unit 6S, Level 3). One worked specimen is a bone bead or tube fragment from Unit 6N, Level 4.

A total of 980 specimens (469.7 grams) appear unmodified and include beaver (n=1), black bear (n=6), catfish (n=5), chipmunk (n=1), dog (n=8), unidentified fish (n=5), frog/toad (n=1), gray squirrel (n=20), hare/rabbit (n=2), large mammal (n=604), medium bird (n=4), medium mammal (n=155), mollusk (n=11), muskrat (n=2), pigeon (n=23), perching bird (n=2), pigeon (n=4), raccoon (n=4), salmon/trout (n=2), small bird (n=3), small mammal (n=47), turkey/pheasant (n=1), deer (n=62), woodchuck (n=7).

Shorthouse Units

The 2005 excavation of units within the shorthouse yielded 452 fragments of mammal remains, totaling 182.0 grams (table 8.10). It is notable that these units together all produced lower faunal frequencies than several

TABLE 8.10. Taxons identified in shorthouse units

ID	Name	Count	Weight	MNI
Ursus americanus	Black bear	1	1.9	1
Canis familiaris	Domestic dog	1	0.3	1
Large mammal	Large mammal	346	133.0	
Medium mammal	Medium mammal	80	12.9	
Small mammal	Small mammal	3	0.4	
Odocoileus virginianus	White-tailed deer	21	33.5	1
Total		452	182.0	3

individual features that were floated. Ninety percent of the shorthouse unit specimens are burned, gnawed, weathered, or show evidence of polish. A total of 362 specimens are calcined (100.6 grams), while 39 are charred (20.2 grams) and 2 have been exposed to some heat (1.1 grams). All burned bones are fragments of unidentified small, medium, and large mammal long bones, vertebra, and ribs, with the exception of deer-mandible and foot-bone fragments. Carnivore gnawing is evident on 1 large mammal long bone and 1 deer-mandible fragment (4.9 grams), and weathering was recorded on 2 specimens of large mammal long bone (2.0 grams). A clear polish was noted on one specimen (0.2 grams) of large mammal long bone, and a possible polish was noted on a similar but charred bone (1.2 grams). Forty-four specimens (53.1 grams) appear unmodified and include black bear (n=1), dog (n=1), large mammal (n=28), medium mammal (n=4), and deer (n=10).

Comparisons between Site Contexts

Bone Modification

Numerous types of bone modification were identified within the faunal assemblage. Because the features included material from flotation, which inflates specimen counts, the weight of each category of modification per unit was used to construct a comparative table and chart of bone modifications across the site. Table 8.11 shows the composition of each unit by raw weight in grams, while the chart shows the normalized contents of each unit by the percentage weight of each bone modification.

By raw weight the features appear to show some differentiation, with Features 1 and 2 containing the most worked bone, Feature 3 containing the most cut and carnivore gnawed bone, Feature 12a containing the most polished bone, and Feature 12b containing the most bone showing digestive damage. The interpretation changes slightly when raw weights are divided by total weight of the bone in each context. Feature 1 now has the most burned and digestive damaged bone, and Feature 12c has the most burned bone. Using either measure, Feature 2 has the most worked bone, Feature 3 has the most cut and carnivore gnawed bone, and Feature 12a has the most polished bone.

TABLE 8.11. Comparison of bone modifications by weight per feature

By weight	F1	F2	F3	F12a	F12b	F12c	F17	Midden	Shorthouse
Calcined	21.1	1.5	30.2	2.8	39.5	3.2	0	389.7	100.6
Charred	21.8	3.9	12.7	2.2	86.3	9.6	0	124.4	20.2
Heat	0.3	0	0	0	5.6	0	0	6	1.1
Digestive	9.4	0.4	10.3	0	17.4	1	0	7.5	0
Carnivore	0.5	1.1	16.6	0	5	0	0	0	4.9
Rodent	0.2	0	0	0	0	0	0	0.2	0
Sun/weather	0	0	0	0	0	0	0	3.5	2
Worked	3.1	3	0	0	0.5	0	0	4.7	0
Cut	0	0	80.8	0	0	0	0	4.7	0
Polished	0	0	0.6	2.1	0	0	0	17.2	1.4
Unmodified	53.1	13	104.7	30.4	231.9	20.9	1.3	469.7	53.1

Interpreting Shorthouse Hearth Feature Differences

One means of interpreting the differences between shorthouse feature contents is that each hearth contains the refuse of different activities that took place in and around the shorthouse. With high amounts of burned and digestive damaged bone, Feature 1 appears to have been a receptacle for general refuse from cooking. Owing to the delay between ingestion and regurgitation of bone that produces digestive damage, it is likely that dogs were active in the vicinity of this feature. The recovery of an awl suggests that leather, fishnet, or basketry work also occurred there. The contents of Feature 2 are very similar to Feature 1, only with more carnivore gnawed than digestive damaged bone. Another awl fragment was also recovered from this context.

The higher amounts of cut bone and lower amounts of burned bone suggest that Feature 3 suggests a butchery location. The overall rates of carnivore gnawing and digestive damage are high here, which also supports this interpretation. Feature 12a contains very little burned bone and no carnivore gnawed or digestive damaged bone. However, this feature contains more polished bone than any other feature. This polish is difficult to interpret beyond an analogy to the shine that is produced on handles of worked bone from skin oils or on objects used in the hide-tanning process. It is possible that some oil-dependent or oil-producing activity occurred near this location. Features 12b and 12c are very similar in their contents to Feature 1, with the exception of not containing worked bone.

Comparison of Midden and Shorthouse Units

When comparing the contents of midden to shorthouse units, the greatest difference appears to be in the higher amounts of calcined and carnivore gnawed bone in the shorthouse. Calcined bone is more common in habitation areas as a by-product of cooking and is scattered during hearth cleanings. The higher amounts of carnivore gnawed bones suggest that dogs were allowed to consume scraps in and around the habitation area and were not relegated to picking through the refuse midden.

Species

The taxonomic contents of the units and features varied across the site. The tables below summarize the raw counts (NISP or total number of fragments) and the relative percentage of each taxonomic category used, per unit or feature.

By raw counts both Feature 12b and 12c appear to have high amounts of fish bone. However, by percentage of feature content it becomes clear that Features 3 and 12c contain much higher percentages of fish than Feature 12b. Similarly, while Feature 12b has the highest frequency of pigeon bones, Feature 2 contains a much higher faunal percentage of pigeon. The frequencies and percentages of small species, such as fish, pigeon, and small rodents, are much lower in the midden and shorthouse units than in the features, but it is likely because of the use of flotation to recover small bones from features.

Tables 8.12 to 8.14 summarize the contents of units and features using much more general taxonomic groupings. This compilation allows the relative components of the features to be examined with less influence from recovery methods. Here the contents of Features 1 and 2 appear more similar, as are the contents of the midden and shorthouse. Features 3 and 12c contain high amounts of fish, and Feature 12a contains a high amount of mollusks but almost no fish.

Conclusion

Features 1 and 2 are very similar in faunal contents and likely represent the general refuse from cooking and sewing, hide working, net weaving, or basket making. Feature 3 mainly contains the precooking refuse from the processing of a variety of food animals, which attracted the site's dogs. Feature 12a seems to be a processing area of mammal and mollusks. The high amounts of polished bone here may be from the processing of an elk hide or similar oil-rich activity. Features 12b and 12c likely represent general cooking activity areas, similar to Features 1 and 2, with 12b being more related to mammal cooking and 12c more related to fish cooking. The midden and shorthouse areas contain mainly calcined and

TABLE 8.12. **Summary of taxons identified as NISP per feature**

NISP	F1	F2	F3	F12a	F12b	F12c	F17	Midden	Shorthouse
Beaver								1	
Black bear								7	1
Bigmouth bass					1				
Carp/minnow	7				25				
Catfish				1	17	11		5	
Chipmunk	3				3	5		1	
Domestic dog			1		2	2		9	1
Elk			2	5					
Fish	36	2	183		228	360		4	
Frog/toad					8	2		1	
Gray squirrel	5	1	9		15	1		22	
Green frog	4		4		1				
Hare/rabbit								2	
Large mammal	65	8	93	26	253	16		1556	346
Medium bird					1			4	
Medium mammal	60	2	195	6	263	42	8	557	80

Mollusk				20	12	8		11
Muskrat								2
Perching bird		2						2
Pigeon	6			6		33	10	4
Raccoon				6		7		4
Rat/mouse								
River otter	1							
Salmon/trout	2			8		6		2
Small bird	40			63		86	79	3
Small mammal	22		3	85	6	760	72	63
Sucker							1	
Sunfish							1	
Toad						1		
Tortoise/turtle	3							3
Turkey/pheasant					1			1
White-tailed deer	11	2		10		21	14	129
Woodchuck	1							7
White-footed mouse				8				

TABLE 8.13. **Summary of taxons identified as percentage NISP per feature**

% NISP	F1	F2	F3	F12a	F12b	F12c	F17	Midden	Shorthouse
Beaver								0.1	
Black bear								0.3	0.2
Bigmouth bass					0.1				
Carp/minnow	2.7				1.4				
Catfish				1.8	1.0	1.8		0.2	
Chipmunk	1.1				0.2	0.8			
Domestic dog			0.1		0.1	0.3		0.4	0.2
Elk			0.3	8.8					
Fish	13.7	11.8	26.4		13.1	58.4		0.2	
Frog/toad					0.5	0.3			
Gray squirrel	1.9	5.9	1.3		0.9	0.2		0.9	
Green frog	1.5		0.6		0.1				
Hare/rabbit								0.1	
Large mammal	24.7	47.1	13.4	45.6	14.5	2.6		64.8	76.5
Medium bird					0.1			0.2	
Medium mammal	22.8	11.8	28.1	10.5	15.1	6.8	100.0	23.2	17.7

Species								
Mollusk	2.3		2.9	21.1	0.5		0.5	
Muskrat							0.1	
Perching bird		11.8					0.1	
Pigeon			0.9		1.9	1.6	0.2	
Raccoon							0.2	
Rat/mouse			0.9		0.4			
River otter	0.4							
Salmon/trout	0.8		1.2		0.3		0.1	
Small bird	15.2		9.1		4.9	12.8	0.1	
Small mammal	8.4		12.3	10.5	43.7	11.7	2.6	0.7
Sucker						0.1		
Sunfish						0.1		
Toad					0.1			
Tortoise/turtle							0.1	
Turkey/pheasant				1.8				
White-tailed deer	4.2	11.8	1.4		1.2	2.3	5.4	4.6
Woodchuck	0.4						0.3	
White-footed mouse			1.2					

TABLE 8.14. **Summary of taxonomic classes identified as percentage NISP per feature**

% NISP	F1	F2	F3	F12a	F12b	F12c	F17	Midden	Shorthouse
Mammal	63.9	76.5	58.2	75.4	75.7	24.7	100.0	98.3	100.0
Fish	17.1	11.8	27.6	1.8	15.9	60.4	0.0	0.5	0.0
Bird	17.5	11.8	10.0	1.8	6.9	14.4	0.0	0.6	0.0
Amphibian	1.5	0.0	0.6	0.0	0.6	0.3	0.0	0.0	0.0
Reptile	0.0	0.0	0.0	0.0	0.0	0.0	0.0	0.1	0.0
Mollusk	0.0	0.0	2.9	21.1	0.5	0.0	0.0	0.5	0.0

charred mammal bone. The midden area contained a much higher diversity of species, although in very low frequencies. The all-mammal contents of the shorthouse proper (not the hearths) may simply be a function of mammal bone resilience to trampling and thus better preservation and recovery in high traffic areas.

9

Botanical Remains

JACK ROSSEN

Detailed analysis of water flotation-collected plant remains from Haudenosaunee sites is rare indeed. This chapter discusses plant remains recovered from twenty flotation samples representing 170 liters of soil. Materials were collected from the three primary intact subplowzone site contexts: shorthouse hearths, posts, and midden (table 9.1). The result was a collection of almost eighteen thousand specimens, dominated by wood charcoal (table 9.2). Also recovered were cultigens (corn, bean, squash, gourd, sunflower, and tobacco), nutshell (thick-shelled hickory, bitternut hickory, acorn, and butternut), and an array of economic wild plant seeds (tables 9.3–9.5). Botanical remains were heavily concentrated in the shorthouse hearths.

The wood charcoal gives insights into the dominating tree species of sixteenth-century forests, as well as preferred species for shorthouse post construction. The morphology of corn shows differences between the Cayuga eight-row variety and contemporary Ohio Valley "Eastern Eight," suggesting some influences from "Midwestern Twelve" varieties of the Midwest. The rare find of a tobacco seed shows morphological similarity to one of two varieties recovered at Caborn-Welborn sites at the confluence of the Wabash and Ohio Rivers (Pollack 2006; Rossen 1994). The presence of pawpaw raises a curious problem. How did this species come to appear in the Corey site, through trade, embedded procurement (collection during long-distance travel), or intentional extension of the growing range? Medicinal plants such as bayberry, hawthorn, bedstraw, and nightshade add to other site evidence of medicinal activities at Corey.

TABLE 9.1. Contexts and literage of Corey site flotation samples

Context	# samples	Liters
Shorthouse hearths	8	91
Posts	7	42
Midden	5	37
Total	20	170

TABLE 9.2. Frequencies, gram weights, and ubiquities of general categories of plant remains

Category	Freq.	%*	Gm wt.	%*
Wood charcoal	14,568	81.3	171.7	93.9
Wild plant seeds**	2,459	13.7	—	—
Cultigens	596	3.3	8.3	4.5
Nutshell	212	1.2	2.5	1.4
Unidentified— general/seed/legume	83	.5	.3	.2
Total plant remains	17,918	100.0	182.8	100.0

*Calculated to nearest 0.1 percent.
**Includes sumac, a possible protected or encouraged plant.

Methods

Botanical remains are produced from archaeological sites using a method known as water flotation. Soil samples are placed in a tank with agitated water, and the lighter charcoal and roots float to the surface and are collected in a nylon bag. Portions of the sample that sink are caught below in fine screen. The samples are passed through a two-millimeter geological sieve before sorting charcoal from uncarbonized contaminants such as roots. In open prehistoric sites like Corey, only carbonized plant remains may be considered archaeological, although a few dessicated blackberry/raspberry and sumac seeds are present in hearths. Materials such as wood and nutshell from the larger than

TABLE 9.3. Corey site botanical remains by individual sample

Sample	Species	Freq.	Gm wt.
Feature 1 hearth bottom	wood (hickory 40%, bark 20%, maple 15%, beech 5%, cedar 5%, birch 5%, sycamore 5%, Am. elm 5%)	1,140	11.4
5 liters	corn—cupule (*Zea mays*)	32	.4
	corn—kernel fragments	4	.0
	hickory (*Carya* sp.)	16	.3
	bitternut hickory (*Carya cordiformis*)	5	.0
	acorn (*Quercus* sp.)	4	.0
	blackberry/raspberry (*Rubus* sp.)	33	—
	bedstraw (*Galium* sp.)	8	—
	sumac (*Rhus* sp.)	5	—
Feature 2 hearth	wood (Am. elm 40%, beech 28%, maple 16%, hickory 12%, ash 4%)	3,440	43.0
13 liters	corn—kernel fragments (*Zea mays*)	30	.8
	corn—cupule	44	.5
	bean (*Phaseolus vulgaris*)	4	.0
	gourd—rind (*Lagenaria* sp.)	6	.0
	gourd—seed	1	—
	hickory (*Carya* sp.)	13	.2
	acorn (*Quercus* sp.)	3	.0
	blackberry/raspberry (*Rubus* sp.)	288	—
	sumac (*Rhus* sp.)	182	—
	hawthorn (*Crataegus* sp.)	1	—
	bedstraw (*Galium* sp.)	1	—
	unidentified—seed (deformed)	2	—
Feature 3 hearth	wood (beech 25%, Am. elm 20%, hickory 20%, sycamore 10%, white oak 10%, maple 10%, pine 5%)	1,764	18.1
15 liters	corn—kernel fragments (*Zea mays*)	110	1.8
	corn—cupule	6	.1
	squash—seed (*Cucurbita pepo*)	1	—

TABLE 9.3. Corey site botanical remains by individual sample (Continued)

Sample	Species	Freq.	Gm wt.
	gourd—rind (*Lagenaria* sp.)	1	.0
	blackberry/raspberry (*Rubus* sp.)	320	—
	sumac (*Rhus* sp.)	242	—
	bayberry (*Myrica pensylvanica*)	1	—
Feature 3 hearth	wood (beech 32%, white oak 16%, pine 16%, Am. elm 8%, sycamore 8%, maple 8%, hickory 4%, Am. chestnut 4%, ash 4%)	2,306	34.9
10 liters	corn—kernel fragments (*Zea mays*)	32	.6
	corn—cupule	51	.8
	bean (*Phaseolus vulgaris*)	2	.0
	gourd—rind (*Lagenaria* sp.)	6	.0
	hickory (*Carya* sp.)	88	1.3
	bitternut hickory (*Carya cordiformis*)	37	.2
	sumac (*Rhus* sp.)	71	—
	blackberry/raspberry (*Rubus* sp.)	54	—
	grape (*Vitis* sp.)	2	—
	unidentified—general (amorphous)	14	—
	unidentified—seed (deformed)	2	—
Feature 7	wood (hickory)	14	.2
post, 2 liters	sumac (*Rhus* sp.)	1	—
Feature 9	wood (cedar 60%, ash 20%, bark 20%)	156	1.4
post, 12 liters	sumac (*Rhus* sp.)	1	—
Feature 10	wood (beech 50%, maple 50%)	214	3.2
post	sumac (*Rhus* sp.)	4	—
5 liters	blackberry/raspberry (*Rubus* sp.)	2	—
	unidentified—general (amorphous)	2	.0
Feature 11 hearth	wood (beech 25%, maple 25%, Am. elm 15%, ash 15%, sycamore 10%, white oak 5%, cedar 5%)	860	8.6
10 liters	corn—kernel fragments (*Zea mays*)	12	.3

TABLE 9.3. Corey site botanical remains by individual sample (Continued)

Sample	Species	Freq.	Gm wt.
	corn—cupule	1	.0
	bean (*Phaseolus vulgaris*)	1	.0
	gourd—rind (*Lagenaria* sp.)	6	.0
	blackberry/raspberry (*Rubus* sp.)	33	—
	sumac (*Rhus* sp.)	20	—
	bayberry (*Myrica pensylvanica*)	3	—
	bedstraw (*Galium* sp.)	2	—
	pawpaw (*Asimina triloba*)	1	—
	tobacco (*Nicotiana* sp.)	1	—
Feature 12a hearth	wood (beech 33%, maple 33%, Am. elm 17%, white oak 17%)	932	9.8
6 liters	corn—kernel fragments (*Zea mays*)	24	.3
	corn—cupule	16	.1
	bean (*Phaseolus vulgaris*)	3	.0
	gourd—rind (*Lagenaria* sp.)	2	.0
	hickory (*Carya* sp.)	3	.1
	butternut (*Juglans cinerea*)	1	.0
	blackberry/raspberry (*Rubus* sp.)	95	—
	sumac (*Rhus* sp.)	28	—
	unidentified—general (amorphous)	9	—
Feature 12b hearth	wood (maple 30%, beech 20%, Am. elm 20%, cedar 10%, hickory 10%, ash 5%, sycamore 5%)	1,016	13.2
15 liters	corn—kernel fragments (*Zea mays*)	20	.4
	corn—cupule	4	.0
	bean (*Phaseolus vulgaris*)	5	.1
	gourd—rind (*Lagenaria* sp.)	1	.0
	sunflower (*Helianthus annuus*)	2	—
	hickory (*Carya* sp.)	4	.3
	blackberry/raspberry (*Rubus* sp.)	460	—
	sumac (*Rhus* sp.)	260	—

TABLE 9.3. Corey site botanical remains by individual sample (Continued)

Sample	Species	Freq.	Gm wt.
Feature 12b hearth	wood (beech 40%, hickory 20%, maple 20%, Am. elm 10%, sycamore 10%)	714	5.0
18 liters	corn—kernel fragments (*Zea mays*)	32	.7
	corn—cupule	10	.1
	bean (*Phaseolus vulgaris*)	13	.1
	gourd—rind (*Lagenaria* sp.)	1	.0
	squash—seed (*Cucurbita pepo*)	1	—
	sunflower (*Helianthus annuus*)	1	—
	hickory (*Carya* sp.)	4	.0
	bitternut hickory (*Carya cordiformis*)	4	.0
	blackberry/raspberry (*Rubus* sp.)	219	—
	sumac (*Rhus* sp.)	71	—
	unidentified—general (amorphous)	7	.0
Feature 15	wood (beech 40%, maple 30%, Am. elm 20%, Am. chestnut 10%)	174	2.2
post	corn—kernel fragments (*Zea mays*)	10	.2
7 liters	bean (*Phaseolus vulgaris*)	5	.0
	gourd—rind (*Lagenaria* sp.)	1	.0
	hickory (*Carya* sp.)	1	.0
	acorn (*Quercus* sp.)	1	.0
	sumac (*Rhus* sp.)	1	—
Feature 15	wood (sycamore 50%, maple 50%)	249	3.1
post	corn—kernel fragments (*Zea mays*)	12	.3
7 liters	hickory (*Carya* sp.)	1	.0
	butternut (*Juglans cinerea*)	1	.0
	sumac (*Rhus* sp.)	12	—
	grape (*Vitis* sp.)	1	—
	unidentified—legume	1	.0
	unidentified—general (amorphous)	4	.0
Feature 16	wood (pine 90%, sycamore 10%)	172	1.5

TABLE 9.3. Corey site botanical remains by individual sample (Continued)

Sample	Species	Freq.	Gm wt.
post	sumac (*Rhus* sp.)	2	—
6 liters	grape (*Vitis* sp.)	1	—
Feature 17	wood (Am. elm 90%, hickory 10%)	734	9.9
post	corn—kernel fragments (*Zea mays*)	2	.0
3 liters	bean (*Phaseolus vulgaris*)	1	.0
	sumac (*Rhus* sp.)	1	—
	unidentified—general (amorphous)	3	.0
Unit 2 Level 5	wood (unidentified 40%, red oak 30%, beech 10%, hickory 10%, maple 10%)	183	1.5
midden	corn—kernel fragments (*Zea mays*)	9	.1
5 liters	corn—cupule	4	.0
	gourd—rind (*Lagenaria* sp.)	1	.0
	hickory (*Carya* sp.)	12	.1
	bitternut hickory (*Carya cordiformis*)	4	.0
	acorn (*Quercus* sp.)	2	.0
	blackberry/raspberry (*Rubus* sp.)	1	—
	bedstraw (*Galium* sp.)	1	—
	unidentified—general (amorphous)	5	.0
Unit 4 Level 5	wood (unidentified 40%, cedar 20%, white oak 10%, maple 10%, pine 10%, sycamore 10%)	150	1.6
midden	corn—kernel fragments (*Zea mays*)	4	.0
7 liters	bean (*Phaseolus vulgaris*)	1	.0
	sumac (*Rhus* sp.)	3	—
	blackberry/raspberry (*Rubus* sp.)	1	—
Unit 5 Level 5	wood (unidentified 30%, hickory 20%, pine 15%, beech 15%, cedar 10%, white oak 5%, sycamore 5%)	484	4.6
midden	corn—kernel fragments (*Zea mays*)	17	.1
7 liters	corn—cupule	9	.0
	gourd—rind (*Lagenaria* sp.)	2	.0

TABLE **9.3.** **Corey site botanical remains by individual sample (Continued)**

Sample	Species	Freq.	Gm wt.
	hickory (*Carya* sp.)	3	.0
	sumac (*Rhus* sp.)	7	—
	blackberry/raspberry (*Rubus* sp.)	1	—
	unidentified—general (amorphous)	7	.0
Unit 6 Level 5	wood (white oak 40%, maple 30%, unidentified 20%, beech 10%)	440	4.4
11 liters	corn—kernel fragments (*Zea mays*)	17	.4
	corn—cupule	2	.0
	bean (*Phaseolus vulgaris*)	8	.1
	gourd—rind (*Lagenaria* sp.)	1	.0
	hickory (*Carya* sp.)	3	.0
	sumac (*Rhus* sp.)	9	—
	blackberry/raspberry (*Rubus* sp.)	4	—
	grape (*Vitis* sp.)	1	—
	unidentified—general (amorphous)	24	.2
Unit 7 Level 4	wood (unidentified 50%, maple 20%, beech 20%, white oak 10%)	107	.6
midden	corn—kernel fragments (*Zea mays*)	4	.0
7 liters	corn—cupule	1	.0
	acorn (*Quercus* sp.)	2	.0
	sumac (*Rhus* sp.)	3	—
	blackberry/raspberry (*Rubus* sp.)	1	—
	unidentified—general (amorphous)	3	.0

two-millimeter sample were identified, counted, and weighed. Sievings smaller than two millimeters were carefully scanned for seeds. This procedure is followed because fragments of wood and nutshell smaller than two millimeters are difficult to reliably identify. Specimens larger than this size are representative of smaller specimens, with the possible exceptions of acorn, squash rind, and gourd rind (Asch and Asch

TABLE 9.4. Corey site wood charcoal

Species	Freq.	%*	Gm wt.	%*
American beech (*Fagus grandifolia*)	3,544	24.3	42.1	24.5
American elm (*Ulmus americana*)	3,228	22.2	39.6	23.1
maple (*Acer* sp.)	2,520	17.3	28.8	16.8
hickory (*Carya* sp.)	1,294	8.9	14.5	8.4
white oak group (*Quercus* sp.)	1,085	7.4	12.8	7.5
sycamore (*Platanus occidentalis*)	807	5.5	9.4	5.4
pine (*Pinus* sp.)	701	4.8	8.8	5.1
ash (*Fraxinus* sp.)	441	3.0	5.4	3.1
birch (*Betula* sp.)	410	2.8	4.2	2.4
cedar (*Juniperus virginiana*)	374	2.6	3.9	2.3
American chestnut (*Castanea dentata*)	109	.7	1.6	.9
red oak group (*Quercus* sp.)	55	.3	.6	.3
Total identified wood charcoal	14,568	100.0	171.7	100.0
unidentified wood charcoal	421	3.9		
bark	259	2.6		
Total wood charcoal	15,248	178.2		

*calculated to nearest 0.1%

1975). Sieving thus saves considerable laboratory sorting time without information loss.

The samples were examined under a light microscope at magnifications of 10x to 30x. Identification of materials was aided by a comparative collection of both archaeological and modern specimens, along with standard catalogs (Delorit 1970; Martin and Barkley 1973; Panshin and de Zeeuw 1970; US Department of Agriculture 1948). Specimens were sorted by species, counted, and weighed to the nearest tenth of a gram. Macroscopic wood characteristics were observed from specimen cross-sections. Changes in the visibility of macroscopic characteristics that occur during carbonization were also accounted for, to ensure maximum accuracy of identification (Rossen and Olson 1985). Very small wood specimens or

TABLE 9.5. Corey site botanical remains

Plant type/species	Freq.	Gm wt.	Ubiquity
Cultigens			
corn—kernel fragment	339	6.0	.80
corn—cupule (*Zea mays*)	180	2.0	.60
bean (*Phaseolus vulgaris*)	43	.3	.50
gourd—rind (*Lagenaria* sp.)	28	—	.55
sunflower (*Helianthus annuus*)	3	—	.10
squash (*Cucurbita pepo*)	2	—	.10
tobacco (*Nicotiana* sp.)	1	—	.05
Nutshell			
thick-shelled hickory (*Carya* sp.)	148	2.3	.55
bitternut hickory (*Carya cordiformis*)	50	.2	.20
acorn (*Quercus* sp.)	12	.0	.25
butternut (*Juglans cinerea*)	2	.0	.10
Wild plant seeds			
blackberry/raspberry (*Rubus* sp.)	1,312	—	.70
sumac (*Rhus* sp.)	1,123	—	.95
bedstraw (*Galium* sp.)	12	—	.20
grape (*Vitis* sp.)	5	—	.20
bayberry (*Myrica pensylvanica*)	4	—	.10
pawpaw (*Asimina triloba*)	1	—	.05
hawthorn (*Crataegus* sp.)	1	—	.05
Miscellaneous			
unidentified—general	78	.3	
unidentified—seed fragments	4	—	
unidentified—legume	1	—	

specimens that were badly deformed during the carbonization process were classified as "unidentified." Similarly, nonwood specimens that were badly deformed were classified as "unidentified—general," and deformed or fragmented seeds were classified as "unidentified—seeds."

Frequencies for seed or wood lots containing more than four hundred specimens represent carefully constructed estimates and not exact figures. Actual frequencies were recorded for lots containing fewer than four hundred specimens. Estimates were derived in the following manner. Two hundred specimens were counted, this subsample was weighed, and the weight of the total sample was divided by the subsample. This number was then multiplied by two hundred. Estimates of the species composition of each sample were derived by identifying between fifteen and fifty specimens. An estimate of the relative percentage of each species represented was then used to calculate the estimated frequency of each species in a sample. This system is believed to be a reliable and efficient method for handling large lots of wood charcoal (Rossen 1991).

Preservation

Archaeobotanical preservation varies greatly between sites for reasons that are only partially understood. Two factors that influence preservation are soil drainage and the chemical composition of soil deposits (such as soil pH and ash content). The circumstances surrounding plant carbonization, including firing temperature and the amount of oxygen reduction present, also influence preservation. Soil particle size and inclusions affect whether carbonized plant remains are eroded or destroyed by mechanical grinding.

Preservation of carbonized plant material was variable at Corey. The shorthouse hearths and posts contained excellent preservation, with nutshell and seeds displaying clear surface reticulations and little evidence of erosion. The presence of small carbonized seeds such as tobacco and nightshade also indicates excellent preservation. Botanical materials were present but were more fragmented and eroded in the midden samples.

Wood Charcoal

Twelve species of wood charcoal were recovered (see table 9.4). The three dominating species are American beech (*Fagus grandifolia*), American elm

(*Ulmus americana*) and maple (*Acer* sp.). The second tier of species includes hickory (*Carya* sp.), white oak group (*Quercus* sp.), sycamore (*Platanus occidentalis*) and pine (*Pinus* sp.). Tertiary species in this collection are ash (*Fraxinus* sp.), birch (*Betula* sp.), eastern red cedar (*Juniperus virginiana*), American chestnut (*Castanea dentata*), and red oak group (*Quercus* sp.).

A few environmental comments may be made on this wood charcoal collection. There is some variation in the preferred habitats of the recovered species, suggesting the active foraging of different environments surrounding the site. Sycamore, the largest native tree species in the Northeast, tends to pioneer on upland slopes, ash prefers valleys and slopes with well-drained soils, but American chestnut and American elm live in moister soils, while chestnut prefers uplands and elms are usually in valleys and floodplains. Pines tend to colonize in more acid soils, while beech, maples, and oaks grow in a wide variety of habitats, including moist lowlands and upland valleys (Little 2004).

In aggregate, the wood charcoal suggests a mixed beech-elm-maple-hickory forest with a variety of secondary and tertiary species. Beech and elm are better represented in the archaeological collection than in the present nearby forests, with Dutch elm disease having decimated local elm populations. American chestnut was probably better represented in sixteenth-century forests than in the Corey site. The archaeological percentages may partially represent species preferences as much as environmental proportions. However, the heavy mixing of wood species in all fire-hearth samples indicates that firewood was randomly collected without great attention to species. Some posts give clear indication of the species chosen for shorthouse construction, and several species were utilized, including hickory (Feature 7), cedar (Feature 9), pine (Feature 16), and American elm (Feature 17).

Plant-Food Remains

Prehistoric plant-food remains from Corey include cultigens, nutshell, and a variety of wild economic plant seeds (see tables 9.3 and 9.5). The foundation of Haudenosaunee agriculture was the Three Sisters, corn, beans, and squash, grown together in mounds of symbolic and agronomic symbiosis (Mount Pleasant 2006).

Corn (Zea mays)

Corn, the first of the Three Sisters, is nearly ubiquitous in the collection. Recovered were cupules, the outer structural layer of the cob that holds kernels in place, and kernels. The cupules are thick walled and vary from open to partially closed, with spongy, segmented bottoms generally typical of the "Eastern Eight" variety. The specimens range in size from 6 to 12.5 millimeters in cupule width (measured around the cob circumference) and 3.8 to 4 millimeters in cupule length (measured along the length of the cob). Kernels are low, broad, and crescent shaped, with the few complete specimens ranging from 10.5 to 11 millimeters in width and 8 to 8.5 millimeters in height (figure 9.1). These are all typical measurements for the Eastern Eight variety, considered to be a forerunner of the eight-row Iroquois White corn that is still grown by Haudenosaunee people today (Mount Pleasant 2011). Some of the cupules, however, are not as open as Eastern Eight specimens from the Ohio Valley, particularly from the contemporary Fort Ancient culture (Rossen 1992; Rossen and Edging 1987) and also exhibit heavier glumes and spongier, less clearly segmented or unsegmented cupule bottoms. These traits suggest some influence from the twelve-row Mississippian corn variety known as Midwestern Twelve.

Eastern Eight corn is generally an eastern US phenomenon stretching from the Fort Walton Mississippian sites of the Florida panhandle to New England, New York, and southern Ontario and Quebec (Riley, Edging, and Rossen 1990). In Kentucky there is a distinctive separation between Fort Ancient (AD 1000–1750) peoples in the eastern and central portions of the state who used Eastern Eight corn and their contemporaries, western Kentucky Mississippian groups who used a closed-cupule, twelve-row type known as Midwestern Twelve (Rossen and Edging 1987). I previously discussed the implications for the archaeological distribution of corn varieties throughout the eastern United States and commented that the easterly distribution of Eastern Eight suggests a Caribbean diffusion route of entry into the eastern United States (Riley, Edging, and Rossen 1990). Other scholars view all eastern woodlands corn as having diffused from the southwestern United States (Lusteck 2006). Whatever its diffusion route, the corn recovered at Corey, while not an exact match, is more

9.1. Botanical remains, including bean (*top*) and squash seed (*bottom*). (Courtesy of Jack Rossen)

closely aligned morphologically with Fort Ancient–style (Ohio Valley) Eastern Eight corn than other varieties (Rossen 1992).

The collection is dominated by kernel fragments, which represent food processing and waste. Kernels appear in three times the quantity of cupules, the inedible waste product that generally represents simple discard. The ubiquity index allows for a general suggestion of the intensity of corn use at Corey. Ubiquity is the percentage of total analyzed samples containing a given plant remain, and kernels are present in 80 percent of analyzed samples, while cupules are present in 60 percent of samples (see table 5). Hearth Features 11 and 12B are notably dominated by corn kernels, while hearth Feature 1 is dominated by cupules, potentially separating areas of food waste versus processing discard within the shorthouse. However, other shorthouse hearths such as Features 2, 3, and 12A contain a balanced amount of both kernels and cupules.

Bean (Phaseolus vulgaris)

Beans appear in ten (50 percent) flotation samples, including hearth, post, and midden contexts. The most notable concentration is eighteen beans recovered from the two Feature 12B (shorthouse hearth) samples. Beans are clearly recognizable from their shape, cotyledon interiors, and pebbly outer surface texture. The appearance and use of *Phaseolus* beans in the prehistoric eastern US woodlands has been a topic of debate. The high frequencies in Fort Ancient sites of the Ohio Valley have long been known (Rossen 1992; Wagner 1983, 1987). Fort Ancient cultures adopted and heavily used *Phaseolus* beans, while their contemporary Mississippian neighbors to the west did not (Rossen and Edging 1987; Rossen 2008). This difference in bean use may represent an east-west divide along the Eastern Seaboard, suggesting a Caribbean entry route (Riley, Edging, and Rossen 1990).

In terms of entry date, it has been asserted that *Phaseolus* beans diffused into the eastern United States relatively late, ca. AD 1300, instead of the earlier ca. AD 1000 date that was previously generally accepted (Hart and Scarry 1999). Early Fort Ancient sites like Muir, in central Kentucky, with their beans and associated eleventh-century radiocarbon dates, will be further evaluated to test the hypothesis of late-arriving beans. Whatever arrival date is decided on based on future research, it is clear that *Phaseolus* beans were essential to the sixteenth-century Cayuga economy.

Bean specimens from Corey vary from 8 to 11 millimeters in length with reniform shapes, virtually identical to Ohio Valley specimens (see figure 9.1).

Squash (Cucurbita pepo)

The third of the Three Sisters, squash, was recovered from Features 3 and 12B. These seeds measure 12 millimeters in length by 6 to 7 millimeters in width (see figure 9.1). Prehistoric squashes in the eastern United States were hard shelled, and most archaeologists believe they were used primarily for their edible seeds, along with use as containers and fishing floats (Hart, Daniels, and Sheviak 2004; Hudson 2004). However, the ancient Tuscarora squash (Boston Marrow) variety that is grown in Three Sisters mounds at the Cayuga-SHARE Farm is a large variety with delicate flesh.

Squash appears early in the archaeological record, having been recovered sporadically in Archaic period contexts seven to eight thousand years ago (W. Cowan et al. 1981; Kay, King, and Robinson 1980; Marquardt and Watson 1977). There is ongoing debate if the early specimens were cultivated or wild and whether squash had native North American origins (see Heiser 1989; B. Smith 1987; Watson 1989 on this debate). Allozyme, morphology, and phytogeography studies convinced more scholars that squash was independently domesticated in the eastern United States from wild populations in Arkansas and Missouri (Decker-Walters 1990; see discussion in Edging 1995, 170). Whether squash was cultivated during Archaic times or not, by Haudenosaunee times it was certainly a farm plant.

Gourd (Lagenaria sp.)

A total of twenty-eight specimens of gourd rind are distributed in eleven samples (ubiquity = .55), including hearth, post, and midden contexts. Gourd is of possible African or Asian origin (Erickson et al. 2005), used for edible seeds and as containers and fishing floats. It is commonly thought that the use of gourds diminished throughout the eastern United States with the adoption and increasing use of ceramics during the Woodland period. Their use at Corey is emphasized by the underrepresentation of these fragile remains in the archaeological record relative to their importance (Asch and Asch 1975), and thus the high ubiquity measure is more indicative than the raw frequency. At the eighteenth-century Seneca site of Townley-Read, an abundance of gourd rind suggests that it retained importance even through the abandonment of ceramics and adoption of brass kettles (Jordan 2008; Rossen 2006a). There is also ample evidence that gourds continued to be used at historic Euro-American and African American sites as well, in poor and slave households (Doddridge 1989

[1824], 88; Ferguson 1992, 97–98), and at military forts during the Revolutionary and Civil Wars (Rossen 2000a, 102).

Sunflower (Helianthus annuus)

Three sunflower achenes were recovered from two analyzed samples of Feature 12B. The independent domestication of sunflower in the lower Ohio Valley area is supported by genetic evidence (Harter et al. 2004). The cultivation of sunflower in that region is demonstrated by a steady increase in seed size from the Late Archaic through the Woodland and Late Prehistoric periods. Yarnell considered the case of sunflower in detail in his now-classic study, noting that original wild sunflower achene lengths range from 4.5 to 5 millimeters and that modern ruderal sunflowers have mean achene lengths of 4 to 7 millimeters, which is intermediate between wild and fully domesticated varieties (Yarnell 1978, 291). According to Yarnell's compilations, the Kentucky prehistoric trajectory of sunflower achene growth was as follows: sunflowers from Late Archaic to Late Woodland all exhibit achenes varying from 7 to 10 millimeters in length (C. Cowan 1979; C. Cowan et al. 1981; Yarnell 1969, 1978, 292), and sunflower domestication further intensified during the Late Prehistoric period at Mississippian sites (contemporary to Corey) in Missouri and Ohio, where mean achene length reached 10 to 12 millimeters (Yarnell 1978, 293). All Corey specimens are partial, but one sunflower achene fragment is 7 millimeters in length, suggesting a domesticated specimen.

Tobacco (Nicotiana sp.)

One tobacco seed was recovered from Feature 11, a shorthouse hearth. The seed may be compared with specimens recovered from the contemporary Late Mississippian, Caborn-Welborn Phase site of Slack Farm in Kentucky. At that site, tobacco seeds exhibit two distinctive morphologies. One group of seeds (Type 1) presents slightly raised reticulations, while in a second group (Type 2), the area bounded by each reticulation is itself raised, producing an overall lumpy effect to the seed (Rossen 1994). The Corey seed is a match for the Type 2 seed from Slack Farm. Most eastern US woodlands archaeological sites have not produced sufficient tobacco collections to undertake detailed identification to species level, and these specimens are extremely rare in the Northeast (Wagner 2000). It is thus not known whether these differences represent morphological variability within one species (usually assumed to be *Nicotiana rustica*) or two distinctive species.

Prehistoric tobacco is probably native to the eastern Andean slopes of South America (Wilbert 1987), although there are indigenous North American varieties (Haberman 1984). Though the minute seeds are difficult to recover, tobacco has been documented at more than ninety prehistoric sites of eastern North America, ranging from the Caribbean to Ontario (Riley, Edging, and Rossen 1990; Wagner 2000). The earliest eastern US tobacco appears in Middle Woodland sites of Illinois near the confluence of the Illinois and Mississippi Rivers (Asch and Asch 1985; Chapman and Shea 1981; Johannessen 1984; Wagner 1991).

According to the ethnographic and ethnohistoric literature of the Americas, tobacco was often utilized in healing and ritual settings (Wilbert 1987). Plant remains discarded from specialized or ritual contexts might be expected to be found in a particular area of a site or in association with special features and not in association with staple-food debris. This situation does not appear to be the case at Corey, where the tobacco seed is associated with typical food refuse in the shorthouse. Tobacco use may represent an element of medicinal activity at Corey.

Nutshell

Thick-shelled hickory (*Carya* sp.), bitternut hickory (*C. cordiformis*), acorn (*Quercus* sp.), and butternut (*Juglans cinerea*) nutshell were recovered. Thick-shelled hickory, recovered in eleven samples (ubiquity = .55), is the most abundant nut, while acorn, an underrepresented species owing to its thin fragile shells, and butternut were recovered in only trace amounts.

During much of the Archaic and Woodland periods throughout the eastern US woodlands, hickory was a focal resource. Hickory nuts were valuable for their high protein and fat content and relative ease of collection, preparation, and storage. Swanton (1946) reviewed at length the ethnographic data on use of hickory nuts by southeastern Native Americans. One common use was in a "hickory nut soup," prepared by cracking nuts and placing them into a pot of boiling water, where the nutshell would settle to the bottom, leaving an oily white broth.

Bitternut hickory is a native thin-shelled pecan hickory. It is identified by the lobe thickness of slightly under one millimeter (Lopinot 1982, 700–702). The nuts are extremely bitter and astringent because of their high tannin content and are thus considered inedible even for squirrels (Elias 1972). The Haudenosaunee, however, have a tradition of soaking the nuts in a lye solution of ashes or maybe calcite to leach the tannins (Parker 1994 [1910], 99–101; Waugh 1973 [1916], 122).

Butternut is widespread in the eastern US archaeological record in small amounts. The nutmeats contain considerable protein and fat (Lopinot 1982, 858–59). Butternut trees, however, produce good harvests only every two or three years, so it may not fit into a seasonal collecting strategy as well as other nut-bearing species that produce consistent harvests (Krochmal and Krochmal 1982; US Department of Agriculture 1948, 110, 202).

Nutshell Densities

The Corey nutshell densities are very low in comparison with earlier and contemporary sites of the Ohio River (not enough systematic archaeobotany has been conducted in New York to make this comparison). Densities from the Archaic through Early Woodland periods in the eastern woodlands commonly range from 15 to 40 specimens per liter of floated soil (Rossen 2000b). Mississippian sites of Kentucky, contemporary to Corey, where nut use was maintained and maybe even tree silviculture occurred (Munson 1973), average 10.9 specimens per liter. The neighboring Fort Ancient sites, where nut use was heavily de-emphasized, average 1.7 specimens per liter. In contrast, Corey has 1.2 nutshell specimens per liter of floated soil. Subtract the single concentration of nutshell in a Feature 3 sample, and the nutshell density plummets to 0.5 specimens per liter. These values suggest that nuts were a supplemental and not a focal food source at Corey.

Wild Plant Seeds

Wild plant seeds recovered represent a host of probable and possible utilized plants. These seeds represent a wild plant collecting component of the diet, along with some medicinal plants.

The fleshy fruits blackberry/raspberry (*Rubus* sp.), sumac (*Rhus* sp.), and grape (*Vitis* sp.) are present. The great frequencies of carbonized blackberry/raspberry and sumac seeds in the hearth features strongly suggest fire drying for storage (see Bartram 1955 [1791]: 321). Sumac in particular is a pervasive plant in the archaeological record throughout the eastern US woodlands. This bush or small tree grows in disturbed land but is not common in undisturbed forests. Sumac berries are best known for their prehistoric use in a high vitamin C tea and as a high-energy food source and medicine (Gilmore 1931, 47–48; Vogel 1982, 378). Fire drying for storage is ethnographically documented (Swanton 1946, 606) as well as use as a flavoring for the hickory nut soup described above (C. Cowan 1979, 9). In the Ohio Valley, sumac became particularly important to Fort Ancient people during the time contemporary to Corey, when it may have been a protected or encouraged plant (Rossen 1992, 196–99).

Bedstraw or cleavers (*Galium* sp.) was recovered in four samples. Some archaeobotanists consider the persistent presence of bedstraw in the archaeological record to represent accidental inclusions, because the seeds readily stick to clothing and hair (Asch, Ford, and Asch 1972). Bedstraw has now been recovered in high frequencies at many Ohio Valley sites (Dunn 1984; Henderson 1992; Rossen 1992, 194). At the Fort Ancient village of Capitol View in Kentucky, bedstraw was recovered in distinctive spatial distributions inside houses (Henderson 1992). As the archaeological occurrences proliferate, it becomes clear that bedstraw must be viewed as a prehistoric economic plant of considerable importance. As its name suggests, bedstraw could be used as bedding material, as suggested by its spatial distribution at Capitol View. The plant may also be eaten in salads and used as a dye. In other regions of the United States, the plant was historically used as a diuretic by the Ojibwa and a perfume among the Omaha and Ponca (Gilmore 1931, 63).

Pawpaw (*Asimina triloba*) is a small tree that is common in the Southeast, with a natural range extending north to central Pennsylvania, extreme western New York along the southern shores of Lake Ontario, and southern Ontario Province of Canada (Little 2004). The creamy fruit has been compared in some respects to bananas and mangos. Pawpaw is beyond its natural range at the Corey site. Is this a case of exchange, embedded procurement (procurement during long-distance travel), or planting to extend the natural range?

Medicinal Plants: Bayberry (Myrica pensylvanica)
and Hawthorn Crataegus sp.)

Two recovered plants have primarily medicinal uses. Bayberries were recovered from two shorthouse hearths, Features 3 and 11. The plant, found commonly in contemporary Mississippian sites, has various medicinal uses, as an astringent to combat intestinal tract diseases, diarrhea, and colitis, and to fight colds and flu, sometimes in combination with raspberry (Hutchens 1991, 30, 231). Hawthorn contains active ingredients, including tannins, flavonoids, and phenolic acids, used in traditional medicine for digestion and to strengthen cardiovascular functions. It is also mentioned as an agent to both generate and cure witchcraft (Herrick 1995, 143, 161).

Conclusion

The archaeological plant collection from the Corey site adds to our understanding of environment, construction preferences, activities, diet, and medicine. The wood charcoal is our best evidence of the area's sixteenth-century mixed hardwood-softwood forests, featuring beech, elm, maples, and oaks. Hickory, cedar, pine, and elm were used for posts. Plant-related activities include cultivating the Three Sisters plus gourd, sunflower, and tobacco, along with fire-drying berries and processing and use of medicinal plants. Nuts were collected, and bitter acorns and bitternut hickory were leached of their tannins. Pawpaw is an intriguing plant found beyond its natural range, suggesting an effort to add to the local diet, either through long-distance procurement or adaptation of foreign plants to the local setting.

10

Other Artifact Assemblages

MACY O'HEARN AND SARAH WARD

Other artifact assemblages include excavated materials that do not fall into the previously discussed categories. These objects range in function from production by-products to artifacts with utilitarian and possibly recreational and symbolic uses. A total of 277 miscellaneous artifacts (table 10.1) were recovered during the 2003 and 2005 field seasons at the Corey site. Materials discussed in this chapter are temper for ceramics, calcite, daub, ceramic pipe fragments, possible gaming pieces, and very low-frequency oddities such as drilled stones, petrified wood, and a Herkimer diamond.

Temper (n=122)

The most numerous type of miscellaneous material found at the Corey site is stone temper (figure 10.1), a raw material crushed and mixed with clay in the production of ceramics to improve stability during the firing process. Recovered chunks of white and off-white granitic stone closely match temper materials seen in the petrographic analysis of Corey ceramics, identified as quartz monzonite and feldspar (see chapter 4). The recovered chunks (n=122) thus appear to be discarded temper, with specimens ranging in weight from less than 1 to 66 grams, for a total of 707 grams. These materials were evenly distributed between the midden area (379 grams) and the shorthouse (328 grams). The identified temper is available in local glacial tills (Lajewski, Patterson, and Callien 2003).

Calcite (n=104)

Chalky calcite ($CaCo_3$) or calcium carbonate is found in association with limestone and chert deposits (Boggs 2006). A total of 18 pieces of calcite

TABLE 10.1. Frequencies of miscellaneous artifacts

Miscellaneous artifact type	Frequency
Temper	122
Calcite	104
Daub	32
Ceramic pipe fragments	9
Gaming pieces?	6
Drilled stones	2
Petrified wood	1
Herkimer diamond	1
Total	277

were recovered from the site. The collection weighs 206 grams, with individual fragments ranging from 1 to 72 grams. Calcite was recovered from both midden and shorthouse contexts. The midden area, however, contains a higher percentage of calcite fragments (n=91, 87.5 percent) than the shorthouse (n=13, 12.5 percent).

Calcite could be used as a white pigment or low-hardness abrasive. There are references in the Great Lakes to soaking dry corn in lime water with calcium carbonate dissolved in it, a process that softens corn for use and releases vitamin B3, which otherwise remains bound in the grain. The Cayuga used wood ash and ash sifter baskets to make a lime or weak lye for soaking their corn (Parker 1994 [1910], 51, 69; Waugh 1973 [1916], 62), a practice presently conducted by Dan Hill at the Cayuga-SHARE Farm in Union Springs, New York. Lye solutions were also used to soak bitternut hickory to leach its bitter tannins (Parker 1994 [1910], 99–101; Waugh 1973 [1916], 122). The exact function of calcite at the site is unknown. Calcite may have been procured at the Onondaga Escarpment chert quarries in coordination with the collection of high-quality cherts (chapters 5 and 6) (Lajewski, Patterson, and Callien 2003).

Daub (n=32)

Daub is unfired and untempered clay often used in coordination with sticks and branches. A total of 32 daub fragments were found at the site, weighing approximately 123 grams and ranging between 1 and 17 grams. All daub fragments were recovered as a diffuse scatter across ten excavation units of the shorthouse area. Use of the wattle-and-daub technique for house construction has been documented among Native American groups in the southeastern United States, including the Cherokees and Creeks (Pavao-Zuckerman 2007; Sears 1955), in structures that differ from Haudenosaunee shorthouse or longhouse construction techniques (Driver and Massey 1957). Despite the routine use of the term *wattle-and-daub construction* by archaeologists, the archaeological evidence of daub use on structures in the eastern US woodlands is rare (Knight 2007). The purpose of daub at the Corey site remains undetermined. The recovered amount is probably not enough to represent a major aspect of shorthouse construction, unless it was used in a limited way to line the interior roof for fire protection, a technique known among Mississippian peoples in the southeastern United States (Brennan 2007).

Ceramic Pipe Fragments (n=9)

A total of 9 decorated and undecorated ceramic pipe fragments were recovered (figure 10.1b). These materials were equally divided between midden and shorthouse contexts, with 4 pipe fragments spread across 3 units of the midden and 5 fragments in the shorthouse, each from a different unit. There is 1 square-collared bowl fragment of black finish with decoration along the side of the rim and 1 slightly flared trumpet pipe-bowl fragment with small punctates along the side of the rim (Rutsch 1973, 154–58, 167). The third decorated pipe-bowl fragment was cross-mended from 2 separate fragments from the same midden unit, with 1 recovered from Level 3 (20–30 cm) and the other from Level 5 (40–50 cm). This cross-mend could mean that midden accumulated rapidly or that a fragment was displaced through a root hole or crack. This specimen exhibits diagonal and horizontal incising, resembling in form a bulbous basket-bowl pipe described by Rutsch (ibid., 133–37). In addition, a single undecorated bowl fragment, 2 pipe stems with intact mouthpieces, and 4 pipe-stem fragments were recovered.

Pipe smoking occurred in a variety of sacred, secular, and social occasions. It is probable that tobacco (*Nicotiana rustica*) was smoked in ceramic

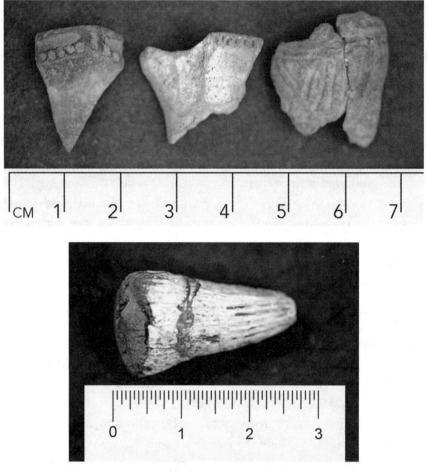

10.1. Decorated pipe bowl fragments: black ware square collared (*top left*) and red ware basket bowl (*top right*), plus ground antler tine (*bottom*). (Courtesy of Jack Rossen)

pipes, but a variety of other smoking materials were known in the Northeast, including sumac (*Rhus* sp.), arrowroot (*Maranta* sp.), cherry and birch bark, and mullein (*Verbascum* sp.) (ibid., 31–32).

Possible Gaming Pieces (n=6)

Six possible gaming pieces were recovered, ranging from 3 to 18 grams in weight. The specimens are all from four excavation units of the northern zone of the site that was identified as a ground stone processing area. The artifacts that have been identified as gaming pieces are characterized by their small size and two flat, parallel surfaces. They were intentionally cut and smoothed into rectangular or subrectangular shapes. Though their precise function remains unknown, the pieces loosely resemble the ones used in a contemporary Haudenosaunee game of chance called Atenaha, or the Seed Game (T. Porter 2008, 215). In addition to amusement, this game is played "to honor someone who has passed away, or to help settle family disagreements by putting decision-making into the hands of the Creator" (Iroquois Indian Museum n.d.).

Drilled Stones (n=2)

Two drilled stones were recovered from the shorthouse. One specimen is limestone, and the other is gray shale. They may have been large necklace beads. Another possibility is that they were spindle whorls of a friction pump or bow drill used to make fire (Beauchamp 1905, 91–92, 199; Parker 1994 [1910], 39; Waugh 1973 [1916], 50).

Petrified Wood (n=1)

One piece of petrified wood, weighing 7 grams, was recovered from the midden. The only known New York location of petrified wood, representing the genus *Wattieza*, a fern-like tree 385 million years old, is the Gilboa Fossil Forest in Schoharie County, located 112 miles east southeast of Corey (Golding 1927; Stein et al. 2007). This piece may have been an exchange item, collected curio, or symbolic artifact.

Herkimer Diamond (n=1)

A single Herkimer diamond weighing 2 grams was recovered from the shorthouse. This is a double-terminated, eighteen-facet, six-sided quartz crystal from the exposed dolostone of Herkimer County in the Mohawk Valley, about 86 miles east-northeast of Corey. The crystals, found near Herkimer in large quantities in stream sediments and field cavities, closely resemble true diamonds in their surface texture and clarity (Whipple 2007). Mohawk Valley farmers opened their fields to tourist prospecting in 1955, an activity that continues to the present day with as many as five hundred daily summer visitors (Herkimer Diamond Mines n.d.). The Corey site specimen may have served as a symbolic item, an exchange piece, or a curio collected from a long-distance trip.

Discussion

The neglect of minor assemblages by archaeologists in the Northeast has lost opportunities for insights into site activities. Even the cursory reporting of these materials leads to unanswered issues, such as the use of calcite that was procured, brought to the site, and discarded. It is hoped that the reporting of these assemblages will inspire other archaeologists to report and explore the meaning of similar collections. Daub fragments, drilled stones, and the Herkimer diamond were recovered only from the shorthouse, while most calcite was recovered from the midden zone. Possible gaming pieces were present in the ground stone workshop zone where unfinished celts were also recovered, suggesting a range of manufacturing activities in that northern site sector.

The revelation that ceramic temper was procured from a substantial distance raises questions. Has the value of ceramic temper material been underestimated? Perhaps experimental archaeology could illuminate the tempering qualities of feldspar compared to other locally available materials and address why feldspars were procured from afar for ceramic tempering. Also, what is the meaning of the small amounts of daub at the site? There is no direct evidence of daub pit linings, and the amounts could at most represent a limited role in shorthouse construction.

Why are there so few smoking pipes at Corey, especially as compared to the nearby tenth- to eleventh-century Levanna site, where almost two hundred pipes were recovered from a similar excavation effort? Why and in what ways was pipe smoking de-emphasized? Conversely, what activities or circumstances produce a great number of smoking pipes on some Cayuga sites and very few on others? As examples, according to conversations with our Native friends, the raising or condolence of a new chief could rapidly produce many pipes, or perhaps a shift occurred in the use of tobacco and other smoking materials. Pipes also indicate diplomacy and interregional interaction in ways that other distant materials may not (Drooker 2004). Pipes are regionally plentiful in Haudenosaunee country

(Trubowitz 2004), as well as at earlier Cayuga sites like Levanna (see chapter 11).

If the small, carefully cut, and smoothed rectangular and subrectangular artifacts are not gaming pieces, what other use or purpose could they have had? Finally, what meanings did the fragments of petrified wood and the Herkimer diamond hold for Cayuga people living at Corey? These materials, along with the granitic pottery temper, were either procured or exchanged from Mohawk territory and may have represented social relationships, along with the spiritual and symbolic power that distant items often hold, with greater distance often meaning more potent power (DeBoer 1998).

11

Corey Village and the Cayuga World from the Tenth to the Sixteenth Centuries

Jack Rossen

The Corey site excavations give insight into a small and intimate but dynamic sixteenth-century Cayuga village just prior to European contact. The outstanding and conspicuous feature of the site is its earthen double embankment and ditch that encompassed about one-fifth of the site boundary near the steep cliff above Paines Creek. The village contained two side-by-side longhouses facing true north-south. These are actually short longhouses, or "shorthouses," as described for the Townley-Read site in Seneca country (Jordan 2003, 2008) and at the Atwell Fort site in Onondaga territory (Ricklis 1967; Tuck 1971). Posthole evidence favors rigid-pole construction, and there may have been a thin layer of daub on or under the roof, perhaps to protect against fire (Brennan 2007, 78). Other areas of the site were used for working ground stone and other outdoor activities. There was a general shallow sheet midden over much of the site, but deeper midden deposits accumulated in a narrow band along the western and southern site edges. Other outstanding features of the site are a ground stone workshop area and a pathway to an herb area below in the Paines Creek gorge.

The geophysical survey set the tone for the key 2005 site excavations. Following the 2003 field season, which was necessarily confined to the site perimeter by farming activities, the geophysical work reinforced the walkover survey by correlating subsurface anomalies with surface-artifact concentrations, indicating the presence of intact features and feature clusters. This survey ultimately led to the definition of the two side-by-side shorthouses and a research design emphasizing village layout and activity areas.

The core of this book aims at detailed analysis of artifact assemblages, including the ones that have been underemphasized in Haudenosaunee archaeology. Lithic analysis has traditionally emphasized projectile points, but the scarcity of points on this site led to our focus on unifacial tools such as scrapers. The analysis was enhanced by the special study of quarry sites along the Onondaga Escarpment, which clarified the differences between streambed cobble cherts located near the site and quarried material that must be acquired at least fourteen miles north of the site. This analysis in turn led to the model of gendered lithic use, with women primarily making many cutting and scraping unifacial tools from streambed cobbles of Seneca chert, which was removed and redistributed by glaciers. Projectile points, most of which were presumably made and used by men, are made of the in situ stratified quarry cherts that were not affected by glaciers: Moorehouse, Clarence, Nedrow, and Edgecliff. However, even the discard and replacement of broken projectile points may be viewed as a female activity at Corey.

The ceramic analysis takes a possibly controversial stance in roughly equating ceramic styles with ethnicities (Cruz 2011). Although this approach is out of favor in some regions, there is precedence in recent regional studies (Birch and Williamson 2013) as well as ethnoarchaeological literature on style as social information and boundary maintenance between social groups (DeBoer 1990; Hodder 1991; Weissner 1983). Within this framework, the analysis displayed the dominance of key Cayuga ceramic types known as Richmond Incised and Cayuga Horizontal. The accompanying petrographic analysis established a local baseline of paste and temper composition that will hopefully spur future comparative studies. With few exceptions, all ceramics were locally made and are of uniform composition, reinforcing the probability of few manufacturing specialists. The petrographic analysis definitively matched the quartz monzonite and feldspar temper with the discarded chunks recovered during excavation. The ceramics also suggest information exchange, interaction, and even intermarriage with Seneca sites to the west, as styles often associated with neighboring areas appear to have been locally made.

The remarkable analysis of the faunal assemblage highlights the broad-spectrum use of hunting, snaring, and trapping of animals of all sizes and contradicts the simplistic notion of the Cayuga as deer hunters. Few detailed Haudenosaunee faunal assemblages have been collected and reported, resulting in a bias toward large mammal bones and thus the deer-hunter stereotype (Beisaw 2006; Hertzberg 1970, 68). An analysis of faunal remains collected by Marian White during the 1968 to 1970 test excavations of Corey emphasized large mammals and prompted speculation that the Cayuga had ceased to fish in the sixteenth century (Somerville 2013). However, the faunal remains presented here, including small bones picked from flotation samples, display the true diversity of animal exploitation at Corey.

The present analysis is also notable for the attention paid to combinations of fauna in individual features that led to the association of particular shorthouse features with elk-hide processing, basket making or net weaving, precooking food processing, mammal cooking, and fish cooking. Even the free-roaming activity of dogs around the site is evident. Furthermore, the analysis of characteristics of faunal specimens, including calcinization, charring, burning, digestive damage, rodent knawing, sun bleaching, cutting, working, and heat treatment rules out accidental inclusion for species such as chipmunks and frogs. Based on ethnographic analogy, the latter may be associated with magical and medicinal practices (Beisaw 2006). The Cayuga historically placed frogs in a medicinal stew or broth to feed children to ensure that they would never get any illness. Ground antler tines are also suggestive of medicinal production, which is interesting given the controversy of deer-antler extract use by professional athletes such as football star Ray Lewis and golfer Vijay Singh (Lallanilla 2013; Wilhalme 2013). Deer antler contains small amounts of IGF-1 (insulin-like growth factor), a growth and healing chemical similar to HGH (human growth hormone), a substance banned by the National Football League and Professional Golf Association as a performance-enhancing drug. The burned dog remains attest to the multiple purposes of man's best friend. Consumption of dog was linked to curing disease and warding off misfortune among the Haudenosaunee (Kerber 1997, 90). The sacrifice, decoration, and burning of a white dog as part of the Midwinter or New Year Ceremony was witnessed and described by Lewis Henry Morgan and others (1993 [1851], 210–19; Tooker 1965). Finally, the presence of black bear, elk, and passenger pigeon attests to ecosystem changes and extinctions owing to Euro-American settlement and hunting. Passenger pigeon is a strong indicator of spring occupation, as they are most easily taken during their nesting season (Beisaw 2006).

The botanical remains, which are not often systematically collected, analyzed, and reported from Haudenosaunee sites, highlight the environment and mixed economy of cultivated and wild species. Wood-charcoal identifications give insights into the mixed hardwood and softwood forest, along with preferred tree species for building materials. The Three Sisters complex of corn, beans, and squash was well established (Hart 2008), along with cultivation of gourd, sunflower, and tobacco. Seasonal collection, leaching, and storage of nuts, along with fire drying of blackberry, raspberry, and sumac, are indicated. Medicinal plants like hawthorn, bayberry, and bedstraw add to medicinal activities at the site suggested by other assemblages. The recovery of pawpaw presents a mystery of either long-distance procurement or adaptation of outside plants to the local setting.

Ground stone and other assemblages are usually given little attention by archaeologists, if they are analyzed at all. The analysis of ground stone implements was central to defining a major activity zone of the site, and the overall emphasis on small pallets in the assemblage led, along with the layout and pathway of the village, to the hypothesis of partial occupational specialization involving medicinal treatment. Other minor assemblages are noteworthy, including the quartz monzonite and feldspar chunks used for ceramic temper and calcite, whose exact use remains unknown, although soaking of corn and bitternut hickory is a possibility. The relative scarcity of smoking pipes is notable. Considering the great frequency and density of pipes at earlier sites in the area (see the discussions of the Levanna and Myers Farm sites below) and at sixteenth-century sites elsewhere in Haudenosaunee country (Trubowitz 2004, 154), it must be asked why local smoking-pipe manufacture and use so greatly diminished between the tenth and sixteenth centuries or whether this phenomenon is site specific. Smoking-pipe frequencies may indicate relative levels of diplomacy or interregional interaction in a different way than other distant materials at a site (Drooker 2004).

The Levanna Site (Tenth or Eleventh Century)

Since excavations were completed at the Corey site, I have conducted fieldwork at two other Cayuga villages. The Levanna site was occupied sometime between the tenth and eleventh centuries. Levanna thus falls within the time period designated as Owasco (AD 900–1300) by William A. Ritchie (1944, 1980 [1965]). The term *Owasco* has become controversial as an indicator of any unified cultural phenomenon. Specifically, the ceramics, corn-beans-squash agriculture, and longhouse architecture of this period may have formed or arrived at different time periods (Hart and Brumbach 2003; see also the discussion in the epilogue).

The Levanna site deposits are shallow, between 15 and 30 centimeters of midden, with fine-grained patterns of features in yellow sandy-clay subsoil. That is, features such as pits and posts are clearly aligned in rows and patterns without overlapping or intrusion, a pattern that along with shallow deposits usually indicates a short-term site occupation (Binford 1978, 483–95). Much of the site is unplowed, a testimony to the stewardship of landowners who continue to believe in the site's significance and farmed around it for decades. The firm soil texture and presence of features to the surface, along with eight-inch pottery sherds and large intact animal bones, confirm the unplowed nature of the site. During the three field seasons, we excavated 140 square meters, revealing sixty-nine features, including hearths, pits, and posts. Rows of hearths and post patterns revealed the remains of a long, narrow building, at least ten meters long and three meters wide, with an entrance at one end just a few meters from the sloping edge of the site. The other end stops abruptly in the disturbed area of the 1930s excavations of Harrison Follett. We call this structure a "proto-longhouse," because it does not manifest the formalized paired-post longhouse construction of later times, such as the excavated Corey site shorthouse. In fact, the contrast between the small posts at Levanna and the larger, more widely spaced posts at Corey suggest a shift from flexed-pole to rigid-pole "pi-frame" construction techniques (Beauchamp 1905, 207; Engelbrecht 2003, 75; Lacquement 2007). The close proximity of the Levanna proto-longhouse entrance to the site perimeter, along with extensive trenching along the natural site edges where streambeds run, provided evidence that the site had no palisade. Despite the large horizontal area excavated, no evidence of round structures was found to corroborate Follett's (1957) earlier report.

Although only a shallow site, the black midden of Levanna contains high artifact densities. One-square-meter units, excavated in five-centimeter levels, commonly produced one hundred artifacts, dominated by lithics, ceramics, and fauna, again indicating an intensive but relatively brief occupation. Preliminary ceramic and lithic analysis suggests no meaningful artifact differences between five-centimeter excavation levels. A total of thirty-one projectile points were recovered, including Levanna (the type site for this projectile), Madison Triangle, small-stemmed, and Jack's Reef Corner-Notched types. Three Middle Archaic points, including two Normanskill and one Lamoka specimen, all recovered from inside the proto-longhouse, attest to the collection and curation of earlier artifacts. A large Archaic site with these point types is located less than one mile from Levanna.

Several thousand potsherds were recovered. Detailed ceramics analysis has been conducted. Nina Rogers (University of Denver) investigated ceramics from the proto-longhouse, while Macy O'Hearn (Ithaca College) is analyzing other decorated ceramics (Rogers 2014). Stylistic analysis indicates a meshing of ceramic types of the classic MacNeish (1952) typology. Commingled types found within the proto-longhouse include at least twelve types traditionally associated with Owasco occupations and six types often associated with earlier Point Peninsula occupations (MacNeish 1952; Ritchie and MacNeish 1949; Rogers 2014). The stylistic variety in this short-term occupation site suggests substantial social-group interaction, which for the Haudenosaunee could include clan-based hospitality, work parties, medicine societies, and intermarriage.

Recent research has found that types and manufacturing techniques overlap much more in time and span far greater time periods than previously thought, suggesting overlapping transitions in the ceramic sequence of types (Hart and Brumbach 2009). The Levanna site analyses exhibit consistent correlation of different types and are thus a single-site and single-occupation synchronic corroboration of those findings (Rogers 2014). The results could be interpreted as supporting a form of in situ development model, with the Haudenosaunee developing over the long term in the northeastern United States, versus the in-migration model of an intrusive Haudenosaunee that led to the Levanna site's early characterization as Algonkian (Ritchie 1928; see also Snow 1995, 1996; Crawford and Smith 1996; and the epilogue of this volume on this issue).

The Levanna site assemblages include 182 fragmented smoking pipes. They are widely scattered throughout the midden, though a distributional analysis indicates concentrations in the proto-longhouse and in two toss areas just outside it. Identified to me by Native leaders are Haudenosaunee images of Hado:ih, the great healer (a false-face image), a flying head, a corn-husk person (the little people of Haudenosaunee folklore), a healer wearing a wolf mask, and animals (Canfield 1904; Cusick 2004 [1825], 25–26; Johnson 2010 [1881]; Schoolcraft 2002 [1846], 265–66; for pipe comparisons, see Wonderley 2002). We know that pipes were produced at Levanna because of the presence of unfinished and unfired specimens, both stems and partial bowls, discarded in a midden area distant from the proto-longhouse. One pipe stem shows a line with five sets of ascending chevrons surrounded by radial emanating lines. This symbol has been described to me by Native friends as an early version of the Tree of Peace, a central Haudenosaunee symbol related to the formation of the confederacy (Parker 1912; figure 11.1). The five sets of chevrons symbolize the five needles of the white pine (Schroeder 1992).

As with Corey, close attention will be paid to artifact assemblages and subassemblages that are not often analyzed in the Northeast. A large collection of more than two hundred fishnet sinkers includes specimens at several stages of manufacture, which are being analyzed for size, weight, and reduction sequence. Tiny polished specimens may represent children's toys. Ethnographic analogy may be made with Inuit groups in Arctic Canada who still make and use similar stone sinkers. Fishhooks and bone barbed-harpoon points that were recovered from the midden are being analyzed for design and size, particularly in juxtaposition with the large collection of fishbone. Chunks of pottery temper and discarded clay in the midden may illuminate manufacturing processes and activity areas.

11.1. Levanna site pipe stem with Tree of Peace design. (Courtesy of Theodora Weatherby)

We are early in the artifact analysis. Unifacial lithic tools, utilized flakes, and debitage will produce a detailed understanding of tool kits. Michael Spears (2010) of Ithaca College conducted microscopic use-wear and polish analysis of lithic tool edges, along with an experimental replication study. Our detailed lithic analysis has already been greatly aided by the study of Joseph Winiarz of a series of chert quarries along the Onondaga Escarpment that passes north of the site (chapter 5). The site contains materials from these quarries along with tools and flakes made from stream cobbles. Almost all unifacial tools and scrapers at the site are made from lower-quality stream cobbles. As with Corey, it is suspected that for the most part, lithic tool and raw material use were gendered, that is, (male) projectiles were made from quarried chert, while (female) unifacial cutting and slicing implements were made from stream cobbles (see Albright 1999; Bird 1993; Gero 1991a, 1991b; Gorman 1995 for models of lithics and gender). There are small amounts of exotic cherts and banded green-slate gorgets that are still under comparative analysis.

Extensive X-ray florescence on ceramics and pipes is under way in order to separate locally made from nonlocal specimens and ultimately understand the nature and extent of pipe trading. Unfinished, unfired pipes should provide a local trace-element baseline. Faunal preservation at the site is excellent, and sites in this area tend to show a wide variety of fish, terrestrial animals, and birds. The intensive water flotation of complete features along with blocks from all levels and my analysis of these materials will provide a detailed archaeobotanical profile.

The Myers Farm Site (Fifteenth Century)

During the summers of 2011, 2013, and 2014, I conducted excavations at the Myers Farm site. This site, located nine miles from Levanna and five miles from Corey, immediately surprised. Recorded by Robert Deorio in 1973, the site was thought to have been a "transitional," or Oak Hill Phase, village (Deorio 1980, 71). Our excavations rapidly indicated that the site is a small hilltop farmstead with a black midden barely 10 meters in diameter. The outstanding feature of the site discovered in the first field season is a large stratified roasting pit 1.5 meters in diameter and 1.3 meters deep. Among the large quantity of materials in the pit were thirty-two limestone hoe blades, some of which were placed around the pit edge as a lining (Ward 2014a). The pit also contained a complete (fragmented) pot and large quantities of faunal and botanical remains. The first radiocarbon date is 400+/-20 BP or 1466+/-18 calibrated. During the second and third field seasons, a square building with chinked double-corner posts surrounding the large fire pit and an elaborate system of multichambered storage pits outside the building were defined.

Ceramic analysis revealed that along with the site-wide preponderance (68 percent) of local (Cayuga) types and prototypes, there was a concentration of various types near the fire pit that are stylistically associated with regions to the west (Seneca), east (Mohawk), and north (Ontario) (O'Hearn 2013a, 2013b). Further analysis, involving both petrographics and XRF, aim to determine whether or not these were locally made. The forty limestone hoe blades vary greatly in size, suggesting use by both adults and children, or at least a variety of agricultural techniques (Ward 2014a, 2014b). Hundreds of grinding slabs and hand grinders, small ceramic serving plates, and more than thirty smoking pipes attest to the large-scale food production, consumption, and communal gatherings that occurred at the site. Ground penetrating radar was conducted by Michael Rogers (see chapter 2), including several hundred meters surrounding the midden zone. The preliminary interpretation of Myers Farm is that it represents a fifteenth-century farmstead and agricultural station surrounded by cultivated fields where communal feasts were conducted for people who converged for planting and harvesting.

War or Peace in Cayuga History?

In Haudenosaunee oral history, the Peacemaker, along with his companions Hiawatha and the woman Jigonsaseh, convinced the five original nations to end centuries of brutal warfare and form a confederacy and the Great Peace (Wallace 1994). The question is when this occurred and can archaeologists document landscapes of war and peace? Furthermore, how do Haudenosaunee landscapes appear during the crucial time period from the tenth to the sixteenth centuries?

We might also ask if archaeologists prefer war to peace when reconstructing the past. There are case studies like Rapa Nui (Easter Island) where long-held assumptions of a past filled with violence and warfare have not held up to the careful scrutiny of archaeological correlates

(Boersema 2015; Hunt and Lipo 2012). More regionally, the Haudeno-saunee have long been characterized as relentlessly violent:

> They were a fierce and war-like race. They extended their conquests from Quebec to the Carolinas, and from the western prairies to the forests of Maine. On the south, they forced tribute from the conquered Delaware, and on the east, the Indians of New England fled at the first peal of the Mohawk war-cry. It was not the Indian race alone who quailed before their ferocious valor. All Canada shook with the fury of their attack, and the people fled to forts for refuge. The Conquerors roamed like wolves among the burning settlements, and the colony felt itself on the brink of ruin . . . so great was their power that there is little doubt that if Europeans had not interfered, the Iroquois would have gained possession of the entire North American continent. (Proctor 1930, 1–2)

However, in their final discussion of the Mantle site, a sixteenth-century ancestral Wendat (Iroquoian) community in Ontario, Jennifer Birch and Ronald E. Williamson state: "The shadow of the historic conflict between the Wendat and Iroquois has been projected back in time in such a way that archaeologists have restrained themselves from seeking evidence of more amicable relations between Iroquoian communities in Ontario and New York State, such as ties of kinship and intermarriage or trade and exchange" (Birch and Williamson 2013, 162).

In Cayuga territory, warfare narratives dominate the archaeological and historical literature (Parmenter 2013). The three major sites I investigated over the last decade have all in one way or another been associated by archaeologists with warfare and wartime. The tenth-or eleventh-century Levanna site was inaccurately presented by investigators from Arthur C. Parker to Harrison Follett as a defensively located hilltop village with palisades (Schulenberg 2002, 158). The fifteenth-century Myers Farm site was thought to be a hilltop nucleated village. The earliest descriptions of the Corey site referred to it as being "defended" by cliffs and earthworks (Macauley 1829, 111). The Corey site was locally known as "the fort," and the major research effort of Marian White (1969) that included Corey featured a study of the settlement pattern attributes and effects of warfare.

Excavations on all three sites have thus far given no indications of wartime activities in terms of archaeological correlates. The Levanna site is situated below the cliff lines, lower and closer to Cayuga Lake than where defensive settlements might be expected. Like Corey, the defensive positioning of Levanna has been greatly overstated. Ritchie discussed the site as "on a naturally fortified piece of ground" with "steep embankments" (1928, 9). In reality, the creek banks at the site boundaries are gently sloping and easily traversed, and the site is flat and open to the east and west. Also contrary to statements made by earlier investigators, our excavations did not produce evidence of a palisade, despite our substantial efforts to locate the post rows along the site perimeter. Early photos of the supposed reconstructed palisade excavated in the 1930s show a sinewy line of narrow posts winding through the middle of the site.

Careful analysis of the extensive materials from the re-excavation of Levanna may bear on this question of war versus peace. The x-ray florescence of ceramics and pipes may isolate clusters of trade pipes from other Haudenosaunee areas. Some of the baseline chemical signatures of clay that may be useful for comparison have been established (Kuhn 2004; Wonderley 2002, 2005). Are trade pipes present and can they be associated with other Haudenosaunee regions? The XRF signatures of these pipes are being compared within the site to other pipes containing more typical "Owasco" geometric and curvilinear symbols. Preliminary distributional analysis of artifacts in and around the proto-longhouse has indicated fine-grained patterns of use and toss areas, and future analysis should provide more details. New excavations at other sites contemporary to Levanna may be helpful in corroborating the more unusual finds.

The fifteenth-century Myers Farm site presents another aspect to the wartime-peacetime debate. It has long been assumed by archaeologists that the Cayuga lived exclusively in nucleated defensive villages. Once thought to be another two-acre nucleated village, investigation at Myers Farm instead depicts a small isolated farmstead where communal gatherings associated with agricultural work occurred. How could an undefended small site surrounded by agricultural fields operate in a wartime landscape?

Within this framework, the Corey site is an intriguing case study. A GIS study of the distribution of sixteenth-century Cayuga sites rejects defense as a reason for settlement location across the landscape (Birnbaum 2011). The Corey site superficially fits a wartime model with its clifftop locale and double earthen embankment and ditch. However, the embankment abuts the steepest cliff line, while the level eastern side was open and undefended. During visits to the site, Haudenosaunee clan mothers immediately saw these earthworks as protection from the cliff and not for defense. Freida Jacques in particular noted that the site has cliffs, a village, and children, so she saw no mystery to the purpose of the earthwork. She also thought the ditch between embankments would be perfect for food storage. As discussed below, among sixteenth-century Cayuga sites, only the Indian Fort Road and Klinko sites on the western side of Cayuga Lake have confirmed palisades. Do these sites represent a period of social tension on the periphery of Cayuga territory prior to the abandonment of the western lakeside in favor of the more peaceful eastern lakeside?

The shorthouses of Corey provide further evidence. At the eighteenth-century Townley-Read site, a Seneca village excavated under the direction of Kurt Jordan, the architectural analysis and definition of shorthouses were made. Jordan believes that short longhouses, or shorthouses, were an indicator of the peaceful and prosperous "Seneca Restoration" of 1715–54, with people feeling secure enough to spread out their living quarters while maintaining the social and clan relationships of longhouses (Jordan 2003, 2008). Finally, the scarcity of projectile points at all three sites does not advance a wartime scenario through time in the eastern lakeside Cayuga territory.

It has been tempting to think of these peacetime sites, especially Levanna, as early indicators of the Great Peace associated with the formation of the Haudenosaunee Confederacy. Can archaeologists find evidence of the age of the confederacy? There has been substantial disagreement among archaeologists, historians, and Native oral historians as to the confederacy's age (Cusick 2004 [1825]; Fenton 1998, 68–71). This issue is discussed in more detail in the epilogue that follows this chapter. For the moment, it suffices to state that early "Owasco" sites such as Levanna have been considered difficult to directly connect with the ethnographic Haudenosaunee. This difficulty has led to "braided stream," "branching tree," and "multiscalar" models that emphasize regional variation and change instead of cultural continuity and connection (Hart and Engelbrecht 2012; Miroff and Knapp 2009).

The Levanna site materials, particularly the smoking pipes, raise the possibility of coordinating the archaeological record with the oral history of the Haudenosaunee. In this case, cultural continuity between archaeological settlements and the Haudenosaunee appears stronger than is described in the braided-stream, branching-tree, and multiscalar models. The Corey site could thus be a village that was occupied several hundred years after the formation of the confederacy and the adoption of the Great Peace.

The direct contact period that ensued shortly after the occupation of the Corey site brought unprecedented social upheaval to Cayuga country (Parmenter 2010), culminating in the scorched-earth destruction wrought by the William Butler detachment of the Sullivan Campaign in 1779 (Cook 2000 [1887]; Mann 2005). This era is discussed below in terms of the Wells Barn or Peachtown site, the destruction of the famous fifteen-hundred-tree peach orchard, and the contributions of the site to our knowledge of Cayuga lifeways.

Energy Confluence and Occupational Specialization at Corey

Even prior to the site excavations, Haudenosaunee clan mothers warned me of the unusual power and energy confluence associated with the Corey site. The dramatic positioning of the site on cliff lines, the earthwork construction, and the confluence of creeks below are indeed impressive. Heeding the warnings of the clan mothers, we proceeded slowly and carefully with our excavations. One day we were caught on site by a surprise thunderstorm, and a tree fell within inches of the supply tent where we had taken refuge. On another day, as a clan mother asked about the signs we were observing as we worked, a swarm of monarch butterflies descended on us. The discovery of the built pathway down to the gorge, the study revealing the unusual variety and density of medicinal herbs there (Keemer and Williams 2003), along with the frog and burned dog faunal remains, a few medicinal plants in the archaeobotanical collection, and the ground stone pallets and ground antler tines together led us to consider the role of medicine and healing at the village as a source of the site's perceived power.

Occupationally specialized villages are known ethnographically in places such as Mexico, Ecuador, Peru, and Japan (Bruhns 1994, 83; Iwasaki-Goodman and Freeman 1994; Price 1967). On the Big Island of Hawai'i, the site of Lapakahi was known as a site of medicinal specialists, including adjacent herb gardens (J. Clark 2002, 210; Kirch 1996, 83). The site remains a center for *lapa'au*, traditional Hawaiian medicine, and the setting for international conferences on integrative medicine. The ethno-archaeological parameters for understanding occupationally specialized villages have been explored (David and Kramer 2001). They include the substantial devotion of space to the production of materials related to specialized activities, the increasing standardization of material culture, and the differentiation of material culture between contemporary sites of a region (David and Kramer 2001; Mohr-Chavez 1992).

The evidence of at least partial occupational specialization for the Corey site can only be suggestive. There is a ground stone working area that covers a substantial portion of the northern site sector, where the manufacture of unusual small pallets, too small to grind corn, was emphasized. A substantial effort was made in the construction of a pathway down to the gorge sixty feet below the site where the densest herbal zone yet identified in central New York still exists. Furthermore, the accumulation of a deep midden on the site edge above the herb area, instead of tossing the debris over the cliff, suggests respect for the herb zone below. The consumption of frog and dog and the grinding of antler tines are also evidence of medicinal activities. At least two plants that were recovered, bayberry and hawthorn, have exclusively medicinal uses, while others, such as sumac and raspberry, have corollary medicinal properties (Herrick 1995). Only detailed case studies of other Cayuga village sites could shed further light on the issue of differentiation of material culture between villages. Specifically, do other contemporary villages manifest a similar high visibility of evidence for medicinal activities in their site structure and artifact assemblages?

An additional case of occupational specialization in Cayuga territory may be the Wells Barn or Peachtown site in Aurora, New York. Wells Barn is an eighteenth-century site that probably corresponds to the site of Chonodote or Peachtown in the Sullivan Campaign soldier journals. Though occupied two centuries after Corey in a world heavily pressured by Euro-American settlement, Wells Barn displays interesting patterns of specialization. To begin, it is the only Cayuga settlement located near the lakeshore, while other sites are a half mile to one and a half miles east of the lake, either below the cliff lines like Levanna or above the cliffs like Corey. The site is located in a low-lying warm-protected microzone near Cayuga Lake where temperatures are substantially higher than in surrounding areas. It was associated with a huge fifteen-hundred-tree peach orchard that was destroyed by William Butler's troops during the Sullivan Campaign on September 23 and 24, 1779 (G. Grant in Cook 2000 [1887], 113). Perhaps the site was chosen as the best place to grow the introduced and adopted peaches. Soldier descriptions describe the village as "chiefly old buildings" (compared to the "large and commodious" Cayuga Castle), including twelve to fourteen houses, probably an indicator that the site was only seasonally occupied, perhaps during the peach harvest (T. Grant in Cook 2000 [1887], 143).

Archaeological excavations at Wells Barn produced little habitational debris but lenses of thick crude sherds of storage vessels and agglomerated waster sherds associated with repeated pit firings of ceramics. My interpretation of the site has been that it was a specialized peach-growing and -processing site only temporarily occupied each year (Rossen 2006b, 257–58). This specialized station would hypothetically have fire-dried, jarred, and traded peaches throughout Cayuga country and beyond. In terms of understanding the Cayuga world, the eighteenth-century Wells Barn site suggests foreknowledge of the structure and organization of occupational site specialization.

The Woods and Clearing Model

The Woods and Clearing Model is prominent in Haudenosaunee symbolic thought and daily activities. The clearing was primarily the domain of women, including the village and agricultural fields, while the woods and hunting grounds were primarily the domain of men, who spent less time in the village and were considered visitors (Hertzberg 1970, 23–34; Green 1997, 14; Richter 1992, 23). Haudenosaunee leaders recognize both gender separation and cooperation. According to Peter Jemison, "The domain of women was really the village itself; the home belonged to the woman. The gardens, the fields were also the responsibility of the women, and they spent the time that it took to plant, to weed, and to harvest" (Ferrero 2001). Some scholars have cautioned about taking the gender differentiation of woods and clearing literally, stating that this structure was not rigid and that the mobility of women and mixed-gender activities such as fishing obscured gender separation in reality (Green 1997). Onondaga clan mother Audrey Shenandoah emphasized gender cooperation in activities such as braiding and hanging corn (Ferrero 2001). Haudenosaunee life has been best characterized as both gendered and balanced, both different and equal, with a practical and flexible structure (Venables 2010). Within this framework, there is evidence for the degree to which the woods and clearing dichotomy conceptually structured Haudenosaunee life, including women's ownership of farming equipment (Tooker 1996 [1984]), the tasks of daily life (Venables 2010), and the way that land rights and treaties were perceived (Venables 2000, 93–98).

Does the Corey village show evidence of female dominance in accordance with the Woods and Clearing Model? Archaeological evidence at Cayuga sites like Parker Farm and Carman and at Seneca sites like Townley-Read have successfully examined gendered activities, finding them to be dominated by women's activities despite the presence of men's activities and the lack of spatial segregation of male and female work zones (Allen 2010; Jordan 2014). At Corey the great frequencies of ceramics and scrapers made of locally available Seneca streambed chert cobbles, considered primarily female products, and the scarcity of projectile points, usually a male product associated with travel to the Onondaga

Escarpment quarries, provide some archaeological support for the model. Even the low-frequency presence of (only) broken projectile points in the midden may be relatable to female repair and replacement activity. The wide range of faunal remains, including a range of small animals that would be trapped or snared, also suggests the dominance of female and children activities in the Corey archaeological record. On the other hand, ground stone tool production focused on celts is usually thought of as a male activity related to land clearing and field preparation. Even in this case, the production of small pallets in the activity area, probably associated with grinding herbs and pigments, is not a clearly gendered activity.

Was the medicinal activity at Corey related to women? The evidence is circumstantial. Herb growing or collecting would be a natural outgrowth or correlate of female agriculture and plant gathering. In historic times into the present, there were no restrictions against women participating in medicine societies (Brown 1996 [1970]), and most herbalists in Haudenosaunee country today are women. In terms of providing a stable and sedentary base for medicinal activities and the production of medicinal technology and herbs, including a direct chain between cultivation, processing, and practice, it is logical to think of the medical practitioners of Corey as women.

Sixteenth-Century Neighbors

Some comparisons may be made between the Corey village and neighboring sixteenth-century settlements. In Cayuga country the best comparisons may be made with the Klinko, Indian Fort Road, Parker Farm, and Carman sites (Allen 2009; Baugher and Clark 1998; Nelson 1977; Sanft 2013; Stout 2012a, 2012b). These sites on the western side of Cayuga Lake are thought to represent a sequence of village movements. Cayuga longhouses on both sides of Cayuga Lake appear to be much narrower than (barely half the width of) structures elsewhere in Haudenosaunee territory (Michaud-Stutzman 2009). This difference in size may reflect the overall smaller population of the sixteenth-century Cayuga than their Haudenosaunee contemporaries.

Whereas the Carman site (2 acres) is the same size as Corey, and Parker Farm (2.4 acres) and Klinko (3.4 acres) are slightly larger, Indian

Fort Road (5.9 acres) is nearly three times larger than Corey, making it the largest village of the period (Sanft 2013). This knowledge raises questions. If the four sites represent a sequence of a single village's movements, why is Indian Fort Road larger than the others? One possibility is that the two villages fused during a coordinated village movement. It is notable that Indian Fort Road and Klinko are the only sites with confirmed palisades (D. Jones and A. Jones 1980; Nelson 1977). In contrast, efforts to locate expected palisades at Carman and Parker Farm have not been successful (Allen 2010, 60; Conger and Allen 2013). Second, this set of sites appears to represent a relatively brief single-century Cayuga occupation of the "west bank" of Cayuga Lake, as opposed to the longer-term use of the "east bank" heartland (including Corey) by the primary Cayuga population (Allen 2009). Thus, the principal Cayuga settlements would have been on the eastern side of the lake both before and after the sixteenth century, with a more dispersed population on both sides of the lake during the sixteenth century. Was there more social tension and defense west of Cayuga Lake than on the eastern side at this time, perhaps associated with a partial and temporary population movement out of the eastern lakeside heartland?

A settlement model of principal and satellite sites has been presented for the Haudenosaunee (Jordan 2013; Wray et al. 1987). Satellite settlements both near to and distant from principal settlements were used to maintain contact with distant Haudenosaunee people and integrate outsiders into local villages. Could the four "west bank" Cayuga sites represent pairs of primary and satellite sites instead of a four-village movement sequence? More directly relevant to the present study, does the Corey village fit into a satellite-system model? In presenting his version of the satellite model as a response to the pressures of Euro-American contact, Kurt Jordan emphasized the seventeenth- and eighteenth-century historical period, when Haudenosaunee expansion was at its zenith (Parmenter 2010). Jordan also suggests that the principal settlement and satellite system had prehistoric antecedents. If we accept the premise of a highly fluid Cayuga population around Cayuga Lake, and are not bothered by the distance to the "west bank" sites, then the Corey village could be viewed as a satellite village. Alternatively, there may have been local principal sites on the eastern lake side like the Colgan site (Jordan, personal communication, 2013).

To the west, sixteenth-century Seneca villages have also been modeled by Charles Wray and his collaborators as larger settlements paired with small satellite villages about one mile away. The detailed study of the Adams and Culbertson sites presents this case in detail. Adams was about ten acres in size, whereas Culbertson was about five to eight acres. These sites were paired with the two- to three-acre Alva Reed and Johnston sites, respectively (Wray et al. 1987, 229–38). Proposed village movement sequences were plotted. These sites date to relatively late in the sixteenth century and unlike Corey contain European contact materials.

To the east, about eight contemporary Onondaga villages are well known. Villages may have been paired in alliance, although the term *satellite* has not been used by scholars, and some villages were palisaded while others were not (Tuck 1971). Three larger villages (Temperance House, Quirk, and Chase) are estimated at four to five acres in size, about twice the size of Corey, while five smaller villages (Atwell Fort, Pickering, Sheldon, Dwyer, and Brewerton) are estimated as between two and three acres, more comparable in size to Corey (Bradley 2005, 49–50). Population density may have been relatively comparable between the Onondaga and Cayuga, with the Onondaga having a few larger and more populated villages. A broader demographic study lists only six of twenty-one villages occupied from AD 1500–1700 as having palisades (E. Jones 2010, 394).

The starkest contrast can be made with sixteenth-century Mohawk territory (Funk and Kuhn 2003). Three large villages (Klock, Smith-Pagerie, and Garoga) are considered the sequential result of periodic village movement. Klock and Smith-Pagerie are about four acres in size, twice the size of Corey, while Garoga is two and a half acres, comparable to Corey. However, in comparison to Corey's two shorthouses, there are at least twenty-one known longhouses among the three villages: at least seven at Klock, five at Smith-Pagerie, and nine at Garoga. Most of these structures were more than 150 feet long, with the longest being the 230-foot House 1 at Smith-Pagerie (ibid., 148).

Population estimates of the Mohawk villages were made based on midline hearths, family compartments, and pit-feature density. These techniques produced a range of estimates, from 370 to 845 for Klock, 1,760 to 2,325 for Smith-Pagerie, and 1,400 to 3,000 for Garoga. Although the Mohawk villages are not much larger in area than Corey, they were much denser and more heavily built. Contrasting the lowest Mohawk village estimates with the highest estimate for Corey (sixty), contemporary Mohawk villages were six to twenty-three times greater in population, although barely twice the area. Also in contrast with Corey, the Mohawk villages had defensive palisades (Funk and Kuhn 2003).

Last, in terms of size and structure, a contrast may be made between the Corey village and the Iroquoian longhouse settlements of Ontario. By the time of the sixteenth-century occupation of Corey, settlements in Ontario had been through a multidimensional intensification process (Birch and Williamson 2013; Creese 2011; Kapches 1994; Warrick 2000). This process included village fusion, growth, and consolidation of longhouses, sometimes surpassing 300 feet (91 meters) in length (Kapches 1994), regularization of village spatial proxemics, and increasing tension between the need for leadership and organization of more concentrated populations and the continuing social ethic of egalitarianism (Birch 2008, 2010; Creese 2011; Kapches 1990).

Ontario Haudenosaunee villages grew from an average size of one-half acre to an average of four acres (Creese 2011, 132–34). The Mantle site, an ancestral sixteenth-century Wendat (Iroquoian) village, archaeologically displayed ninety superimposed longhouses (both long and short types) on its seven acres (2.9 ha) and may have been the fusion product of as many as eight small villages. Its village plan changed from having an open plaza to having little or no open space (Birch and Williamson 2013). In contrast, in central New York Cayuga territory, the tenth-or eleventh-century Levanna site and the sixteenth-century Corey site are both two-acre villages (2.0 for Levanna and 2.2 for Corey) with open space and short longhouses or shorthouses, leaving no evidence of processes of growth, fusion, crowding or consolidation. Yet between the times of Levanna and Corey, there was village reorganization that suggests formalization of longhouse architecture and spatial proxemics, more discrete activity and workshop areas, and at least partial occupational specialization.

What accounts for the differences in sixteenth-century village size, density, and layout across Haudenosaunee territory? Mohawk and Seneca villages may have been more defensive, although they also may have been placed for wind protection (Engelbrecht 2003, 92). The density of large longhouses in Mohawk villages as well as their configuration within the village may reflect tensions along the outside borders of the confederacy. Populations appear to have risen in Seneca, Onondaga, Mohawk, and Oneida territories during the sixteenth century at annual rates of between 1.2 and 3.2 percent, with the Mohawk showing the greatest growth rate (E. Jones 2010). Excepting the Indian Fort Road and Carman sites, Cayuga villages like Corey were smaller, intimate, and more spacious with an open layout. Even the two larger Cayuga villages appear to have had more open space and narrower longhouses or shorthouses than their Haudenosaunee contemporaries (Allen 2009; Baugher and Clark 1998).

The sixteenth-century Cayuga maintained a relatively small population, while Haudenosaunee peoples around them steadily grew (Engelbrecht 1987). Could occupational specialization of small villages be considered an alternative Cayuga pathway, instead of growth, fusion, and consolidation, within the increasingly complex Haudenosaunee world? Could the Corey village represent the somewhat specialized makeup of satellite villages within a developing system in which incorporation of outsiders and communication with distant relations were becoming of increasing importance?

Cayuga Circulations

The Cayuga world on the eve of European contact can be viewed as a series of human and material circulations. It is a cross-cutting and interwoven series of movements, both shorter and longer term in space and time, with some being regular and predictable, others being daily, sporadic, or rare in an individual lifetime. The woods-clearing model with its gendered foundation, both conceptual and practical, provides a foundation to work from, including prescriptions for bases of operations within and beyond the village and corresponding tasks and responsibilities.

The placement of sixteenth-century Cayuga villages has been studied, including topography, elevation for defense, and proximity to building wood, limestone outcrops, hunting grounds, transportation routes, and wetlands (Allen 1999, 2009). A GIS study of these settlements rejects defensive positioning as a key factor. The study instead favors a strategic combination of positioning near good agricultural land complemented by access to wetlands (Birnbaum 2011). Although not specified, the assumption is that "good agricultural land" is equated with the Honeoye silt-loam soil type that surrounds the Corey village. The pattern of placement of Cayuga villages on and near islands of this soil type, which constitutes only 18 percent of Cayuga County, has long been obvious to me. For instance, at the Cayuga-SHARE Farm, crops, berries, and trees grow vigorously on an island of Honeoye silt loam. We have found numerous limestone hoe blades at the farm, evidence of Cayuga agricultural fields located west of the large eighteenth-century settlement of Goiogouen (Cayuga Castle). Archaeologists are just beginning to understand the traditional environmental knowledge of the Cayuga, including the nature and geography of soil types.

The periodic movement of Haudenosaunee villages has long been recognized, with movements usually described as between ten to thirty years (Allen 2009; Engelbrecht 2003; Wray et al. 1987). For this reason, the archaeological sites generally contain shallow middens and fine-grained feature patterns with little overlap, well-defined activity areas, and discrete spatial patterning of artifacts. We may add the isolated farmstead with seasonal work groups like Myers Farm (and, later, the fruit orchard and processing station) as splinter populations outside of villages, with concomitant gatherings of workers for planting, harvest (in the later case of Wells Barn processing for exchange), and feasting.

The Corey village was particularly well prepared and equipped for medicinal activities. People may have traveled there to seek medical specialists with their unusually well-endowed herb gardens. As early as Levanna in the tenth or eleventh century, smoking pipes with Haudenosaunee iconography suggest the presence of medicine societies and travel for medical attention. If the eighteenth-century Wells Barn site is any indicator of earlier patterns, there was substantial movement of people with exchange goods. Men were traveling to hunt and walking fourteen to thirty miles to quarry sites along the Onondaga Escarpment for high-quality chert and calcite. The corresponding more local movement of women to garner stream-cobble chert led to the gendered acquisition and use of raw lithic materials. One Herkimer diamond suggests procurement or exchange 85 to 112 miles to the east in Mohawk territory. Plants like pawpaw represent procurement during travel or exchange or extension of natural plant ranges through local planting. The sporadic presence of green-banded slate from the Ohio Valley (at Levanna) and cherts from the Mohawk and Hudson Valleys and perhaps farther afield hints at the less systematic long-distance movements that were accomplished.

This outline of a complex, interwoven, and overlapping series of human and material circulations in the Cayuga world, fully developed by the time of the Corey site occupation, also hints at the disruptions that were to come with Euro-American land occupation. Does the absence of high-quality chert at the Wells Barn (Chonodote) site suggest that trips to the Onondaga Escarpment quarry sites were no longer possible by the middle of the eighteenth century? The economic, political, and spiritual power of the peach orchard is indicated by the amount of effort expended by American soldiers on its destruction during those two September days in 1779 (T. Grant in Cook 2000 [1887], 143).

Haudenosaunee Concepts and Archaeology

At this point, I think it is worthwhile to briefly revisit some Haudeno-saunee concepts that were discussed in the introduction. The good mind is a well-trained and balanced mind that is aware of each thought and its consequences. In much the same way, the archaeologist considers all pieces of information from a site in a disciplined way in order to understand their interrelationships and produce a complete and logical story. Within the framework of indigenous archaeology, the archaeologist gratefully adds the participation, concepts, guidance, and interpretative ideas of Native people, along with an awareness of the past and present impacts of archaeology. There is much work to be done for archaeologists working in Haudenosaunee territory to build relationships and overcome the painful history of archaeology. Perhaps one of the greatest obstacles is telling the archaeological stories in English, the imperfect language that is one-dimensional in comparison with Haudenosaunee languages.

The interpretations presented here embrace a vision of the thriving Cayuga world as lived in a dynamic peacetime village with a broad-spectrum economy of farming, fishing, hunting, trapping, snaring, and collecting. This view of the Cayuga lifeway includes multidimensional circulations of people, sophisticated if not specialized occupations (partic-ularly medicine), regular long-distance social and procurement contacts, and perhaps centuries of experience with confederacy relationships. As the clan mothers advised me at the onset of research, the Corey village was and is a place of unusual power. As I complete this work, I think back on another concept they taught me—how archaeologists do not find any-thing, but are conduits and have stories revealed to them when the time is socially and politically correct. Why is the time right for the Corey site story to be told? That is a story for the epilogue.

Epilogue

Challenging Dominant Archaeological Narratives of the Haudenosaunee

JACK ROSSEN

I began working in Haudenosaunee archaeology and community activism at a midcareer point after twenty years as a South American archaeologist in Peru, Chile, and Argentina. In this sense I developed an outsider's perspective on New York archaeology. During my work with the Cayuga people and their history, I found in central New York State a set of both deeply entrenched and emerging narratives that were produced and reproduced by regional organizations and mass media, along with some local historians and regional academics (Mann 2003, 2005). Over time these narratives were reinforced by political objectives associated with local resistance to Native cultural revitalization and land claims (Harnden 2000). Challenging most of these narratives involves careful archaeological research within the perspective that has come to be known as indigenous archaeology (Watkins 2000). In this epilogue, I briefly describe four key dominant narratives and how they are being challenged.

Narrative 1: The Europeans arrived in central New York and found an empty wilderness.

This assertion appears in local histories written by regional, county, or village historians (Edmunds 2000, 1). The empty-wilderness narrative is widespread, and I have encountered versions of it in various places, including Kentucky and Vermont (Channing 1977; Lacy 1999). In the New York case, the empty-wilderness narrative is associated with submersion of the Sullivan Campaign of 1779, when George Washington sent General John Sullivan and approximately one-third of the Continental army north to conduct a scorched-earth destruction of Haudenosaunee villages, crop fields, and fruit-tree orchards. My many visits to local secondary schools (fourth grade to high school) indicate that most schools do not teach about the campaign, which should be considered the single most important event of Finger Lakes history.

One event that began to change this situation was the republication of the long-out-of-print journals of the expedition's soldiers (Cook 2000 [1887]). A regional organization, Upstate Citizens for Equality, utilizes the empty-wilderness narrative to support Narrative 2, discussed below. During the Cayuga Land Claim hearings of 2001, a Canadian historian invoked the narrative to claim that Canada was actually the Cayuga homeland. The lack of interest by professional archaeologists in Cayuga history, including the absence of archaeologists in the key eastern region of Cayuga Lake from 1970 to 2000 following the work of Marian White, reinforced the narrative. Despite more than a decade of archaeological research in the region clearly showing a long Cayuga chronology, the narrative of the empty wilderness persists or is transformed into Narrative 2.

Narrative 2: The Cayuga arrived late in central New York (ca. 1600s), displacing earlier people, or the formation of a recognizable Cayuga people or ethnicity occurred very late in prehistory (or both).

This narrative is a reworked version of the first one and can also be referred to as the "braided stream," "branching tree," or "multiscalar" model of the development of Haudenosaunee ethnicities. In this narrative, cultural interaction and exchange between groups led to a late postcontact or early contact-period development of the peoples we today recognize as Cayuga, Seneca, Onondaga, Oneida, and Mohawk. The model challenges the labeling of particular ceramic types as being associated with single ethnic groups. It has depended on research conducted on museum archaeological collections. I fear that this narrative may be associated with an indirect and unstated resistance to repatriating human remains to Native nations through the Native American Graves Protection and Repatriation Act of 1990. This law currently depends on demonstrating cultural affiliation to repatriate human remains and funerary artifacts to Native peoples. How-ever, New York State's long-standing policies on NAGPRA and affiliation are based on the conviction that precontact cultures cannot be affiliated with existing Native groups like the Cayuga (Beisaw 2010).

A close relative to the late-arrival narrative is the idea that the Haude-nosaunee in-migrated to central New York, displacing Algonkian-speak-ing peoples who inhabited the region (Ritchie 1932). During the 1930s and '40s, archaeological sites like Levanna were routinely labeled as "Algonkin" or "Algonkian," referring to the Algic speakers of New Eng-land, southern Canada, and the Great Lakes that surrounded Iroquoian speakers of the Northeast at the time of European contact (Ritchie 1928, 1932). Arthur C. Parker referred to the Levanna site as being associated with the "Third Period Algonkin." The in-migration and displacement idea fell out of fashion in the 1950s with Richard MacNeish's study of ceramic types (MacNeish 1952; Ritchie and MacNeish 1949). Dean Snow (1995) revived the theory of in-migration of Haudenosaunee groups into the Northeast in the 1990s, leading to brisk debate. He readjusted his in-migration hypothesis from AD 1000 to AD 700 based on critiques (Craw-ford and Smith 1996; Snow 1996).

The Levanna site (chapter 11) was reclassified within the time period designated as Owasco (AD 900–1300) by Ritchie (1944, 1980 [1965]; Follett 1957; Ritchie and MacNeish 1949; Schulenberg 2002). This chronological and cultural term has been declared useless and "dead" (Hart and Brum-bach 2003). According to this line of thinking, the cultural traits defin-ing Owasco, its ceramics, corn-beans-squash agriculture, and longhouse architecture all appear to have formed or arrived at different time peri-ods. There is also substantial variation between groups that have been placed under the regional and temporal umbrella of Owasco. In its place, scholars have suggested a concept of branching, braided, or interwoven cultural development that led to a relatively late development of the rec-ognizable Haudenosaunee tribes (Hart and Engelbrecht 2012). Multiscalar archaeological models are also emphasizing regional variation over cul-tural continuity and connections (Miroff and Knapp 2009).

I too dislike the term *Owasco,* but for very different reasons. I believe the term disengages these archaeological cultures from and obscures their connections to the historical and present-day Haudenosaunee. The use of disengaging terms to refer to archaeological periods connected to present-day Native peoples may be considered a long-term subnarrative of oppression. The process of renaming is central to recovering sacred meaning and revitalizing cultures (LaDuke 2005). I have come to believe it is more accurate to refer to peacetime sites like Levanna and Myers Farm, in the heart of Cayuga territory with Haudenosaunee art, symbolism, and architecture, as "Early Cayuga." The forthcoming detailed analyses of these sites will add to our local understanding of the timing of the introduction of various cultural traits of this time period and continue to challenge the dominant narrative.

Narrative 3: The Haudenosaunee Confederacy is a relatively recent phenomenon, having occurred just before European contact, or it occurred after European arrival as a response to pressure from the contact situation.

There has been substantial discussion and disagreement as to the age and origins of the Haudenosaunee Confederacy (Bonaparte 2006, 47–52; Fenton 1998, 68–71). The Haudenosaunee themselves have long maintained in oral histories that their confederacy is more than one thousand years old (Cusick 2004 [1825]). In contrast, one argument made by archaeologists is that evidence of smoking trade pipes at the confederacy edges, between the Seneca to the west and the Mohawk to the east, suggests a functioning confederacy did not exist before 1650 (Kuhn and Sempowski 2001) or even the 1700s, if it existed at all (Starna 2008). This time line would make the confederacy a post–European contact phenomenon. Supporting this perspective, historian Jon Parmenter states that the "completion of the process of League formation reflected an increasing concern with . . . unprecedented, revolutionary and spiritually powerful phenomena," specifically the intrusion of Europeans. The Peacemaker epic story of confederacy formation thus represents "protocols pertaining to the transformation of a cultural context of intergroup hostility and suspicion to one in which freedom of movement and peaceful communication prevail" (Parmenter 2010, xliv–xlv).

A significant discrepancy is raised by this perspective. If the confederacy with its Great Peace was formed on the principles of ending centuries of warfare as Europeans arrived, why did a postcontact formation set off (according to Parmenter) a period of aggression against both Natives and Europeans? Was there never truly a Great Peace? Why were the Peacemaker and his companions Hiawatha and Jigonsaseh, supposedly late-sixteenth- or early-seventeenth-century people in this account, not known as historical figures? The confederacy undoubtedly passed through various stages of development and reorganization, so why not view the contact period as one more stage or incarnation of an established confederacy? A confederacy with time depth might better explain the power and organization of the Haudenosaunee as they confidently navigated the tumultuous and fragmenting times of the contact era.

Other archaeologists have accepted a relatively late precontact date in the early 1400s, largely based on settlement-pattern data showing five site clusters by that time (Snow 1994). Meanwhile, ethnohistorians have matched aspects of oral history to astronomical events such as eclipses, specifically the black sun that appeared as the Seneca debated in council on joining the confederacy in some versions of the Peacemaker epic (Canfield 2013 [1902], 206; Wallace 1994), to posit earlier dates such as AD 1142 (Mann and Fields 1997). According to oral accounts, "The sun went out and for a little time there was complete darkness . . . when the corn was getting ripe" (Bonaparte 2006, 49). The eclipse of August 18, 909, may best fit the criteria of the oral history and corroborate the tenth- to eleventh-century evidence from Levanna (NASA Eclipse Tables, figure 12.1). The 12:48 p.m. eastern standard time occurrence matches the midday time of Seneca council meetings, while the path of the AD 909 eclipse passed through both Ganondagan, where the Seneca council was held, and Onondaga, where it was also observed.

Following my discussion of the origins of the confederacy and the black-sun sky-sign event at the Ho Tung Visualization Laboratory at Colgate University, a computerized reenactment of the 909 eclipse designed by Joe Eakin, their senior visualization designer, was displayed. Whereas many solar eclipses do not display strong darkening of the sky, this

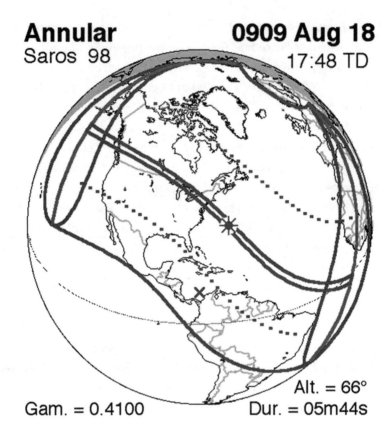

Annular   **0909 Aug 18**
Saros 98   17:48 TD

Alt. = 66°
Gam. = 0.4100   Dur. = 05m44s

Five Millennium Canon of Solar Eclipses (Espenak & Meeus)

12.1. Path and timing of the August 18, 909, eclipse. The time of day listed is Greenwich mean time, which translates to 12:48 p.m. eastern standard time. (Eclipse predictions by Fred Espenak, NASA/GSFC)

planetarium visualization exhibited an unusually dramatic darkening and the appearance of stars, matching the "complete darkness" of the oral history (Rossen 2013; Wallace 1994). However, while intrigued by the black-sun story, Native scholars remind us that it does not appear in all versions of the Peacemaker epic (Richard Hill Sr., personal communication, 2013). It has even been suggested that the black-sun reference is derived from Jesuit eclipse stories (Bonaparte 2006, 40).

Can archaeologists find evidence of the age of the confederacy? What might the emerging Cayuga archaeological record tell us about this controversy? Already, the peacetime archaeological correlates of Levanna, Myers Farm, and Corey challenge the dominant warfare narrative and support the oral history. Longhouse architecture, intertribal medicine-society pipes, an absence of palisades, and an emphasis on elaborate detailed artwork suggest that at least some Haudenosaunee people were living in peaceful conditions during the tenth or eleventh century. The presence of isolated undefended farmsteads like Myers Farm in the fifteenth century with its communal feasting also contradicts expectations of wartime settlement patterns. Close examination of the earthworks and positioning of Corey does not justify its local reputation as a "fort."

The complete artifactual analyses and reports on the Levanna and Myers Farm sites will further explore this narrative (see chapter 11). New excavations at other sites contemporary to Levanna may be helpful in producing a broader context for constructing new narratives. In particular, the discovery and investigation of more undefended villages and agricultural stations would reinforce this perspective. In terms of understanding confederacy formation, scholars have raised issues of delineating the processes of ideology versus political realities, suggesting that the conceptual and political realities of confederacy may have occurred at different dates (Starna 2008). An early view of the confederacy may thus emphasize early conceptual and political advances toward the union during a long-term process of consolidation.

Narrative 4: The Cayuga were justly punished for supporting the British during the American Revolution by losing their land.

Though not directly related to the present archaeological research, this narrative is deeply rooted in New York, powerfully affecting perceptions of the Cayuga in central New York. As discussed above, in August and September 1779, George Washington sent one-third of the Continental army into what is now central New York to burn villages, crop fields, and fruit-tree orchards in what is widely recognized as a scorched-earth campaign. As the Sullivan Campaign reemerged from historical obscurity with the republication of the campaign's soldiers' journals (Cook 2000 [1887]), the "punishment" narrative developed to justify the brutal destruction and displacement of the Cayuga people. According to this popular narrative, the Cayuga loss of land and denials of land rights are justified punishment for supporting the British during the American Revolution.

The truth is more complex. The Cayuga were delicately positioned between world powers, first the British and the French and then the British and the Americans, negotiating their survival as a balance between expedient support for one, the other, or both groups (Jordan 2008). Documentation has been compiled that a majority of Cayuga leadership, including their leading chiefs and clan mothers, officially stated neutrality at the onset of the American Revolution. There was a letter from the American-supporting Oneida requesting leniency for the Cayuga in advance of the Sullivan Campaign (Mann 2005, 102–4).

The struggles of maintaining neutrality and the pressures from both sides of the war, especially as the Seneca, Oneida, and Mohawk generally took sides and dismembered the confederacy, are well documented (Fenton 1998, 582–98). Eventually, one contingent of Cayuga led by Fish Carrier fought with the British, while another chief, Teguttelawan, claimed that half the tribe favored the Americans. John Cantine, an American Revolutionary War general, knew of a "good Indian," a Chief Wheelock, who led a Cayuga village in what is now Ellis Hollow near Ithaca and supported the Americans. Chief Wheelock, it was stated, "would fight with the Americans again if a second war came" (Gallagher 1937, 5). Chief Wheelock apparently died in action fighting alongside the Americans against the British in 1813, at which time his village dispersed (Kone 1994, 19; Lounsbery 1909).

Peter Whiteley has compiled the most detailed documentation of Cayuga actions during the American Revolution. He notes that Teguttelawan's claim "may be true, but did not entail any active engagements." He characterized the notion that the Cayuga were enemies of the patriots as "an oversimplification" and that some were "evidently neutral or in sympathy with the Americans" (2000, 26). This work was compiled as background research in the Cayuga Land Claim trial hearings of 2001, as the court grappled with Cayuga history and its relevance to a

long-running (1980) land claim. Since completing this document, Whiteley has had more than a decade to reflect on the role of the Cayuga in the
Revolutionary War:

> Of course the Cayuga attempted to defend their homelands; insofar
> as they thought of their best shot of doing that lay in siding with their
> age-old allies, the British Crown and its Loyalist supporters—or alter-
> natively, in remaining actively neutral. Why should this have anything
> to do with their land claim against an illegal taking by New York State?
> We know that the state and the regional anti-Indian organization UCE
> [see introduction] continually return to the notion that the Cayuga were
> "enemies" during the war, ergo somehow "deserved" to lose their land.
> But that argument rests on misconceived atavistic emotion (do we still
> "blame" the Japanese as a nation for Pearl Harbor, and seek to penalize
> them accordingly?), not on historical facts or context. It is hard for me to
> see that any Haudenosaunee would have fought out of some supposed
> ideological sympathy to the policy aims of either Loyalists or Patriots
> (even supposing they would have understood them in anything like the
> same way as their protagonists). So ultimately, I think the question is
> moot, and approaches the history from the wrong angle. (personal com-
> munication, 2013)

Conclusion

Deeply entrenched narratives of the Haudenosaunee are designed to
revise, minimize, oversimplify, or erase their history. In Cayuga territory these narratives conflict with detailed analysis of historical records
and complexities of historical reality or with oral histories of ethnicity
and a confederacy that emphasizes time depth of at least one thousand
years and a deep connection to the Cayuga Lake landscape. The dominant
narratives often deny connections between modern peoples and ancient
groups in the same geographical area and their corresponding land rights.
Within some of these debates, archaeological indicators of ethnicity and
Confederacy (that is, longhouses, dispersed settlement pattern, absence
of palisades, medicine-society artifacts) are in danger of become moving
targets in a process of denial. That is, some archaeologists are changing

their opinions of what archaeological traits represent the Haudenosaunee, based on the dominant narratives, particularly as "multiscalar" archaeology and "rhizotic" braided-stream or branching-tree models emphasize regional variation and de-emphasize the connections between the present, history, and prehistory. There are also justifications for the Cayuga loss of land and subsequent dispersal.

Much appears to be at stake in these contradictions of narratives, including new challenges to the existing dominant ideas: hegemony over the process of knowledge construction, the historical validity of oral history, the extension back in time of affiliation for NAGPRA-based repatriation, the development and maintenance of respectful and productive relationships between Native people and archaeologists, and, ultimately, the acceptance of the legitimacy of people like the Cayuga as they return to live in their ancestral homeland. Constructing new narratives is a time-consuming process of detailed research, analysis, and presentation. It is a collaborative process that archaeologists must undertake in cooperation with Native chiefs and clan mothers, who have significant contributions to make to site and artifact investigations and interpretations.

Archaeology is transforming from a discipline that has had profoundly negative effects on Haudenosaunee people ("Theft from the Dead" 1986; Benedict 2004; Jemison 1997) to one that can have positive results by shedding light on the darkness of historical revision and erasure (Hansen and Rossen 2007; Rossen 2006b, 2008). The perspectives of indigenous archaeology provide one framework and philosophy for opening new research vistas. These perspectives challenge dominant narratives while producing more multidimensional narratives that account for the complexity and depth of history and the present-day issues produced by it. When the clan mothers state that it is time to tell more stories of Cayuga history and archaeology, I take it to mean that it is time to challenge dominant narratives that separate the Haudenosaunee from their history, land, and rights.

Works Cited

◆

Contributors

◆

Index

Works Cited

Abel, Timothy J. 2000. "The Plus Site: An Iroquoian Remote Camp in Upland Tompkins County, NY." *North American Archaeologist* 21, no. 3: 181–215.

Albright, Sylvia. 1999. "A Working Woman Needs a Good Toolkit." In *Feminist Approaches to Pacific Northwest Archaeology*, edited by Kathryn Bernick. Northwest Anthropological Research Notes, vol. 33. Moscow, ID: Coyote Press.

Allen, Kathleen M. S. 1999. "Considerations of Scale in Modeling Settlement Patterns Using GIS: An Iroquois Example." In *Practical Applications of GIS for Archaeologists*, edited by K. L. Westcott and R. J. Brandon, 101–12. Philadelphia: Taylor and Francis.

———. 2009. "Temporal and Spatial Scales of Activity among the Iroquois: Implications for Understanding Cultural Change." In *Iroquoian Archaeology and Analytic Scale*, edited by Laurie E. Miroff and Timothy D. Knapp, 153–78. Knoxville: Univ. of Tennessee Press.

———. 2010. "Gender Dynamics, Routine Activities, and Place in Haudenosaunee Territory: An Archaeological Case Study from the Cayuga Region of Central New York State." In *Archaeology and Preservation of Gendered Landscapes*, edited by Sherene Baugher and Suzanne M. Spencer-Wood, 57–77. New York: Springer.

Arnold, Dean E. 1985. *Ceramic Theory and Cultural Process*. Cambridge: Cambridge Univ. Press.

Arnold, Dean E., Ronald L. Bishop, and Hector Neff. 1991. "Compositional Analysis and 'Sources' of Pottery: An Ethnoarcheological Approach." *American Anthropologist* 93, no. 1: 70–90.

Asch, David L., and Nancy B. Asch. 1975. "Appendix V: Plant Remains from the Zimmerman Site—Grid A; A Quantitative Perspective." In *The Zimmerman Site: Further Excavations at the Grand Village of Kaskaskia*, edited by M. I. Brown. Report of Investigations, no. 23. Springfield: Illinois State Museum.

———. 1985. "Prehistoric Plant Cultivation in West-Central Illinois." In *Prehistoric Food Production in North America*, edited by Richard I. Ford, 149–204.

Anthropological Papers, no. 75, Museum of Anthropology. Ann Arbor: Univ. of Michigan.

Asch, Nancy B., Richard I. Ford, and David L. Asch. 1972. *Paleoethnobotany of the Koster Site*. Report of Investigations, no. 24. Springfield: Illinois State Museum.

Bartram, William. 1955 [1791]. *Travels through North and South Carolina, Georgia, East and West Florida*. Dover, NY.

Baugher, Sherene, and Sara Clark. 1998. *An Archaeological Investigation of the Indian Fort Road Site, Trumansburg, New York*. Ithaca, NY: Cornell Univ.

Beauchamp, William M. 1901. *Aboriginal Occupation of New York*. Official Bulletins of the New York State Museum, Frederick H Merrill, Director, nos. 32, 34, 36. Vol. 1, pt. 1. Albany: State Univ. of New York.

——. 1905. *Aboriginal Use of Wood in New York*. New York State Education Department Bulletin 89. Albany: New York State Museum.

Behrensmeyer, A. K. 1978. "Taphonomic and Ecologic Information from Bone Weathering." *Paleobiology*: 150–62.

Beisaw, April M. 2000. "Cultural Influences on the Differential Decomposition of Animal Bone." Paper presented at the annual meeting of the Society for American Archaeology, Philadelphia.

——. 2006. "Deer, Toads, and Frogs: A New Interpretation of the Faunal Remains from the Engelbert Site, Tioga County, New York." *Northeast Anthropology* 72: 1–24.

——. 2010. "Memory, Identity, and NAGPRA in the Northeastern United States." *American Anthropologist* 112, no. 2: 244–56.

——. 2012. *Identifying and Interpreting Animal Bones: A Manual*. College Station: Texas A&M Univ. Press.

Bender, Susan J. 1994. "Marian E. White: Pioneer in New York Archaeology." In *Women in Archaeology*, edited by Cheryl Claassen, 85–95. Philadelphia: Univ. of Pennsylvania Press.

——. 1999. "Alternative Networks in the Career of Marian E. White." In *Assembling the Past: Studies in the Professionalization of Archaeology*, edited by Alice B. Kehoe and Mary Beth Emmerichs. Albuquerque: Univ. of New Mexico Press.

Benedict, Salli M. Kawennotakie. 2004. "Made in Akwesasne." In *A Passion for the Past: Papers in Honour of James F. Pendergast*, edited by J. V. Wright and J. Pilon, 435–54. Gatineau, QC: Canadian Museum of Civilization.

Betts, Ian M. 1991. "Thin-Section and Neutron Activation Analysis of Brick and Tile from York and Surrounding Sites." In *Recent Developments in Ceramic*

Petrology, edited by A. Andrew Middleton and Ian C. Freestone, 39–55. Occasional Paper, no. 8. London: British Museum.

Bilharz, Joy. 1978. *Nunamiut Ethnoarchaeology*. New York: Academic Press.

———. 1979. "Organization and Formation Processes: Looking at Curated Technologies." *Journal of Anthropological Research* 35: 255–73.

———. 1989. "An Alyawara Day: Making Men's Knives and Beyond." *American Antiquity* 51: 547–62.

———. 1998. *The Allegany Senecas and Kinzua Dam: Forced Relocation through Two Generations*. Lincoln: Univ. of Nebraska Press.

Binford, Lewis R. 1973. "Interassemblage Variability: The Mousterian and the 'Functional Argument.'" In *The Explanation of Cultural Change: Models in Prehistory*, edited by Colin Renfrew, 227–54. London: Duckworth.

———. 1977. "Forty-Seven Trips: A Case Study in the Character of Archaeological Formation Processes." In *Stone Tools as Cultural Markers: Change, Evolution, and Complexity*, edited by R. V. S. Wright, 24–36. Canberra: Australian Institute of Aboriginal Studies.

———. 1978. *Nunamiut Ethnoarchaeology*. New York: Academic Press.

———. 1980. "Willow Smoke and Dogs' Tails: Hunter-Gatherer Settlement Systems and Archaeological Site Formation." *American Antiquity* 44, no. 3: 4–20.

Birch, Jennifer. 2008. "Rethinking the Archaeological Application of Iroquoian Kinship." *Canadian Journal of Archaeology* 32, no. 2: 194–213.

———. 2010. "Coalescence and Conflict in Iroquoian Ontario." *Archaeological Review from Cambridge* 25, no. 1: 29–48.

Birch, Jennifer, and Ronald F. Williamson. 2013. *The Mantle Site: An Archaeological History of an Ancestral Wendat Community*. London: Altamira Press.

Bird, C. M. F. 1993. "Woman the Toolmaker: Evidence for Women's Use and Manufacture of Flaked Stone Tools in Australia and New Guinea." In *Women in Archaeology: A Feminist Critique*, edited by Hilary Du Cros and Laurajane Smith, 22–30. Canberra: Australian National Univ.

Birnbaum, David. 2011. "Using GIS to Determine the Influence of Wetlands on Cayuga Iroquois Settlement Location Strategies." BA honors thesis, Univ. of Central Florida.

Blitz, John H. 1988. "The Adoption of the Bow and Arrow in Prehistoric North America." *North American Archaeologist* 9, no. 2: 123–45.

Boersema, Jan J. 2015. *The Survival of Easter Island: Dwindling Resources and Cultural Resilience*. Cambridge: Cambridge Univ. Press.

Boggs, Sam, Jr. 2006. *Principles of Sedimentology and Stratigraphy*. 4th ed. Englewood Cliffs, NJ: Prentice Hall.

Bonaparte, Darren. 2006. *Creation and Confederation: The Living History of the Iroquois*. Ahkwesáhsne, Mohawk Territory: Wampum Chronicles.

Bradley, James W. 1987. *Evolution of the Onondaga Iroquois: Accommodating Change, 1550–1655*. Lincoln: Univ. of Nebraska Press.

———. 2005. *Evolution of the Onondaga Iroquois: Accommodating Change, 1500–1655*. Lincoln: Univ. of Nebraska Press.

Brennan, Tamira K. 2007. "In-Ground Evidence of Above-Ground Architecture at Kincaid Mounds." In *Architectural Variability in the Southeast*, edited by Cameron H. Lacquement, 73–100. Tuscaloosa: Univ. of Alabama Press.

Brown, Judith K. 1996 [1970]. "Economic Organization and the Position of Women among the Iroquois." In *Iroquois Women: An Anthology*, edited by W. G. Spittal, 182–98. Ohsweken, ON: Iroqrafts.

Bruchac, Margaret M., Siobhan M. Hart, and H. Martin Wobst. 2010. *Indigenous Archaeologies: A Reader on Decolonization*. Walnut Creek, CA: Left Coast Press.

Bruhns, Karen. 1994. *Ancient South America*. Cambridge: Cambridge Univ. Press.

Canfield, William Walker. 1904. *The Legends of the Iroquois, Told by "the Cornplanter."* New York: A. Wessels.

———. 2013 [1902]. *The Legends of the Iroquois, Told by "the Cornplanter."* San Bernardino, CA: Ulan Press.

Channing, Steven A. 1977. *Kentucky: A Bicentennial History*. New York: W. W. Norton.

Chapman, Jefferson, and Andrea B. Shea. 1981. "The Archaeobotanical Record: Early Archaic to Contact in the Lower Little Tennessee River Valley." *Tennessee Anthropologist* 6: 61–84.

Clark, John R. K. 2002. *Hawai'i Place Names: Shores, Beaches, and Surfs*. Manoa: Univ. of Hawai'i Press.

Clark, Sara. 1998. "Ceramic Analysis." In *An Archaeological Investigation of the Indian Fort Road Site, Trumansburg, New York*. Vol. 1, *Text*, by Sherene Baugher and Sara Clark, 52–84. Ithaca, NY: Cornell Univ.

Cleland, Herdman Fitzgerald. 1903. *A Study of the Fauna of the Hamilton Formation of the Cayuga Lake Section in Central New York*. Washington, DC: Government Printing Office.

Colwell-Chanthaphonh, Chip. 2009. *Inheriting the Past: The Making of Arthur C. Parker and Indigenous Archaeology*. Tucson: Univ. of Arizona Press.

Colwell-Chanthaphonh, Chip, and T. J. Ferguson. 2008. *Collaboration in Archaeological Practice: Engaging Descendant Communities.* Rowan and Litchfield, NY: Alta Mira Press.

Comrie, Bernard. 1990. *The World's Major Languages.* Oxford: Oxford Univ. Press.

Conger, Megan A., and Kathleen M. S. Allen. 2013. "Considering Gendered Domains: Gender, Space, and Archaeological Interpretation in Central New York." Paper presented at New York State Archaeological Association Conference, Watertown, NY.

Cook, Frederick. 2000 [1887]. *Journals of the Military Expedition of Major General John Sullivan against the Six Nations of Indians in 1779 with Records of Centennial Celebrations.* Bowie, MD: Heritage Books.

Cowan, C. Wesley. 1979. "Excavations at the Haystack Rockshelters, Powell County, KY." *Midcontinental Journal of Archaeology* 4: 3–33.

Cowan, C. Wesley, et al. 1981. "The Cloudsplitter Shelter, Menifee County, KY: A Preliminary Report." *Southeastern Archaeological Conference Bulletin* 24: 60–76.

Cowan, Frank. 1987. "Heat-Treating Experiments with Onondaga Chert: Preliminary Results." Ethnoarchaeology Graduate Course, State Univ. of New York, Buffalo.

Crawford, Gary W., and David G. Smith. 1996. "Migration in Prehistory: Princess Point and the Northern Iroquoian Case." *American Antiquity* 61, no. 4: 782–90.

Creese, John L. 2011. "Deyughnyonkwarakda—'At the Wood's Edge': The Development of the Iroquoian Village in Southern Ontario, A.D. 900–1500." PhD diss., Univ. of Toronto.

Cruz, M. Dores. 2011. "'Pots Are Pots, Not People': Material Culture and Ethnic Identity in the Banda Area (Ghana), Nineteenth and Twentieth Centuries." *Azania: Archaeological Research in Africa* 46, no. 3: 336–57.

Cusick, David. 2004 [1825]. *Sketches of Ancient History of the Six Nations.* Bristol, PA: Evolution.

Daniels, Robert A. 1996. *Guide to the Identification of Scales of Inland Fishes of Northeastern North America.* Bulletin 488. Albany: New York State Museum.

David, Nicholas, and Carol Kramer. 2001. *Ethnoarchaeology in Action.* Cambridge: Cambridge Univ. Press.

Day, Peter M., et al. 1999. "Group Therapy in Crete: A Comparison between Analyses by NAA and Thin Section Petrography of Early Minoan Pottery." *Journal of Archaeological Science* 26, no. 8: 1025–36.

DeBoer, Warren. 1990. "Interaction, Imitation, and Communication as Expressed in Style: The Ucuyali Experience." In *The Uses of Style in Archaeology*, edited by M. Conkey and C. Hastorf, 82–104. Cambridge: Cambridge Univ. Press.

———. 1998. "Figuring Figurines: The Case of Chachi, Ecuador." In *Recent Advances in the Archaeology of the Northern Andes: In Memory of Gerardo Reichel-Dolmatoff*, edited by Augusto Oyuela-Caycedo and J. Scott Raymond, 121–28. Monograph 39, Institute of Archaeology. Los Angeles: Univ. of California.

Decker-Walters, Deena. 1990. "Evidence for Multiple Domestications of *Cucurbita pepo*." In *Biology and Utilization of the Cucurbitaceae*, edited by David M. Bates, Richard W. Robinson, and Charles Jeffrey, 96–101. Ithaca, NY: Cornell Univ. Press.

Delly, John G. 1988. *Photography through the Microscope*. Rochester, NY: Eastman Kodak.

Delorit, R. J. 1970. *Illustrated Taxonomy Manual of Weed Seeds*. River Falls, WI: Agronomy Publications.

Deorio, Robert N. 1980. "Perspectives on the Prehistoric Cayuga, Post Owasco Tradition, through the Correlation of Ceramic Types with Area Development." In *Proceedings of the 1979 Iroquois Pottery Conference*, edited by Charles F. Hayes III, 65–85. Research Records 13. Rochester, NY: Rochester Museum and Science Center.

Doddridge, Joseph. 1989 [1824]. *Notes on the Settlement and Indian Wars (Wellsburg, Virginia Gazette)*. Parsons, WV: McClain.

Driver, Harold E., and William C. Massey. 1957. "Comparative Studies of North American Indians." *Transactions of the American Philosophical Society* 47, no. 2: 165–456.

Drooker, Penelope B. 2004. "Pipes, Leadership, and Interregional Interaction in Protohistoric Midwestern and Northeastern North America." In *Smoking and Culture: The Archaeology of Tobacco Pipes in Eastern North America*, edited by Sean M. Rafferty and Rob Mann, 73–124. Knoxville: Univ. of Tennessee Press.

Dunn, Mary E. 1984. "Appendix A: Floral Analysis." In *The Archaeology of Taylorsville Lake: Archaeological Data Recovery and Synthesis*, edited by Boyce N. Driskell, 297–308. Archaeological Report no. 85, Program for Cultural Resource Assessment. Lexington: Univ. of Kentucky.

Edging, Richard B. 1995. "Living in a Cornfield: The Variation and Ecology of Late Prehistoric Agriculture in the Western Kentucky Confluence Region." PhD. diss., Univ. of Illinois.

Edmunds, Sheila. 2000. *Aurora: Time Well Spent*. Aurora, NY: n.p.

Edwards, Chief Jake. 2013. "Thanksgiving Address and the Two Row Wampum." Paper presented at American Indian Program Thirtieth Anniversary: Recognition and Two Row Wampum Renewal Conference. Ithaca, NY: Cornell Univ.

Elias, T. S. 1972. "The Genera of Juglandaceae in the Southeastern United States." *Journal of the Arnold Arboretum* 53: 26–51.

Engelbrecht, William. 1987. "Factors Maintaining Low Population Density among the Prehistoric New York Iroquois." *American Antiquity* 87, no. 1: 13–27.

———. 2003. *Iroquoia: The Development of a Native World*. Syracuse, NY: Syracuse Univ. Press.

Erickson, David L., et al. 2005. "An Asian Origin for a 10,000-Year-Old Domesticated Plant in the Americas." *Proceedings of the National Academy of Sciences* 102, no. 51: 18315–20.

Fenton, William N. 1976. "Marian E. White, 1921–1975." *American Anthropologist* 78, no. 4: 891–92.

———. 1998. *The Great Law and the Longhouse: A Political History of the Iroquois Confederacy*. Norman: Univ. of Oklahoma Press.

Ferguson, Leland. 1992. *Uncommon Ground: Archaeology and Early African America, 1650–1800*. Washington, DC: Smithsonian Institution Press.

Ferrero, Pat. 2001. *Iroquois Women: The Three Sisters* (film). Pittsburgh, PA: Museum of Natural History.

Finch, Roy G. 1998 [1925]. *The Story of the New York State Canals: Historical and Commercial Information*. Albany: New York State Canal Corporation.

Fischer, Joseph R. 1997. *A Well-Executed Failure: The Sullivan Campaign against the Iroquois, July–September 1779*. Columbia: Univ. of South Carolina Press.

Fisher, D. W., Y. W. Isachsen, and L. V. Rickard. 1970. "Geologic Map of New York State, Consisting of 5 Sheets: Niagara, Finger Lakes, Hudson-Mohawk, Adirondack, and Lower Hudson." Map and Chart Series, no. 15, scale 1:250000. Albany: New York State Museum and Science Service.

Flick, Alexander C. 1929. "New Sources on the Sullivan–Clinton Campaign of 1779." *Quarterly Journal of the New York State Historical Society* 10: 185–224.

Follett, Harrison C. 1957. *The Algonkian Site of Levanna, New York, on Cayuga Lake*. Supplement 1 to *Yesteryears*. Germantown, PA: Clarion Call Memorial Publications.

Funk, Robert E., and Robert D. Kuhn. 2003. *Three Sixteenth-Century Mohawk Iroquois Village Sites*. New York State Museum Bulletin 503. Albany: State Univ. of New York, State Education Department.

Gallagher, Lyman H. 1937. "The Birth of Caroline." *Ithaca Journal*, May 5, 5.

George-Kanentiio, Doug. 2000. *Iroquois Culture and Commentary*. Santa Fe, NM: Clear Light.

Gero, Joan M. 1991a. "Gender Divisions of Labor in the Construction of Archaeological Knowledge." In *The Archaeology of Gender: Proceedings of the Twenty-Second Annual Conference of the Archaeological Association of the University of Calgary*, edited by Dale Walde and Noreen D. Willows, 96–102. Calgary: Archaeological Association, Univ. of Calgary.

———. 1991b. "Genderlithics: Women's Roles in Stone Tool Production." In *Engendering Archaeology: Women and Prehistory*, edited by Joan M. Gero and Margaret W. Conkey, 163–93. Oxford: Basil Blackwell.

Gero, Joan M., and Margaret W. Conkey. 1991. *Engendering Archaeology: Women and Prehistory*. Hoboken, NJ: Wiley Blackwell.

Gilmore, Melvin R. 1931. *Uses of Plants by the Indians of the Missouri River*. Lincoln: Univ. of Nebraska Press.

Golding, Winifred. 1927. "The Oldest Known Petrified Forest." *Science Monthly* 24: 514–29.

Gorman, Alice. 1995. "Gender, Labour and Resources: The Female Knappers of the Andaman Islands." In *Gendered Archaeology: The Second Australian Women in Archaeology Conference*, edited by Jane Balme and Wendy Beck, 87–91. Canberra: ANH, RSPAS.

Gosselain, Oliver P. 2000. "Materializing Identities: An African Perspective." *Journal of Archaeological Method and Theory* 7: 187–217.

Green, Gretchen L. 1997. "Gender and the Longhouse: Iroquois Women in a Changing Culture." In *Women and Freedom in Early America*, edited by Larry D. Eldridge, 7–25. New York: New York Univ. Press.

Haberman, Thomas W. 1984. "Evidence for Aboriginal Tobaccos in Eastern North America." *American Antiquity* 49, no. 2: 269–87.

Hall, Grant D. 2000. "Pecan Food Potential in Prehistoric North America." *Economic Botany* 54, no. 1: 103–12.

Hansen, Brooke, and Jack Rossen. 2007. "Building Bridges through Public Anthropology in the Haudenosaunee Homeland." In *Past Meets Present: Archaeologists Partnering with Museum Curators, Teachers, and Community Groups*, edited by John H. Jameson Jr. and Sherene Baugher, 127–48. New York: Springer.

Harnden, Philip. 2000. *Whose Land? An Introduction to the Iroquois Land Claims in New York State*. Syracuse, NY: American Friends Service Committee.

Hart, John P. 2008. "Evolving the Three Sisters: The Changing Histories of Maize, Beans, and Squash." In *Current Northeast Paleoethnobotany II*, 87–100. Albany: New York State Museum Bulletin Series 512.

Hart, John P., and Hetty Jo Brumbach. 2003. "The Death of Owasco." *American Antiquity* 68, no. 4: 737–52.

———. 2009. "On Pottery Change and Northern Iroquoian Origins: An Assessment from the Finger Lakes Region of Central New York." *Journal of Anthropological Archaeology* 28: 367–81.

Hart, John P., Robert A. Daniels, and Charles J. Sheviak. 2004. "Do *Cucurbita pepo* Gourds Float Fishnets?" *American Antiquity* 69, no. 1: 141–48.

Hart, John P., and William Engelbrecht. 2012. "Northern Iroquoian Ethnic Evolution: A Social Network Analysis." *Journal of Archaeological Method and Theory* 19: 322–49.

Hart, John P., and C. Margaret Scarry. 1999. "The Age of Common Beans (*Phaseolus vulgaris*) in the Northeastern United States." *American Antiquity* 64: 653–58.

Harter, Abigail V., Keith A. Gardner, Daniel Falush, David L. Lentz, Robert A. Bye, and Loren H. Rieseberg. 2004. "Origin of Extant Domesticated Sunflowers in Eastern North America." *Nature* 430 (July): 201–5.

Haudenosaunee Environmental Task Force. N.d. *Words That Come before All Else: Environmental Philosophies of the Haudenosaunee*. Onondaga Nation: Haudenosaunee Environmental Task Force.

Hayes, Charles F., III. 1980. "An Overview of the Current Status of Seneca Ceramics." In *Proceedings of the 1979 Iroquois Pottery Conference*, edited by Charles F. Hayes III, 87–94. Report no. 14. Rochester, NY: Rochester Museum & Science Center.

Heiser, Charles B. 1989. "Domestication of Cucurbitaceae: *Cucurbita* and *Lagenaria*." In *Foraging and Farming: The Evolution of Plant Exploitation*, edited by David R. Harris and Gordon C. Hillman, 471–80. London: Unwin Hyman.

Henderson, A. Gwynn. 1992. "Capitol View: An Early Madisonville Horizon Settlement in Franklin County, Kentucky." In *Current Archaeological Research in Kentucky*, edited by David Pollack and A. Gwynn Henderson, 2:223–40. Frankfort: Kentucky Heritage Council.

Herkimer Diamond Mines. N.d. *History*. N.p.

Herrick, James W. 1995. *Iroquois Medical Botany*. Syracuse, NY: Syracuse Univ. Press.

Hertzberg, Hazel W. 1970. *The Great Tree and the Longhouse: The Culture of the Iroquois*. London: Collier Macmillan.

Hickman, Warren. N.d. *A Cayuga Chronicle*. N.p.

Hill, Dan. 2013. "Leave It in the Ground: Issues with Archaeology." Public presentation, Wells College, Aurora, NY, Nov. 21.

Hill, Richard W., Sr. 2013. "Between the Two Rows: Reflecting on the Linked Vessels." Paper presented at American Indian Program Thirtieth Anniversary: Recognition and Two Row Wampum Renewal Conference. Ithaca, NY, Apr.

Hodder, Ian. 1991. "The Decoration of Containers: An Ethnographic and Historical Study." In *Ceramic Ethnoarchaeology*, edited by William A. Longacre, 71–94. Tucson: Univ. of Arizona Press.

Holland, John D. 2003. "A Guide to Pennsylvania Lithic Types." *Journal of Middle Atlantic Archeology* 19: 129–50.

Hudson, Jean L. 2004. "Additional Evidence for Gourd Floats on Fishing Nets." *American Antiquity* 69, no. 3: 586–87.

Hunt, Terry, and Carl Lipo. 2012. *The Statues That Walked: Unraveling the Mystery of Easter Island*. Berkeley, CA: Counterpoint.

Hutchens, Alma R. 1991. *Indian Herbology of North America*. Boston: Shambhala.

Hutton, Frank Zinn. 1971. *Soil Survey of Cayuga County, New York*. Washington, DC: Soil Conservation Service.

Iroquois Indian Museum. N.d. *Sports and Games*. N.p.

Iwasaki-Goodman, Masami, and Milton M. R. Freeman. 1994. "Social and Cultural Significance of Whaling in Contemporary Japan: A Case Study of Small-Type Coastal Whaling." In *Key Issues in Hunter-Gatherer Research*, edited by Ernest S. Burch and Linda J. Ellanna, 377–400. Oxford: Berg Press.

Jacques, Freida. 1991. "Discipline of the Good Mind." *Northeast Indian Quarterly* (Cornell Univ.) (Summer).

Jarvis, Hugh. 1988. "INAA Characterization of Onondaga Chert: A Preliminary Study in Western New York." Master's thesis, State Univ. of New York, Buffalo.

Jemison, G. Peter. 1997. "Who Owns the Past?" In *Native Americans and Archaeologists: Stepping Stones to Common Ground*, edited by Nina Swidler, Kurt E. Dongoske, Roger Anyon, and Alan S. Downer, 57–63. Walnut Creek, CA: Altamira Press.

———. 2013. "The Two Row or Gaswenta." Paper presented at American Indian Program Thirtieth Anniversary: Recognition and Two Row Wampum Renewal Conference, Ithaca, NY, Apr.

Johannessen, Sissel. 1984. "Paleoethnobotany." In *American Bottom Archaeology*, edited by Charles J. Bareis and James W. Porter, 197–224. Urbana: Univ. of Illinois Press.

———. 1988. "Plant Remains and Culture Change: Are Paleoethnobotanical Data Better than We Think?" In *Current Paleoethnobotany: Analytical Methods and Cultural Interpretations of Archaeological Plant Remains,* edited by C. A. Hastorf and V. S. Popper, 145–66. Chicago: Univ. of Chicago Press.

Johnson, Elias. 2010 [1881]. *Legends, Traditions and Laws of the Iroquois, or Six Nations, and History of the Tuscarora Indians.* London: Forgotten Books.

Jones, David, and Anne Jones. 1980. "The Defenses at Indian Fort Road, Tompkins County, New York." *Pennsylvania Archaeologist* 50: 61–71.

Jones, Eric E. 2010. "Population History of the Onondaga and Oneida Iroquois, A.D. 1500–1700." *American Antiquity* 75, no. 2: 387–407.

Jordan, Kurt. 2003. "An Eighteenth-Century Seneca Iroquois Short Longhouse from the Townley-Read Site, ca. A.D. 1715–1754." *Bulletin: Journal of the New York State Archaeological Association* 119: 49–63.

———. 2008. *The Seneca Restoration, 1715–1754: An Iroquois Local Political Economy.* Gainesville: Univ. Press of Florida.

———. 2013. "Incorporation and Colonization: Postcolumbian Iroquois Satellite Communities and Processes of Indigenous Autonomy." *American Anthropologist* 115, no. 1: 29–43.

———. 2014. "Enacting Gender and Kinship around a Large Outdoor Firepit at the Seneca Iroquois Townley-Reas Site, 1715–1754." *Historical Archaeology* 48, no. 2.

Kapches, Mima. 1990. "The Spatial Dynamics of the Ontario Iroquoian Longhouses." *American Antiquity* 55, no. 1: 49–67.

———. 1994. "The Iroquoian Longhouse: Architectural and Cultural Identity." In *Meaningful Architecture: Social Interpretations of Buildings,* edited by M. Locock. Worldwide Archaeology Series, no. 9. Aldershot, Hampshire, UK: Avebury.

Kapuni-Reynolds, Halena. 2014. "Curating Ali'i Heritage: Responsibility and Sensibility in Museums and Archaeology." Paper presented at the annual Society for Hawaiian Archaeology conference, Hilo, HI, Oct.

Kay, Marvin, Francis B. King, and Christine K. Robinson. 1980. "Cucurbits from Philips Spring: New Evidence and Interpretations." *American Antiquity* 45, no. 4: 802–22.

Keemer, Kelly, and Amanda Williams. 2003. *Medicinal Herb Resource Guide: SHARE Farm, 2003.* Union Springs, NY: SHARE.

Kerber, Jordan E. 1997. "Native American Treatment of Dogs in Northeastern North America: Archaeological and Ethnohistorical Perspectives." *Archaeology of Eastern North America* 25: 81–96.

———. 2007. *Archaeology of the Iroquois: Selected Readings and Research Sources.* Syracuse, NY: Syracuse Univ. Press.

Kimmerer, Robin W. 2011. "Restoration and Reciprocity: The Contributions of Traditional Ecological Knowledge to the Philosophy and Practice of Ecological Restoration." In *Human Dimensions of Ecological Restoration*, edited by David Egan. Chicago: Island Press.

———. 2013. "The Fortress, the River and the Garden: A New Metaphor for Cultivating a Relationship between Scientific and Traditional Ecological Knowledge." Paper presented at American Indian Program Thirtieth Anniversary: Recognition and Two Row Wampum Renewal Conference, Ithaca, NY, Apr.

Kirch, Patrick V. 1996. *Legacy of the Landscape: An Illustrated Guide to Hawaiian Archaeological Sites.* Manoa: Univ. of Hawai'i Press.

Knight, Vernon J. 2007. "Conclusions: Taking Architecture Seriously." In *Architectural Variability in the Southeast*, edited by Cameron H. Lacquement, 186–92. Tuscaloosa: Univ. of Alabama Press.

Kone, Barbara B. M. 1994. *A History of the Town of Caroline, Tompkins County, New York, United States of America.* Caroline, NY: Caroline Bicentennial Committee.

Kooyman, Brian P. 2000. *Understanding Stone Tools and Archaeological Sites.* Albuquerque: Univ. of New Mexico Press.

Krieger, Alex D. 1954. "A Comment on 'Fluted Point Relationships' by John Witthoft." *American Antiquity* 19, no. 3: 273–75.

Krochmal, Arnold, and Connie Krochmal. 1982. *Uncultivated Nuts of the United States.* Agricultural Information Bulletin, no. 450. Washington, DC: USDA.

Kuhn, Robert D. 2004. "Reconstructing Patterns of Interaction and Warfare between the Mohawk and Northern Iroquoians during the A.D. 1400–1700 Period." In *A Passion for the Past: Papers in Honour of James F. Pendergast*, edited by James V. Wright, 145–66. Mercury Series, Archaeological Paper, no. 164. Gatineau, QC: Canadian Museum of Civilization.

Kuhn, Robert D., and Martha L. Sempowski. 2001. "A New Approach to Dating the League of the Iroquois." *American Antiquity* 66, no. 2: 301–14.

Lacquement, Cameron H. 2007. *Architectural Variability in the Southeast.* Tuscaloosa: Univ. of Alabama Press.

Lacy, David. 1999. "Myth-Busting and Prehistoric Land Use in the Green Mountains of Vermont." In *The Archaeological Northeast*, edited by M. A. Levine, K. E. Sassaman, and M. S. Nassaney. Westport, CT: Bergin & Garvey Press.

LaDuke, Winona. 2005. *Recovering the Sacred: The Power of Naming and Claiming*. Cambridge, MA: South End Press.

Lajewski, C. K., William Patterson, and C. W. Callien. 2003. "Historic Calcite Record from the Finger Lakes, New York." *GSA Bulletin* 115: 373–84.

Lallanilla, Marc. 2013. "Ray Lewis and Deer-Antler Spray: What Does the Science Say?" *Huffington Post*, Feb. 1.

Lacquement, Cameron H. 2007. *Architectural Variability in the Southeast*. Tuscaloosa: Univ. of Alabama Press.

Lima, Pûlama, Windy McElroy, James Bayman, and Ty Kâwika Tengan. 2014. "Training the Next Generation of Hawaiian Archaeologists: A View from the North Shore Archaeological Field School." Paper presented at the annual Society for Hawaiian Archaeology conference. Hilo, HI, Oct.

Lippert, Dorothy. 2010. "Echoes from the Bones: Maintaining a Voice to Speak for the Ancestors." In *Being and Becoming Indigenous Archaeologists*, edited by George Nicholas, 184–90. Walnut Creek, CA: Left Coast Press.

Little, Elbert. 2004. *National Audubon Society Field Guide to North American Trees*. New York: Alfred A. Knopf.

Lopinot, Neal H. 1982. "Plant Macroremains and Paleoethnobotanical Implications." In *The Carrier Mills Archaeological Project: Human Adaptation in the Saline Valley, Illinois*, edited by Richard W. Jefferies and Brian M. Butler, 2:671–860. Research Paper no. 33. Carbondale: Southern Illinois Univ., Center for Archaeological Investigations.

Lounsbery, Cantine. 1909. "Early History of Brookton Village, Settled by John Cantine, a Revolutionary War General." *Ithaca Daily Journal*, Aug. 10, 5.

Low, Sam. 2013. *Hawaiki Rising: Hôkûle'a, Nainoa Thompson, and the Hawaiian Renaissance*. Waipahu, HI: Island Heritage.

Luedtke, Barbara E. 1992. "Lithic Sources in New England." *Bulletin of the Massachusetts Archaeological Society* 54, no. 2: 56–60.

———. 1993. "An Archaeologist's Guide to Chert and Flint." Univ. of California Archaeological Research Tools, no. 7. Institute of Archaeology, UCLA, Los Angeles.

Lusteck, Robert. 2006. "The Migrations of Maize into the Southeastern United States." In *Histories of Maize: Multidisciplinary Approaches to the Prehistory, Linguistics, Biogeography, Domestication, and Evolution of Maize*, edited by John Staller, Robert Tykot, and Bruce Benz, 521–28. Walnut Creek, CA: Left Coast Press.

Lyman, R. L. 1994. *Vertebrate Taphonomy: Cambridge Manual in Archaeology*. Cambridge: Cambridge Univ. Press.

Lyons, Oren, John Mohawk, and Vine Deloria Jr. 1992. *Exiled in the Land of the Free: Democracy, Indian Nations and the U.S. Constitution*. Santa Fe, NM: Clear Light.

Macauley, James. 1829. *The Natural, Statistical and Civil History of the State of New York in Three Volumes*. Vol. 2. New York: Gould and Banks; Albany, NY: William Gould.

MacCarald, Clara. 2014. "Archaeology Helps Tell the Story of the Cayuga Nation." *Ithaca Times*, Sept. 8.

MacNeish, Richard S. 1952. *Iroquois Pottery Types: A Technique for the Study of Iroquois Prehistory*. Bulletin 124, Anthropological Series, no. 31. Ottowa: National Museum of Canada.

Makowski, Krzysztof. 2008. "Andean Urbanism." In *Handbook of South American Archaeology*, edited by Helaine Silverman and William H. Isbell, 633–57. New York: Springer.

Mann, Barbara A. 2000. *Iroquoian Women: The Gantowisas*. New York: Peter Lang.

———. 2003. *Native Americans, Archaeologists, and the Mounds*. New York: Peter Lang.

———. 2005. *George Washington's War on Native America*. Westport, CT: Praeger.

Mann, Barbara A., and Jerry L. Fields. 1997. "A Sign in the Sky: Dating the League of the Haudenosaunee." *American Indian Culture and Research Journal* 21, no. 2: 105–63.

Marquardt, William H., and Patty Jo Watson. 1977. "Excavation and Recovery of Biological Remains from Two Archaic Shell Middens in Western Kentucky." *Southeastern Archaeological Conference Bulletin* 20.

Martin, Alexander C., and William D. Barkley. 1973. *Seed Identification Manual*. 2nd ed. Berkeley: Univ. of California Press.

McManamon, Francis P. 1995. "Special Report: The Native American Graves Protection and Repatriation Act." *Federal Archaeology, Offprint Series* (Fall–Winter).

Michaud-Stutzman, Tracy S. 2009. "The Community and the Microhousehold: Local Scales of Analysis within an Iroquois Village." In *Iroquoian Archaeology and Analytic Scale*, edited by Laurie E. Miroff and Timothy D. Knapp, 131–52. Knoxville: Univ. of Tennessee Press.

Milisauskas, Sarunas. 1977. "Marian Emily White, 1921–1975." *American Antiquity* 42, no. 2: 191–95.

Miroff, Laurie E., and Timothy D. Knapp. 2009. *Iroquoian Archaeology and Analytic Scale*. Knoxville: Univ. of Tennessee Press.

Moerman, Daniel. 1998. *Native American Ethnobotany*. Portland, OR: Timber Press.

Mohr-Chavez, Karen L. 1992. "The Organization of Production and Distribution of Traditional Pottery in South Highland Peru." In *Ceramic Production and Distribution: An Integrated Approach*, edited by George J. Bey and Christopher A. Pool, 49–92. Boulder, CO: Westview Press.

Morell, Sally Fallon, and Mary Enig. 2000. *Guts and Grease: The Diet of Native Americans*. Washington, DC: Weston A. Price Foundation.

Morgan, Lewis Henry. 1993 [1851]. *League of the Iroquois*. Secaucus, NJ: Citadel Press, Carol Publishing Group.

Mount Pleasant, Jane. 2006. "The Science behind the Three Sisters Mound System: An Agronomic Assessment of an Indigenous Agricultural System in the Northeast." In *Histories of Maize: Multidisciplinary Approaches to the Prehistory, Linguistics, Biogeography, Domestication, and Evolution of Maize*, edited by John Staller, Robert Tykot, and Bruce Benz, 529–37. Walnut Creek, CA: Left Coast Press.

———. 2011. *Traditional Iroquois Corn: Its History, Cultivation, and Use*. Ithaca, NY: Plant and Life Sciences.

Muller, Ernest, and Donald Caldwell. 1986. "Geomorphic History of Central New York." In *Surficial Geological Map of New York, Fingers Lake Sheet*. Albany: New York State Museum.

Munson, Patrick. 1973. "The Origins and Antiquity of Maize-Beans-Squash Agriculture in Eastern North America: Some Linguistic Evidence." In *Variations in Anthropology*, edited by Donald W. Lathrap and Jodi Douglas, 107–35. Urbana: Illinois Archaeological Survey.

Nelson, Carol. 1977. "The Klinko Sie: A Late Woodland Component in Seneca County, New York." Master's thesis, State Univ. of New York, Buffalo.

Niemczycki, Mary Ann Palmer. 1984. *The Origin and Development of the Seneca and Cayuga Tribes of New York State*. Report no. 17. Rochester, NY: Rochester Museum & Science Center.

O'Hearn, Macy. 2013a. "A Critical Examination of the Existing Typology for Haudenosaunee Ceramics and an Analysis of the Decorated Ceramics Assemblage from the Myers Farm Site, King Ferry, New York." Senior honors thesis, Ithaca College.

———. 2013b. "Emerging Issues in the Ceramics Analysis of Myers Farm, a 15th Century Cayuga Farmstead." Paper presented at annual meeting, New York State Archaeological Association. Watertown, NY, Apr. 29.

Orlandini, J. B. 1996. "The Passenger Pigeon: A Seasonal Native American Food Source." *Pennsylvania Archaeologist* 66, no. 2: 71–77.

Panshin, A. J., and Carl de Zeeuw. 1970. *Textbook of Wood Technology*. 3rd ed. New York: McGraw-Hill.

Parker, Arthur C. 1912. "Certain Iroquois Tree Myths and Symbols." *American Anthropologist* 14, no. 4: 608–20.

———. 1922. *The Archaeological History of New York*. Albany: State Univ. of New York.

———. 1990 [1913]. *The Code of Handsome Lake, the Seneca Prophet*. New York: Iroqrafts.

———. 1994 [1910]. *Iroquois Uses of Maize and Other Food Plants*. Education Department Bulletin 144, New York State Museum. Ohsweken, Ontario: Iroqrafts.

Parmenter, Jon. 2010. *The Edge of the Woods: Iroquoia, 1534–1701*. East Lansing: Michigan State Univ. Press.

———. 2013. *The Edge of the Woods*. East Lansing: Michigan State Univ. Press.

Parry, William J., and Robert L. Kelly. 1987. "Expedient Core Technology and Sedentism." In *The Organization of Core Technology*, edited by Jay K. Johnson and C. A. Morrow, 285–304. Boulder, CO: Westview Press.

Pavao-Zuckerman, Barnet. 2007. "Deerskins and Domesticates: Creek Subsistence and Economic Strategies in the Historic Period." *American Antiquity* 72, no. 1: 5–33.

Pettingill, Harry. N.d. "The History and Origin of the Five Nations (Iroquois Tribes): The Five Nations Were Immigrants to New York State Too, Same as the Whites." http://www.upstate-citizens.org/Iroquois-origin.htm.

Pollack, David. 2004. *Caborn-Welborn: Constructing a New Society after the Angel Chiefdom Collapse*. Tuscaloosa: Univ. of Alabama Press.

Porter, Joy. 2001. *To Be Indian: The Life of Iroquois-Seneca Arthur Caswell Parker*. Norman: Univ. of Oklahoma Press.

Porter, Tom. 2008. *And Grandma Said . . . Iroquois Teachings as Passed Down through the Oral Tradition*. Bloomington, IN: Xlibirs.

Pozorski, Sheila, and Thomas Pozorski. 2008. "Early Cultural Complexity on the Coast of Peru." In *Handbook of South American Archaeology*, edited by Helaine Silverman and William H. Isbell, 607–32. New York: Springer.

Pozorski, Thomas, and Sheila Pozorski. 1996. "Ventilated Hearth Structures in the Casma Valley, Peru." *Latin American Antiquity* 7, no. 4: 341–53.

Price, John. 1967. "A History of the Outcastes: Untouchability in Japan." In *Japan's Invisible Race: Caste in Culture and Personality*, edited by George DeVos and Hiroshi Vaatsuma, 6–30. Berkeley: Univ. of California Press.

Proctor, Mary A. 1930. *The Indians of the Winnipesaukee and Pemigewasset Valleys*. Franklin, NH: Towne and Robie.

Railey, Jim A. 2010. "Reduced Mobility or the Bow and Arrow: Another Look at 'Expedient' Technologies and Sedentism." *American Antiquity* 73, no. 2: 259–86.

Reed, Nelson A. 2007. "Evidence of Curved Roof Construction in Mississippian Structures." In *Architectural Variability in the Southeast*, edited by Cameron H. Lacquement, 12–31. Tuscaloosa: Univ. of Alabama Press.

Rice, Prudence. 1987. *Pottery Analysis: A Sourcebook*. Chicago: Univ. of Chicago:

Richter, Daniel K. 1992. *The Ordeal of the Longhouse: The Peoples of the Iroquois League in the Era of European Colonization*. Chapel Hill: Univ. of North Carolina Press.

Ricklis, Robert. 1967. "Excavation of a Probable Late Prehistoric Onondaga House Site." *Bulletin: Journal of the New York State Archaeological Association* 39: 15–17.

Riley, Thomas J., Richard Edging, and Jack Rossen. 1990. "Cultigens in Prehistoric Eastern North America: Changing Paradigms." *Current Anthropology* 31, no. 5: 525–41.

Ritchie, William A. 1928. *An Algonkian Village Site Near Levanna, New York*. Research Records no. 1. Rochester, NY: Rochester Municipal Museum.

———. 1932. "The Algonkin Sequence in New York." *American Anthropologist* 34, no. 3: 406–14.

———. 1944. *The Pre-Iroquoian Occupations of New York State*. Rochester, NY: Rochester Museum of Arts and Sciences.

———. 1945. *An Early Site in Cayuga County, New York: Type Component of the Frontenac Focus, Archaic Pattern*. Research Records no. 7. Rochester, NY: Rochester Museum of Arts and Sciences.

———. 1971. *New York Projectile Points: A Typology and Nomenclature*. Bulletin 384. Albany: New York State Museum.

———. 1980 [1965]. *The Archaeology of New York State*. Harrison, NY: Harbor Hill Books.

Ritchie, William A., and Richard S. MacNeish. 1949. "The Pre-Iroquoian Pottery of New York State." *American Antiquity* 15, no. 2: 97–124.

Rogers, Nina. 2014. "Rethinking Levanna Ceramics: A Tenth Century Short Term Occupation Site in Central New York." Master's thesis, Univ. of Denver.

Rossen, Jack. 1991. "Kentucky Landscapes: The Role of Environmental Reconstruction in Settlement Pattern Studies." In *The Human Landscape in Kentucky's Past: Site Structure and Settlement Patterns*, edited by Charles Stout and Christine K. Hensley, 1–7. Frankfort: Kentucky Heritage Council.

———. 1992. "Botanical Remains." In *Fort Ancient Cultural Dynamics in the Middle Ohio Valley*, edited by A. Gwynn Henderson, 189–208. Monographs in World Archaeology, no. 8. Madison, WI: Prehistory Press.

———. 1994. "The Archaeobotanical Record of the Late Mississippian Caborn-Welborn Culture." Paper presented at the Fifty-Fourth Annual Meeting of the Southeastern Archaeological Conference, Lexington, KY.

———. 2000a. "Archaeobotanical Remains from Logan's Fort." In *Archaeological Investigations at Logan's Fort, Lincoln County, Kentucky,* by Kim A. McBride and W. Stephen McBride, 95–105. Research Report no. 3. Lexington: Kentucky Archaeological Survey.

———. 2000b. "Archaic Plant Utilization at the Hedden Site, McCracken County, Kentucky." In *Current Archaeological Research in Kentucky, Volume Six,* edited by David Pollack and Kristen J. Gremillion, 1–24. Frankfort: Kentucky Heritage Council.

———. 2006a. "Botanical Remains from the Townley-Read Site." Ms. submitted to Kurt Jordan, Cornell Univ.

———. 2006b. "New Vision Archaeology in the Cayuga Heartland of Central New York." In *Cross-cultural Collaboration: Native Americans and Archaeologists in the Northeastern United States,* edited by Jordan Kerber. Lincoln: Univ. of Nebraska Press.

———. 2008. "Field School Archaeology, Activism, and Politics in the Cayuga Homeland of Central New York." In *Collaborating at the Trowel's Edge: Teaching and Learning in Indigenous Archaeology,* edited by Stephen W. Silliman, 103–20. Tucson: Univ. of Arizona Press.

———. 2013. "Longhouse, Cookhouse, Smoking Pipes, Eclipse: Archaeology of the Cayuga Heartland and the Origins of Confederacy." Invited presentation at Colgate Univ., Hamilton, NY, Sept. 18.

Rossen, Jack, and Richard Edging. 1987. "East Meets West: Patterns in Kentucky Late Prehistoric Subsistence." In *Current Archaeological Research in Kentucky,* edited by David Pollack, 1:225–38. Frankfort: Kentucky Heritage Council.

Rossen, Jack, and James Olson. 1985. "The Controlled Carbonization and Archaeological Analysis of Southeastern U.S. Wood Charcoals." *Journal of Field Archaeology* 12: 445–56.

Rutsch, Edward S. 1973. *Smoking Technology of the Aborigines of the Iroquois Area of New York State.* Madison, NJ: Farleigh Dickinson Univ. Press.

Sanft, Samantha M. 2013. "Beads and Pendants from Indian Fort Road: A Sixteenth Century Cayuga Site in Tompkins County, New York." Master's thesis, Cornell Univ.

Schoolcraft, Henry R. 2002 [1846]. *Notes on the Iroquois.* East Lansing: Michigan State Univ. Press.

Schroeder, Herbert W. 1992. "The Tree of Peace: Symbolic and Spiritual Values of the White Pine." In *White Pine Symposium Proceedings: History, Ecology, Policy and Management,* edited by Robert A. Stine and Melvin J. Baughman, 73–83. Department of Forest Resources, College of Natural Resources and Minnesota Extension Service. St. Paul: Univ. of Minnesota.

Schulenberg, Janet K. 2002. "New Dates for Owasco Pots." In *Northeast Subsistence-Settlement Change, A.D. 700–1300,* edited by J. P. Hart and C. B. Rieth, 153–65. Bulletin 496. Albany: New York State Museum.

Scollar, I., A. Tabbagh, A. Hesse, and I. Herzog. 1990. *Archaeological Prospecting and Remote Sensing.* Cambridge: Cambridge Univ. Press.

Sears, William H. 1955. "Creek and Cherokee Culture in the 18th Century." *American Antiquity* 21, no. 2: 143–49.

Shaw, David L. 2002. "Longhouse in Backyard? Archaeologist Says Firepit Remains in Aurora Point That Way." *Syracuse (NY) Post-Standard,* June 16, B1, B2.

Shero, Brian. 1970. "Flotation of Soil Samples from Iroquois Sites in Cayuga County, New York." Ms. in Marian White Papers, State Univ. of New York, Buffalo.

Sillar, B., and M. S. Tite. 2000. "The Challenge of 'Technological Choices' for Materials Science Approaches in Archaeology." *Archaeometry* 42, no. 1: 2–20.

Silliman, Stephen W., ed. 2008. *Collaborating at the Trowel's Edge: Teaching and Learning in Indigenous Archaeology.* Tucson: Univ. of Arizona Press.

Silver, I. A. 1970. "The Ageing of Domestic Animals." In *Science in Archaeology,* edited by Don Brothwell and Eric Higgs, 250–68. New York: Praeger.

Skinner, Alanson. 1921. *Notes on Iroquois Archaeology.* Indian Notes and Monographs Series, edited by F. W. Hodge. New York: Museum of the American Indian, Heye Foundation.

Smith, Bruce D. 1987. "The Independent Domestication of Indigenous Seedbearing Plants in Eastern North America." In *Emergent Horticultural Economies of the Eastern Woodlands,* edited by William F. Keegan, 3–47. Center for Archaeological Investigations, Occasional Paper 7. Carbondale: Southern Illinois Univ.

Smith, Claire, and H. Martin Wobst. 2005. *Indigenous Archaeologies: Decolonizing Theory and Practice.* London: Routledge.

Snow, Dean R. 1994. *The Iroquois.* Cambridge: Blackwell.

———. 1995. "Migration in Prehistory: The Northern Iroquoian Case." *American Antiquity* 60, no. 1: 59–79.

———. 1996. "More on Migration in Prehistory: Accommodating New Evidence in the Northern Iroquoian Case." *American Antiquity* 61, no. 4: 791–96.

Somerville, Kyle. 2013. "A Preliminary Examination of Faunal Exploitation at Four Sites in the Eastern Cayuga Sequence." Paper present at annual meeting, New York State Archaeological Association, Watertown, NY.

Spears, Michael. 2010. "Microscopic Usewear Analysis of Lithics from the Levanna Site, Cayuga County, New York." Senior honors thesis, Ithaca College.

Speck, Frank G., and Ernest S. Dodge. 1945. "Amphibian and Reptile Lore of the Six Nations Cayuga." *Journal of American Folklore* 58, no. 230: 306–9.

Squier, Ephraim G. 1849. *Aboriginal Monuments of the State of New-York: Comprising the Results of Original Surveys and Explorations, with an Illustrative Appendix.* Washington, DC: Smithsonian Institution.

Starna, William A. 2008. "Retrospecting the Origins of the League of the Iroquois." *Proceedings of the American Philosophical Society* 152, no. 3: 279–321.

Stein, William E., et al. 2007. "Giant Cladoxylopsid Trees Resolve the Enigma of the Earth's Earliest Forest Stumps at Gilboa." *Nature* 446, no. 7138: 904–7.

Stoltman, James. 1989. "A Quantitative Approach to the Petrographic Analysis of Ceramic Thin Sections." *American Antiquity* 54: 147–60.

———. 1991. "Ceramic Petrography as a Technique for Documenting Cultural Interaction: An Example from the Upper Mississippi Valley." *American Antiquity* 56, no. 1: 103–20.

Stoner, Wesley D. 2002. "Coarse Orange Pottery Exchange in Southern Veracruz: A Compositional Perspective on Centralized Craft Production and Exchange in the Classic Period." Master's thesis, Univ. of Kentucky.

Stoner, Wesley D., et al. 2003. "Variation in Coarse Orange Ceramic Production Recipe at Classic Period Matacapan." *La Tinaja* 14, no. 2.

Stout, Andy. 2012a. "Preserving an Unusual Cayuga Village: Conservancy Obtains an Option on the Indian Fort Road Site." *American Archaeology* 16, no. 1: 45.

———. 2012b. "Preserving a 16th-Century Iroquois Village: The Conservancy Adds Another Site to Its Iroquois Preservation Project." *American Archaeology* 16, no. 2: 48–49.

Streckeisen, A. L. 1974. "Classification and Nomenclature of Plutonic Rocks: Recommendations of the IUGS Subcommission on the Systematics of Igneous Rocks." *Geologische Rundschau* 63, no. 2: 773–85.

Swanton, John R. 1946. *The Indians of the Southeastern United States.* Bulletin 137. Washington, DC: Bureau of American Ethnology.

"Theft from the Dead." 1986. In *Art from Ganondagan, the Village of Peace,* 8. Waterford, NY: State Office of Parks, Recreation, and Historic Preservation, Bureau of Historic Sites.

Thomas, Chief Jake. 1994. *Teachings from the Longhouse*. Toronto, ON: Stoddart.

Tobin, Dave. 2002. "George Washington's Campaign of Terror." *Syracuse (NY) Post-Standard*, Aug. 20, B1.

Tooker, Elisabeth. 1965. "The Iroquois White Dog Sacrifice in the Latter Part of the 18th Century." *Ethnohistory* 12, no. 2: 129–40.

———. 1996 [1984]. "Women in Iroquois Society." In *Iroquois Women: An Anthology*, edited by W. G. Spittal, 199–216. Ohsweken, ON: Iroqrafts.

Trubowitz, Neal. 1977. "A Statistical Examination of the Social Structure of Frontenac Island." In *Current Perspectives in Northeastern Archaeology: Essays in Honor of William A. Ritchie*, edited by Robert E. Funk and Charles F. Hayes III, 123–47. Researches and Transactions of the New York Archaeological Association 17, no. 1. Rochester and Albany, NY: New York State Archaeological Association.

———. 2004. "Smoking Pipes: An Archaeological Measure of Native American Cultural Stability and Survival in Eastern North America, A.D. 1500–1850." In *Smoking and Culture: The Archaeology of Tobacco Pipes in Eastern North America*, edited by Sean M. Rafferty and Rob Mann, 143–64. Knoxville: Univ. of Tennessee Press.

Tuck, James A. 1971. *Onondaga Iroquois Prehistory: A Study in Settlement Archaeology*. Syracuse, NY: Syracuse Univ. Press.

Two Bears, Davina R. 2006. "Navajo Archaeologist Is Not an Oxymoron: A Tribal Archaeologist's Experience." *American Indian Quarterly* 30, no. 3: 381–87.

———. 2008. "Íhoosh'aah, Learn by Doing: The Navajo Nation Archaeology Department Student Training Program." In *Collaborating at the Trowel's Edge: Teaching and Learning in Indigenous Archaeology*, edited by Stephen W. Silliman, 103–20. Tucson: Univ. of Arizona Press.

Underhill, Joy. 2001. "Ganondagan: Bridge between Yesterday and Today." *Life in the Finger Lakes* (Geneva, NY) (Summer).

US Department of Agriculture. 1948. *Woody Plant and Seed Manual*. Miscellaneous Publication no. 654. Washington, DC: US Department of Agriculture.

Van Diver, Bradford. 1985. *Roadside Geology of New York*. Missoula, MT: Mountain Press.

Venables, Robert W. 2000. "Some Observations on the Treaty of Canandaigua." In *Treaty of Canandaigua 1794: 200 Years of Treaty Relations between the Iroquois Confederacy and the United States*, edited by Irving Powless Jr., Paul Williams, John C. Mohawk, Oren Lyons, Daniel K. Richter, Robert W. Venables, Doug George-Kanentiio, Laurence M. Hauptman, Joy A. Bilharz, and Ron LaFrance, 84–119. Santa Fe, NM: Clear Light.

————. 2010. "The Clearings and the Woods: The Haudenosaunee (Iroquois) Landscape—Gendered and Balanced." In *Archaeology and Preservation of Gendered Landscapes*, edited by Sherene Baugher and Suzanne M. Spencer-Wood, 21–55. New York: Springer.

Vest, Jay Hansford C. 2005. "An Odyssey among the Iroquois: A History of Tutelo Relations in New York." *American Indian Quarterly* 29, nos. 1–2: 124–55.

Vogel, Virgil J. 1982. *American Indian Medicine*. Norman: Univ. of Oklahoma Press.

Wagner, Gail E. 1983. "Fort Ancient Subsistence: The Botanical Record." *West Virginia Archaeologist* 35: 27–39.

————. 1987. "Uses of Plants by the Fort Ancient Indians." PhD diss., Washington Univ.

————. 2000. "Tobacco in Prehistoric Eastern North America." In *Tobacco Use by Native North Americans: Sacred Smoke and Silent Killer*, edited by Joseph C. Winter, 185–201. Norman: Univ. of Oklahoma Press.

Wallace, Paul A. 1994. *White Roots of Peace: The Iroquois Book of Life*. Santa Fe, NM: Clear Light.

Ward, Sarah. 2014a. "Myers Farm Site: A Case Study on the Significance of Hoe Blades in Haudenosaunee Culture." Independent study paper, Ithaca College.

————. 2014b. "Myers Farm Site: A Case Study on the Significance of Hoe Blades in Haudenosaunee Culture." Paper presented at the annual meeting, Northeast Anthropological Association, Pottsdam, NY.

Warrick, Gary A. 2000. "The Precontact Iroquoian Occupation of Southern Ontario." *Journal of World Prehistory* 14, no. 4: 415–66.

Watkins, Joe. 2000. *Indigenous Archaeology: American Indian Values and Scientific Practice*. Walnut Creek, CA: Altamira Press.

Watson, Patty Jo. 1989. "Early Plant Cultivation in the Eastern Woodlands of North America." In *Foraging and Farming: The Evolution of Plant Exploitation*, edited by David R. Harris and Gordon C. Hillman, 555–71. One World Archaeology, vol. 13. London: Unwin-Hyman.

Waugh, F. W. 1973 [1916]. *Iroquois Foods and Food Preparation*. Canada Department of Mines, Geological Survey. Anthropological Series 12, Memoir 86. Facsimile ed. Ottawa: Government Printing Bureau.

Weissner, Polly. 1983. "Style and Social Information in Kalahari San Projectile Points." *American Antiquity* 48, no. 2: 253–76.

Whipple, Andrew P. 2007. "Oops, That's Not Really a Diamond." *Science* 316, no. 5825: 690–91.

White, Marian. 1969. "The Nature of Warfare and Confederacies among Northern Iroquoians." National Science Foundation grant proposal.

Whiteley, Peter M. 2000. "The Misappropriation of Cayuga Lands: A Brief History." For the US Department of Justice (Indian Resources), intervenors in *Cayuga Nation et al. vs. Pataki et al.* US District Court, Syracuse, NY.

Wichman, Randy, Keao NeSmith, and Dave Wellman. 2014. "Kaneiolouma, Kaua'i: A Renaissance." Paper presented at the annual Society for Hawaiian Archaeology conference, Hilo, HI, Oct.

Wilbert, Johannes. 1987. *Tobacco and Shamanism in South America*. New Haven, CT: Yale Univ. Press.

Wilhalme, Matt. 2013. "Vijay Singh Admits Using Deer Antler Spray, Says He Didn't Know It Was a Banned Substance." *Los Angeles Times*, Jan. 30.

Witthoft, John G. 1952. "A Paleo-Indian Site in Eastern Pennsylvania: An Early Hunting Culture." *Proceedings of the American Philosophical Society* 96, no. 4: 464–95.

Wonderley, Anthony. 2002. "Oneida Ceramic Effigies." *Northeast Anthropology* 63: 23–48.

———. 2005. "Effigy Pipes, Diplomacy, and Myth: Exploring Interactions between St. Lawrence Iroquoians and Eastern Iroquoians in New York State." *American Antiquity* 70, no. 2: 211–40.

Wray, Charles F., et al. 1987. *The Adams and Culbertson Sites*. Report no. 19. Rochester, NY: Rochester Museum & Science Center.

Wray, Charles F., Martha L. Sempowski, and Lorraine P. Saunders. 1991. *Tram and Cameron: Two Early Contact Era Seneca Sites*. Report no. 21. Rochester, NY: Rochester Museum & Science Center.

Wright, James V. 1995. "Three Dimensional Reconstructions of Iroquoian Longhouses: A Comment." *Archaeology of Eastern North America* 23: 9–21.

Yarnell, Richard A. 1969. "Contents of Paleofeces." In *The Prehistory of Salts Cave, Kentucky*, edited by Patty Jo Watson, 41–54. Springfield: Reports of Investigation, Illinois State Museum.

———. 1978. "Domestication of Sunflower and Sumpweed in Eastern North America." In *The Nature and Status of Ethnobotany*, edited by Richard I. Ford, 289–99. Anthropological Papers, no. 67, Museum of Anthropology. Ann Arbor: Univ. of Michigan.

Contributors

April M. Beisaw is an assistant professor of anthropology at Vassar College in New York, where she teaches courses on archaeology and forensic anthropology. She recently summarized lessons learned from fifteen years of faunal analysis in the book *Identifying and Interpreting Animal Bones: A Manual.* Her current research projects focus on the archaeology of twentieth-century abandonment within the New York City watershed and the archaeology and history of the 1916 Susquehanna River Expedition. She also studies ghost hunting to understand how archaeologists can improve their storytelling skills.

Macy O'Hearn is a 2013 graduate of the anthropology bachelor program at Ithaca College in Ithaca, New York. She earned departmental honors for her senior thesis, "A Critical Examination of the Existing Typology for Haudenosaunee Ceramics and an Analysis of the Decorated Ceramics Assemblage from the Myers Farm Site, King Ferry, New York." She is working on a typological analysis of the decorated ceramics from the Levanna site, a tenth-century Cayuga village site in Levanna, New York. She is interested in pursuing graduate studies in indigenous archaeology.

David Pollack is the director of the Kentucky Archaeological Survey and the editor or coeditor of numerous professional publications on Kentucky prehistory. He has analyzed and published on ceramic assemblages from a variety of Native American sites. His book *Caborn-Welborn: Constructing a New Society after the Angel Chiefdom Collapse* assesses the reorganization of people on the landscape following the demise of an earlier Mississippian polity in southern Indiana.

Michael Rogers is an associate professor in the Department of Physics and Astronomy at Ithaca College. He has PhD and master's degrees in physics and an MAIS in archaeology from Oregon State University. His archaeogeophysics research spans Late Bronze Age cities in Cyprus, pre–American

Revolutionary War house forts in New York State, and Haudenosaunee sites in central New York.

Jack Rossen is professor in the Department of Anthropology at Ithaca College. He received his PhD from the University of Kentucky in 1991. He conducted archaeological research in Peru, Chile, and Argentina and has analyzed archaeobotanical materials from throughout South America, the Ohio Valley, and the northeastern United States. He began work on collaborative, indigenous archaeology and community projects with the Cayuga and Onondaga Nations in what is now central New York in 1998. He was one of the original SHARE (Strengthening Haudenosaunee American Relations through Education) group that purchased the seventy-acre SHARE Farm in 2001 and transferred it to the Cayuga Nation in 2005. He cofounded the Native American Studies Program at Ithaca College with Brooke Hansen in 2003.

Martin J. Smith is a 2004 graduate of the anthropology bachelor program at Ithaca College. He currently lives in the Hudson Valley region of New York, where he owns and operates a small landscaping and outdoor design company and works as a historic carpenter and property manager.

Wesley D. Stoner is an assistant professor in the Anthropology Department at the University of Arkansas. His research explores the roles of human interaction systems in the evolution of cultural complexity. He brings together archaeology and methods developed in the physical sciences to reconstruct social, economic, and political intergroup relationships in the past that would otherwise remain invisible to us today. His primary region of research is Mesoamerica, although he maintains significant research interests in eastern North America.

Sarah Ward is a 2014 graduate of the anthropology bachelor program at Ithaca College. She analyzed the hoe blades from the Myers Farm site, producing the independent study paper "Myers Farm Site: A Case Study on the Significance of Hoe Blades in Haudenosaunee Culture." She is interested in pursuing graduate studies in indigenous archaeology.

Joseph F. Winiarz is a PhD candidate in the Public Policy and Administration program at Walden University. Joseph received his master of arts from Norwich University with a concentration in terrorism studies and international relations and a bachelor of science from Empire State College in archaeology. His dissertation, "U.S. Drone Strike Policy: A Terrorist Generating Machine," explores the narrative that noncombatant casualties provide powerful grievances against the United States and thus turn supporters into opponents. Winiarz's research interests also include the intersection of public policy and administration, failed militaristic campaigns, and the social construction of target populations in policy design and implementation.

Index